The Voter's Guide to Election Polls

Sixth Edition

Michael W. Traugott
University of Michigan

Paul J. Lavrakas
*Retired Professor, Northwestern
University and Ohio State University*

ROWMAN & LITTLEFIELD
Lanham • Boulder • New York • London

Executive Acquisitions Editor: Michael Kerns
Assistant Editor: Elizabeth Von Buhr
Sales and Marketing Inquiries: textbooks@rowman.com

Credits and acknowledgments for material borrowed from other sources, and reproduced with permission, appear on the appropriate pages within the text.

Published by Rowman & Littlefield
An imprint of The Rowman & Littlefield Publishing Group, Inc.
4501 Forbes Boulevard, Suite 200, Lanham, Maryland 20706
www.rowman.com

86-90 Paul Street, London EC2A 4NE

Copyright © 2024 by The Rowman & Littlefield Publishing Group, Inc.
Third edition 2004. Fourth edition 2008.

All rights reserved. No part of this book may be reproduced in any form or by any electronic or mechanical means, including information storage and retrieval systems, without written permission from the publisher, except by a reviewer who may quote passages in a review.

British Library Cataloguing in Publication Information Available

Library of Congress Cataloging-in-Publication Data

Names: Traugott, Michael W., author. | Lavrakas, Paul J., author.
Title: The voter's guide to election polls / Michael W. Traugott, Paul J. Lavrakas.
Description: Sixth edition. | Lanham, Maryland : Rowman & Littlefield, 2024. | Includes bibliographical references and index.
Identifiers: LCCN 2023038414 (print) | LCCN 2023038415 (ebook) | ISBN 9781538187388 (cloth) | ISBN 9781538187395 (paperback) | ISBN 9781538187401 (epub)
Subjects: LCSH: Public opinion—United States. | Public opinion polls—United States. | Election forecasting—United States. | Press and politics—United States.
Classification: LCC HN90.P8 T73 2024 (print) | LCC HN90.P8 (ebook) | DDC 303.3/80973—dc23/eng/20231018
LC record available at https://lccn.loc.gov/2023038414
LC ebook record available at https://lccn.loc.gov/2023038415

∞™ The paper used in this publication meets the minimum requirements of American National Standard for Information Sciences—Permanence of Paper for Printed Library Materials, ANSI/NISO Z39.48-1992.

To Santa and Barbara
For their inspiration and support

Contents

Introduction	1
Polling, the News Media, and Politics	3
The Organization of This Book	8
What Is New in This Edition	9
Concluding Comments	10
Chapter 1: What Are Polls and Surveys and Why Are They Conducted?	13
What Is a Survey?	13
How Does a Poll Differ from a Survey?	14
How Many Different Kinds of Surveys Are There?	14
How Well Do Polls Measure Public Opinion?	16
Are There Other Ways to Obtain People's Opinions?	17
When Is a "Survey" Not a Survey?	17
Why Not Just Count Everyone?	18
Why Is Time Such an Important Factor in Polls Conducted for Media?	19
Who Sponsors Surveys?	20
Who Conducts Polls?	20
Do Polls Have an Impact on Those Who Are Exposed to Them?	20
Chapter 2: What Are Election Polls? How Are They Conducted?	23
What Is an Election Poll?	24
How Many Kinds of Election Polls Are There?	25
How Have Exit Polls Changed?	25
How Do Media Organizations Use Election Polls?	26
Are Current Pre-Election Polls Better than Those Conducted in the Past?	26

Are There Special Problems in Conducting Pre-Election Polls?	28
What Is the Appropriate Population to Sample for Pre-Election Polls?	30
How Do Polls Measure Voting Intention?	30
How Do Polls Measure Candidate Support?	31
What Happens to People Who Have Not Decided Yet?	31
What Are Tracking Polls?	32
Are There Special Problems in Conducting Tracking Polls?	33
How Do Tracking Polls Compare to Other Pre-Election Polls?	34
Are There Other Trends in the Reporting of Pre-Election Polls?	35
How Did Bias Appear in Some State Polls?	35
Can the Publication of Poll Results Affect Whether or How Citizens Vote?	36
What Is the Chance that a Pre-Election Poll Will Produce an Incorrect Projection of an Election Outcome?	36
What Are Exit Polls, and What Are They Used For?	39
Who Conducts the Exit Polls?	40
Have There Been Any Special Problems in Conducting and Interpreting Exit Polls to Project Election Winners?	41
What Is the Chance That an Exit Poll Can Produce an Incorrect Projection of an Election Outcome?	44
Are Pre-election Polls Well Suited to Estimating the Outcome of the Electoral College Vote?	45
Do Election Night Broadcasts of Projections Affect Voting?	46
Are Americans Concerned about the Effects of Election Polls?	46
Can the U.S. Government Regulate How Media Organizations Conduct and Disseminate Their Poll Results?	47
What Options Are Available to Learn More about How Polls Are Conducted?	48
Chapter 3: How Do Political Candidates and Organizations Use Poll Data?	**51**
How Do Candidates Use Polls?	52
When Do Candidates Use Polls?	52
Are Polls the Only Research Technique for Collecting Information During a Campaign?	54
Do the Results of Campaign Polls Depend on When They Are Conducted?	55
Do the Results of Campaign Polls Depend on How They Are Conducted?	55
Do Candidates Use Poll Results in Strategic Ways?	56

Can Candidate Polls Be Misleading?	57
Can Media Poll Results Help a Candidate?	58
Can Media Poll Results Hurt a Candidate?	58
How Do Political Parties Use Polls?	58
Why Do Special-Interest Groups Use Polls?	59
Are There Problems with Some Polls Conducted by Special-Interest Groups?	60
Do Elected Officials Pay Attention to Polls?	61
Chapter 4: How Do News Organizations Collect and Report Poll Data?	**63**
Why Do Media Organizations Conduct Polls?	64
How Can Polls Contribute to Good Journalism?	65
Why Do Media Organizations Collaborate on Polling?	66
How Have Business Conditions Affected Media Polling?	66
Are There Special Pressures that Affect Media Polls?	67
What Are the Standard Data Collection Methods Used in Media Polling?	68
Can the Methodology of Media Polls Have an Impact on The Results?	69
How Are Media Polls Analyzed and Disseminated?	70
Do Reports of Poll Results Differ When Presented on Television or in Newspapers?	71
Can Media Polls Conducted by Different News Organizations Produce Different Results?	71
Why Are There So Many Polls Reported in the Media?	73
Chapter 5: Why Do Pollsters Use Samples?	**75**
What Is Sampling?	76
What Is Involved in a Sample Design?	76
What Is the Target Population for an Election Poll?	77
What Is a Sampling Frame?	79
Do Telephone Directories Make a Good Sampling Frame for Election Polls?	80
Do Lists of Email Addresses Make a Good Sampling Frame for Election Polls?	80
What Is the Sampling Frame for a Typical Pre-Election Internet Poll?	81
What is Registration-Based Sampling (RBS)?	82
What Is the Sampling Frame for the Typical Exit Poll?	82
How Large Does a Sample Need to Be?	83

What Is the Margin of Sampling Error (MOSE) for a Particular
   Sample? 84
How Does Sample Size Affect the Precision of a Poll's
   Estimates? 86
Why Are Some Sample Designs Preferable to Others? 87
What Is a Probability Sample? 88
Why and How Do Pollsters Choose Only One Person within a
   Household to Interview? 90
What Is a Nonprobability Sample? 91
Are Nonprobability Samples Ever Combined with Probability
   Samples? 92
What Is a Random Sample? 93
What Is a Systematic Sample? 93
What Is a Stratified Sample? 94
Do You Need a Larger Sample Size with a National Poll than
   You Do in a Statewide or Citywide Poll? 94
What Is the Response Rate to a Survey? 95
How Does the Nonresponse Affect Survey Accuracy? 97
Do the News Media Acknowledge the Issue of Nonresponse in
   Poll Accuracy? 98
What Does It Mean When Poll Data Are Weighted? 100
Why Haven't I Ever Been Interviewed in an Election Poll? 101

Chapter 6: How Are Questionnaires Put Together? 103

Does a Questionnaire Follow a Particular Order and Format? 103
Do Different Survey Questions Serve Different Purposes? 104
Is There More Than One Kind of Format for Survey Question? 105
Are There Other Differences between Open-Ended and Closed-
   Ended Questions? 107
What Is an Unbalanced Question? 108
Does the Wording of a Question Make a Difference in the
   Responses a Respondent Provides? 109
What Is the Problem of Complex Language in a Poll Question? 110
What Is a Double Negative in a Question? 111
What Is a Double-Barreled Question? 112
What Is the Effect of a Leading Phrase in a Question? 113
Are Responses to Questions on Sensitive Topics Affected by
   How They Are Worded? 113
Can the Wording of a Question Be Manipulated to Produce a
   Certain Result? 114
Do the Response Alternatives in a Closed-Ended Question
   Make a Difference in the Responses They Elicit? 115

What If a Respondent Is Undecided, Uncertain, or Doesn't Have an Opinion on a Question?	116
What If a Respondent Gives a "Don't Know" Response to a Question?	117
Does the Order in Which Questions Are Asked Make a Difference in the Responses Elicited?	118
Are Some Questions Typically Asked Early in a Questionnaire and Others Later?	120
What Is the Problem of a "Socially Desirable" Response to a Survey Question?	121
How Do Researchers Know Whether Questions Are Biased?	122
Are There Other Ways to Test for Bias in a Questionnaire?	123
Chapter 7: How Are Data Gathered for Election Polls?	**127**
What Is the Most Common Form of Data Collection in Election Polls?	128
What Other Forms of Data Collection Are There?	130
What Are the Advantages and Disadvantages of Face-To-Face Data Collection?	131
What Are the Advantages and Disadvantages of Video-Assisted Data Collection?	132
What Are the Advantages and Disadvantages of Telephone Data Collection?	132
What Are the Advantages and Disadvantages of Self-Administered Mail and Internet Questionnaires?	134
What Are the Advantages and Disadvantages of Self-Administered IVR Questionnaires?	135
What is Mixed-Mode Data Collection?	137
What Do Pollsters Do about "Missing Data"?	137
Are There Other Non-Survey Methods for Producing Estimates of What Public Opinion Is on a Particular Topic?	138
Who Gets to Be an Interviewer?	139
How Are Interviewers Trained and Monitored?	140
How Does Contact with a Respondent Take Place?	141
How Long Do Election Poll Questionnaires Take to Complete?	143
Can Interviewers Affect the Kinds of Answers Respondents Give?	145
What Happens If Initial Contact with a Respondent Is Unsuccessful?	146
How Does Information from a Respondent Get Recorded into a Computer?	148

Do Respondents Have to Give Their Names When They Are Interviewed?	149
Chapter 8: How Do Media Organizations Analyze Polls?	**151**
What Is a Variable?	152
How Is a Poll Analyzed?	152
What Are the Frequencies?	153
What Is an Estimate?	153
What Is a Relationship Between Two or More Variables?	154
How Do the Media Typically Present Poll Results?	155
What Are Marginals and Can Their Presentation Be Misleading?	157
What Is a Trend?	157
How Are Trends Analyzed?	158
How Can Surveys Measure Change?	159
What Does It Mean that Public Opinion Has Changed?	160
Is It Possible to Compare Data Collected in Different Polls?	160
Chapter 9: How Can I Evaluate Published Poll Results?	**163**
What Do I Need to Know to Understand and Interpret Poll Results?	163
Are There Any Standards for Reporting Poll Results?	164
Why Should I Want to Know Who Sponsored the Poll?	165
Why Should I Want to Know Who Conducted the Poll?	166
Why Should I Want to Know What Mode of Data Collection Was Used?	166
Why Should I Want to Know What Kind of Sample Was Used?	167
Why Should I Want to Know What the Sample Size Was?	168
Why Should I Want to Know if the Responses of Important Subgroups Were Analyzed Separately?	169
Why Should I Want to Know What the Response Rate Was?	169
Why Should I Want to Know When the Data Were Gathered?	170
Why Should I Want to Know the Exact Question Wordings, Including the Response Categories?	171
Why Should I Want to Know the Question Order?	171
Why Should I Want to Know Whether There Are References to Other Polls on the Same Topic?	172
Does the Analysis Suggest that Changes in Opinion Have Occurred, and Are Such Interpretations Justified?	172
Chapter 10: What Are Some Common Problems and Complaints about Polls and the Media's Use of Them?	**175**

Do Polls Measure "Real" Attitudes?	176
Can Polls Be Designed to Find Whatever the Sponsor Wants?	178
When Is a Survey Not a Survey?	179
What Is an Audience Call-In Poll?	180
What Is an Internet Log-In Poll?	181
How Should I Treat Polls That Are Mailed to My Home or Poll Invitations I Receive Via E-Mail?	182
How Accurate Are Insert Polls in Magazines or Newspapers?	183
How Accurate Are Internet Pop-Up Polls?	184
If I Receive a Telephone Call to Be Interviewed, Should I Participate?	185
Suppose I Am Called at a Bad Time, Like When I Am Sitting Down to Dinner or on My Cell Phone While Driving?	186
How Do I Know if a Poll Is Being Conducted by a Reputable Survey Organization?	186
What Can I Do if I Am Contacted by a Pseudo Poll?	187
What Assurances Should an Interviewer Give that Nothing Bad Will Happen to Me if I Participate in a Poll?	187
Epilogue	189
Appendix A: Standards for Disclosing Information about the Methodology of Public Polls	191
Appendix B: Sample Tolerances (Sampling Errors) for Samples of Different Sizes	197
Glossary	199
Selected References	237
The History and Role of Polls in the Media and Democracy	237
How Polls are Conducted	239
Sampling	240
Information about Election and Policy Polls	241
Polls and Political Candidates	242
Presidential Polling, the Media, and Democracy	242
Questionnaire Design	243
Data Collection and Analysis	244
Data Analysis	245
How to Evaluate Polls	246
What Are Some Common Problems and Complaints about Polls?	247

Index	249
About the Authors	259

Introduction

Contemporary American politics is awash in polling data. Everywhere a citizen turns, polls report the standing of the candidates. A constant stream of horse race news stories describes candidates' behavior as strategic acts prompted by the latest polls. And there are frequent expressions of concern about the impact of polls on the public, such as election night projections based on exit polls that are perceived to affect turnout on the West Coast, where the voters still have time to cast their ballots.

After the 1996 Iowa caucuses, millionaire Steve Forbes was criticized by his Republican opponents and many in the media for spending more than $400 per vote he received. But little of the same kind of complaint was directed at a new kind of poll-based programming effort by PBS, which produced a short series of programs based on a deliberative poll involving 459 people who spent a weekend in Austin, Texas—at a total cost of about $10,000 per respondent. In the 2000 campaign, George W. Bush decided to forgo public funds in his primary campaign; he raised and spent as much as he could. By the time the 2004 primaries and caucuses came around, not only did President Bush forgo public funds, but Howard Dean and John Kerry decided to as well. In the 2008 cycle, no candidate accepted public funding; they all raised and spent as much money as they could; Barack Obama's effort exceeded $750 million. The Citizens United decision by the Supreme Court in 2010 essentially produced an era of unlimited spending in American presidential elections, wiping out the public financing provisions initiated in 1976. By the 2012 campaign, Barack Obama and Mitt Romney and their associated "super PACs" raised and spent more than $1,000,000,000 each. In the 2020 presidential campaign, the two main candidates spent a combined $3.65 billion, including funds from super PACs, with Joe Biden's principal campaign committee becoming the first to raise more than $1 billion and Trump $774 million. The very concept of public funding of the presidential campaigns is now over, and the cost of engaging in political discourse is obviously not a good measure of the quality of a democracy.

The 1996 presidential campaign saw instances wherein one form of pseudo poll, called a push poll by candidates and their consultants, was used in attempts to sway supporters and suppress turnout in the early primaries. Forbes, a relative newcomer to presidential politics, and Patrick Buchanan, an older hand, called these "dirty tricks"; other, more experienced Republican candidates described them as a standard campaign tool. The use of "push polls"—a political telemarketing technique—has trickled down all the way to state legislative races and contests for judicial offices. In another new development, citizens' opinions are being solicited on the internet. Such log-in polls often have very large numbers of respondents, but serious concerns have been raised that these are not representative of the general public.

Two other recent phenomena have raised red flags for those who follow political polls closely. One of them is the rare but disconcerting way that some pollsters are judged to make up data to gain visibility in order to build their business rather than fielding polls. The most notable example involved a firm by the name of Strategic Vision LLC, which was censured by the American Association for Public Opinion Research (AAPOR) after analyses conducted by Nate Silver suggested that the data were questionable. David Johnson, the owner, never produced any data or analyses from any of the surveys he said he had conducted. In the 2022 midterm elections, a number of Republican-leaning firms released results suggesting their state-level candidates were doing well, affecting the polling averages in those states and nationally. The second phenomenon is the possibility of "herding," a practice by which some claim that pollsters might adjust their results to align with those from other polls conducted at the same time, minimizing the chances that they will look different and increasing the perception that there is a consensus in the polls for a particular race. This also eliminates the possibility of findings that are labeled "outliers." AAPOR has also commented on this.

These recent occurrences raise two important questions: Is the average citizen supposed to treat all polls as equivalent and accept their findings with alacrity? Or is it possible to acquire a reasonable amount of knowledge about what polls are and how they are conducted and then apply it to distinguish the good from the bad? This is what this book is about.

Our sense of the need for this book came from frequent speaking engagements and presentations about political polling and its link to contemporary journalism. When speaking to students, citizens groups, and other survey researchers, we learned that people are interested in and concerned about the role polls play in political campaigns and the news coverage that is based on them. Within our lifetime, news organizations have increasingly moved from being simple and straightforward conveyors of this information to serving as active purveyors of it through their own polling organizations.

This book was written to help citizens develop a more critical view of how polls do and don't, yet could and should, contribute to a more informed electorate and a better-functioning democracy. An equally important goal is to help students of politics—those still in school and those who are out in the real world but still striving to increase their understanding of how the process of presidential nomination and selection works—appreciate the use of polls, especially during election campaigns.

POLLING, THE NEWS MEDIA, AND POLITICS

Elections have a special place in American journalism, for several reasons. One reason is that we live in a democracy, and public opinion has such a central role in the functioning and legitimacy of our government. Elections, and the campaigns leading up to them, are the defining political act in the United States. They represent a point at which most Americans devote more time to thinking about politics and public affairs than normal. The election of public officials with broad public support—and the mandates that might be involved—provides a critical underpinning of our system of representation.

At the same time, elections make great news. Presidential elections involve important issues and, eventually, well-known figures. They operate under a system of rules that most citizens are familiar with. They occur on a fixed schedule, involve substantial conflict, and usually come to a neat resolution on Election Day with the declaration of winners and losers—with the notable exception of the 2000 election. The 2020 election was also an exception for a different reason: The polls suggested Joe Biden would win the popular vote, and he did. But the events of January 6, 2021, and the public's reactions to the attempt by insurrectionary forces to prevent the peaceful transfer of power were also explained by polls following that event.

Moreover, campaigns are populated by willing sources interested in talking with journalists and having their side of the story presented in the best possible light. For all these reasons, there is a strong symbiotic relationship between journalists and candidates. They rely on each other for success, even though they often seem at odds with each other.

One of their common interests is how the public feels about the campaigns, the issues, and the candidates—what the public mood is. This is complicated by the fact that there is no common or standard definition of what public opinion is. Some believe it is an attribute of an individual that can be expressed out loud or in public. Others believe that it is the aggregated opinions of people, measured and summarized. By this definition, it is not public unless it is disseminated widely and made known to others. Under these circumstances, an accurate poll or survey is the ideal mechanism for measuring public opinion, and the news media are the ideal vehicles for making these opinions known to others.

In the old days, both candidates and journalists relied on various experts for these assessments. They included party leaders, elected officials, and such unobtrusive indicators as the size of crowds that turned out for scheduled events. But the size of a crowd, for example, is an imperfect measure of public opinion because it is often difficult to associate a good measure of valence or affect with sheer numbers of participants or to gauge the intensity of feelings associated with the views that its members hold. For a very long time, what was missing in American politics was a way to produce systematic and reliable measures of public opinion—information that could be used to plan or revise strategy or to contextualize reporting of what the candidates were saying and doing.

Whereas politicians and journalists have always been interested in knowing about public opinion, the extensive application of survey research techniques did not begin until the 1930s, when the founders of election polling, such as George Gallup, Elmo Roper, and Archibald Crossley, began to collect and publish election-related opinion data. From the start, their efforts were possible because of relationships they established with newspapers and magazines. They needed the mass media to serve as outlets for the wide dissemination of their results because their public opinion business was a way of promoting their firms' proprietary work for commercial clients. And these news outlets were always looking for new and timely content.

After World War II, improvements in sampling methods and increasing commercial demand for survey research led to an increase in polling. The candidates themselves turned to public opinion polls as an integral part of their own strategic efforts, using the information to supplement analyses of historical voting patterns. At the same time, the public dissemination of data rapidly accelerated after the important news organizations in the United States—the networks and major metropolitan daily newspapers—began to collaborate on their own independent data collection in the 1970s. Now the news coverage of election campaigns is filled with poll results, both from polls taken before and after debates, leading up to a primary or general Election Day, and then from exit polls of voters leaving their balloting places. The former data are used to predict winners and to explain and dissect the campaign, and the latter are used to provide poll-based explanations of the meaning of the outcome, as well as to project the winners.

News organizations and journalists justified their entry into the polling business because they believed that the use of poll data contributed to their objectivity in producing news about politics. When they purchased results from the Gallup Poll or one of its competitors, they acquired useful nonpartisan content at a reasonable price. Technological shifts that reduced the cost of polling—most notably the penetration of telephones into virtually every American household and the availability of laptop computers and smartphones that serve as low-cost interviewing devices and data analysis machines—raised the prospect of independent data collection activities. And news organizations further justified this on the basis of increased editorial control: they could ask whatever questions they wanted and put studies into the field whenever they wanted if they ran their own polling operations.

The technology of polling is always changing. In the past two decades, changes in a number of telecommunications-related technologies and the public's use of them plus new government regulations have hampered the conduct of telephone surveys. This includes the proliferation of cell phones and federal regulations affecting how they can be dialed; call screening and call blocking; and the plague of telemarketing that led to the advent of Do Not Call List regulations in 2004. The Federal Communications Commission (FCC) is now considering new regulations that would make calls to cell phones even more difficult and expensive. As we describe later in this revised edition, the cell phone–only population in the United States has grown appreciably, and pollsters and other survey researchers are still struggling to understand the proper way to integrate these individuals into election polls that are conducted via telephone.

Separately, starting in the late 1990s, some polling organizations began to use the internet to collect pre-election poll data in an effort to control costs. Many organizations are now using hybrid designs, combining telephone and web-based data collection, as well as using hybrid probability and nonprobability sample designs. The main attraction remains the low cost of data collection on the web, especially as the budgets of news organizations face ongoing reductions. These are issues that are continually being addressed by survey methodologists and samplers. One possible advance for pollsters that use the internet to gather election poll data would be the development of lists of registered voters that include their e-mail addresses. Another is to mail letters to samples of registered voters and provide them with an internet site to use to complete their questionnaire.

But the current regulatory and social environments related to use of the internet are unpredictable, and it is uncertain what the long-term effects will be on political pollsters. In the last few presidential elections, the exit poll operation embodied in what was called the *Voter News Service (VNS)* (with surveying conducted by Edison Research) went through two jarring elections. In 2000, which was the closest presidential election in American history and was beset by a protracted legal battle that started in Florida, the networks and the exit poll operation had a bad outing that prompted congressional hearings. The sponsoring organizations (the five major news networks and the Associated Press) tried to correct their systems before the 2002 election, but there was not enough time.

On election night 2002, they were unable to produce data for projections and analysis, and VNS went out of business, replaced by the *National Election Pool (NEP*, with surveying still conducted by Edison). They built an entirely new software system for the 2004 election coverage that worked well from a statistical standpoint. But their performance was marred by a number of early "leaks" of exit poll data on various internet blogs throughout Election Day (November 2), and this created a good deal of consternation, as the sponsors of the 2004 exit polls had pledged to withhold the release of exit poll data for a particular state until voting ended there. To counter the problem of leaked exit poll data before voting ended in a particular state in 2006, the NEP established a secret "quarantine room" in New York City, in which each of the exit poll sponsors placed two of their representatives until 5:00 p.m. EST. Members of this group were the only ones, other than the NEP itself, who had access to the incoming exit poll data. The room was closely monitored by independent overseers, and none of the sponsors' representatives had any access to a smartphone or any other means of communicating the early exit poll results that day (November 7) outside of the quarantine room. The cost of collecting exit poll data had increased so much by 2012, in the face of methodological issues and changes in election administration, that NEP announced it would not be conducting polls in every state where there was an election for president or other statewide offices.

Another major change took place in 2020, when Fox News and the Associated Press began to work with National Opinion Research Center (NORC) to develop the *AP VoteCast* model for election projections. Utilizing a hybrid design described in detail in chapter 7, this is technically not an exit poll because they do not collect the data solely by in-person interviews with voters leaving their polling site. They employ mixed-mode data collection to gather large samples of mail, telephone, and web-based respondents, which they combine in a complex statistical model.

These technological and business trends have accelerated the production of polling data and their increased use in news making, and they highlight the problems that pollsters and news organizations have overcome. Several firms now offer software to enable individuals to design and field their own surveys, sometimes at no or low cost. The cost of entry into the polling field has dropped dramatically. There is no need to invest in a telephone facility or to hire sampling statisticians or questionnaire designers. Individuals with no formal training in survey methods or any prior experience in the field can organize these "do it yourself" polls at very low cost. They can be fielded without sampling expenses because they are posted on a website; consist of only a single question; and there is no possibility for analysis of the results by subgroups of respondents. Such polls partially explain why we have more polls than ever before, but they do not tell us what difference polls make or what impact they have on American political life. These are more subjective issues, and we do have views on them as we report in this book.

There is a growing body of literature, increasingly compelling in terms of the evidence mustered, that indicates that polls have a substantial impact on the American political process. Poll results have an impact on the vitality and viability of candidacies, affecting who can raise money, organize a field staff, and secure volunteers. News coverage containing poll results has an impact on assessments that citizens make of candidates and how, and even if, they decide to vote. And polls clearly have an effect on how campaigns are covered, as reporters, editors, and producers use this information to make decisions about who to cover and how to frame the coverage. As a result, the American Association for Public Opinion Research (AAPOR) partnered with the Poynter Center for Media Studies to develop an online web-based course for journalists covering elections since 2008, with an eye toward improving the reporting of public opinion. That course has now been extended to coverage of elections in other countries with different political systems, with the cooperation of the World Association for Public Opinion Research (WAPOR) and the World Association for Marketing, Social, and Opinion Research (ESOMAR).

Despite all these issues, we are not opposed to polls and polling; on the contrary, we see election polls in terms of their still largely unfulfilled potential. There is plenty of room for them to make a substantial contribution to levels of citizen knowledge and understanding of the political process, including the provision of information about how fellow citizens see the political world in terms of issues and how they respond to candidates and their campaigns.

Unfortunately, these possibilities go largely unrealized because too much campaign reporting is devoted solely to who is ahead and who is behind—a form of *horse race coverage* to which polls easily lend themselves. Polls are also used to support explanations of campaign strategy and dynamics, rather than focus on the issues that concern voters and their appreciation and understanding of what the candidates have to say about them.

Our hope is that if citizens understand more about how polls are conducted, analyzed, and reported in the media, they will be able to think about other ways in which such information would be useful to them. And on an informed basis, they will be able and want to exert pressure on news organizations to alter some elements of their coverage so they will be more responsive to the informational interests and needs of their readers and viewers.

THE ORGANIZATION OF THIS BOOK

We faced two fundamental issues in organizing this book: What information should we present? And how should we present it? On the first score, we used our extensive backgrounds in survey research, mass communication, and political science to select appropriate topics and organize them in a useful way. On the second score, we adopted a question-and-answer format for presenting the information because our dealings with students and other members of the public suggested that there was a thirst for more information about polls—where they come from, how they are used, and with what effect—that was most commonly expressed to us in question form.

On the matter of content, we have organized the book in ten chapters that highlight the major elements surrounding polls and polling in the United States: their history and adoption by news organizations; the basics of data collection techniques; typical analysis strategies; and, finally, keys to understanding and interpreting poll results based on a critical review of the sources of the data.

These are the main areas of interest and concern that people have expressed when we talk with them. The book begins with an introduction to polls and surveys that provides a broad overview of what they are and where they come from. This set of principles is extended to political polls, and the differences in polls conducted for candidates and media organizations. This first section ends with a general description of how news organizations collect and report election poll data.

In the next section, the four main elements of the design and analysis of polls are discussed. These include sampling procedures, the design of questionnaires, data collection procedures, and data analysis. These chapters cover such topics as scientific and unscientific procedures for selecting respondents, and what difference they make. Then the content turns to how individual questions are written and how they are assembled to form questionnaires. This is followed by a discussion of how data are gathered and the differences between interviewing people face-to-face, by telephone (including interactive voice response methods), or by using a self-administered questionnaire on the web or a printed version that is mailed back to the polling organization. Finally, different elements of analysis are described in a nontechnical way that highlights principles and does not involve the reader's knowledge of any detailed statistical concepts or procedures.

The book concludes with two chapters on evaluating polls and a discussion of common problems and complaints about polls, some of which have merit and others of which do not. Based on the concepts of good and bad practices covered in the preceding chapters, we offer the reader a guide to evaluating polls and poll-based content they might encounter. And we provide a framework for thinking about election polls and the contributions they might make to politics and to an informed citizenry.

Within each chapter, the information is presented in a question-and-answer format intended to simplify the presentation and interpretation of important points. In a certain sense, the formulation of these questions was the easiest part of our task. These are the questions that people always ask us, directly or indirectly, depending on their level of prior knowledge and their ability to formulate their interests and concerns in a particular way.

In some cases, the formulation of the answer to one question led to another question and the need to answer it. Each answer was prepared with a goal of keeping the length relatively short and the language as simple and direct as possible when dealing with a relatively technical subject. As a further aid to the reader, the glossary contains brief definitions of key concepts. And there are appendixes that contain the key provisions of the public disclosure statement of the main organization devoted to public opinion research in the United States, the American Association for Public Opinion Research (AAPOR). The reader will frequently find italicized words in the question answers, indicating that a definition of the term will be found in the glossary at the end of the book.

WHAT IS NEW IN THIS EDITION

The sixth edition has been completely reviewed and revised to account for the changes in the methodology of polls, new technologies, and changes in the US telecommunications environment that have occurred since the previous edition. The basic science that underlies polling methodology has not changed since the last version, but the pace of technological change in data collection methods advances rapidly. The new content about polling methods includes developments in survey sampling related to the pervasive cell phone–only population and the marked increase in the proportion of voters who vote "early" by using absentee ballots, voting at early voting public places like malls or libraries, or where an entire state like Oregon votes only by mail. There is additional discussion of the accelerated decline in survey response rates among the American public and the ways that technologies such as caller identification, call screening, and voice mail and answering machines contribute to that. The use of the internet to collect data has raised new questions about the role of probability sampling, especially in the face of declining response rates overall. The rise of mixed-mode sampling and recruitment designs involving self-administered questionnaires deployed on the internet has created a change from using the term for people "being interviewed" to "from whom data are gathered" throughout the text.

There are a number of new telecommunications technologies for which pollsters have to account, especially the rise of people giving up their landline telephones in favor of becoming cell phone–only or –mainly households. New telephone number portability regulations permit people to keep their telephone number even when they move out of the area code where the number was originally issued. These trends are especially important to polling; for example, the current regulatory environment in the United States does not permit unsolicited calls to cell phones in part because the user could have to pay charges for them. When combined with the advent of Do Not Call Lists, these developments have resulted in a significant change in the relative cost and efficiency advantages of telephone surveys and prompted the need for more costly mixed-mode research designs that may require some face-to-face interviewing, interviewing on landlines, or use of self-administered web interviews. The FCC continues to consider more stringent regulation of survey research conducted on the telephone.

Pre-election polling is also becoming more complicated because the number of Americans voting before the traditional Election Day is growing through the use of new administrative procedures like voting by mail, early voting, and being able to register as a permanent absentee voter and have a ballot delivered to your home. This has also required hybrid sampling designs to estimate election outcomes that combine exit poll interviewing and pre-election phone surveys with early voters, as well as supplemental Election Day interviews on the phone or internet.

The closeness of the 2000 election and the use of electoral maps on network coverage that used high-impact graphics like red states representing Republican presidential victories and blue states to represent Democratic states has also altered the way late campaign polls are conducted. In the 2004 election there was much less emphasis on national tracking polls and greater utilization of statewide polls conducted in the "battleground states," those that are most competitive. This was accompanied by an overall change in patterns of election coverage that focused on the contest in those states more than on the national popular vote. This trend continued through the 2020 presidential election and into key statewide races in the 2022 midterm elections.

CONCLUDING COMMENTS

Any project of this scope requires assistance from a number of people. We discussed the concept with several of our colleagues, and we received useful feedback for the first edition from Eleanor Singer and Warren Mitofsky, a visitor in Ann Arbor in fall 1995. Santa Traugott was a careful reader and editor of early versions. We would like to thank Dan M. Merkle at ABC News for the helpful information he provided to us about the 2020, 2022, and 2024 national and state polls and early voter surveys that were (or will be) conducted by Edison Media Research for the media-funded National Election Pool. We'd also like to thank David Sterrett and Trevor N. Tompson for the helpful information they provided to us about AP VoteCast, a multi-method methodology deployed by NORC at the University of Chicago that used the latest advances in social science research methods to reach and understand voters of every political ideology during the 2020 and 2022 elections. Any errors or problems that remain are, of course, our own responsibility. We are also grateful to Michael Kerns, our editor, and Elizabeth Von Buhr for her work during the editorial process that resulted in the final book.

Chapter 1

What Are Polls and Surveys and Why Are They Conducted?

A *poll* or a *survey* is a method of collecting information from people by asking them questions. Most polls involve a standardized *questionnaire*, and they usually collect the information from a *sample* of people rather than the entire *population*. People with different interests conduct polls and surveys for many different reasons. Sometimes callers even fake polls on the telephone as a way to sell people some product or to raise money for a particular cause.

Candidates use polls as an essential part of the intelligence-gathering operation of their campaign. Polls provide a candidate with information about what the voters are thinking and how they are inclined to vote. Many candidates also use poll results to stimulate contributions to their campaigns or to dissuade people from contributing to another candidate.

Media organizations conduct polls to collect information for use in news stories and to form judgments about what kinds of news coverage to provide. A substantial portion of the news derived from polls involves reporting who is ahead and who is behind, and by how much. At the end of the campaign, media organizations use polls to project the winner of the race.

Political scientists and other researchers interested in the dynamics of campaigns and elections use polls to learn about how the candidates behave and how voters respond to campaign stimuli. They try to explain why voters react to candidates in certain ways, but they are usually not interested in projecting the winner of a race.

WHAT IS A SURVEY?

A survey is a data collection technique that involves a questionnaire administered to a set of individuals usually sampled from a larger population. The questionnaire consists of multiple items, or questions, ranging from just a few that take only minutes to complete to several hundred that could take more than an hour to complete. The questionnaire can be administered by an *interviewer* in a face-to-face setting, on the telephone, via a web video call, in the mail, via the internet, or by handing it to a respondent to fill out.

Questionnaires can include items on a wide variety of topics. The questions can measure behavior (*Did you vote for president in 2020?*), opinions or attitudes (*Do you approve or disapprove of the way Joe Biden is handling his job as president?*), or the personal characteristics of the respondents (*Generally speaking, do you usually think of yourself as a Republican, a Democrat, an Independent, or what?*).

The group of individuals interviewed almost always consists of a sample selected from a larger population. In order to use the sample to make inferences back to the population with confidence, the respondents in the sample must be selected in a scientific way using a probability selection method.

HOW DOES A POLL DIFFER FROM A SURVEY?

In principle, a poll and a survey are the same thing. The term poll is usually applied to shorter surveys done by commercial organizations, including media organizations. A poll typically involves a questionnaire containing relatively few questions, and it is conducted across a brief interviewing period (often just a few days). The *sample size* of a poll usually ranges from 600 to 1,500 respondents.

Academic and government researchers more typically conduct surveys. They usually involve much longer questionnaires, and they sometimes involve much larger sample sizes, numbering up to the tens of thousands of respondents in the case of some government surveys. The interviewing period is often much longer, ranging from several weeks to a few months.

The term "poll" comes from the usage meaning to ascertain preferences. This is the same use as "polling place," referring to the location where people go to indicate their preferences by casting their votes traditionally on Election Day.

HOW MANY DIFFERENT KINDS OF SURVEYS ARE THERE?

Depending on the classification criteria, there are several kinds of surveys. One way to classify surveys is by the technique (*mode*) used to gather the data. During the past three decades, most pre-election polls have been conducted by interviewers on the telephone, but studies (including exit polls) are conducted in-person using *self-administered* questionnaires. Face-to-face interviews, which are the most expensive to conduct, are usually limited to academic and government research projects. Starting in the late 1990s, many polling firms began to use the internet to collect self-administered questionnaire data about candidate preferences. According to a recent *AAPOR* report (2022), there are six American probability-based online panels that also conduct some pre-election studies.[1] But there are many more nonprobability-based online panels that use the internet to gather data, but most sample and recruit their panel members in unscientific means. These online polls present special challenges for data collection, discussed in detail in chapter 10. In the past two decades there has also been a growth in the use of *Interactive Voice Response* (*IVR*) procedures to conduct pre-election polls. The IVR approach also can present special data quality problems, as discussed in chapter 7.

Another way to classify surveys is according to their sampling design, especially in the way that they can be used to measure change. It is common to talk about *cross-sectional surveys* (surveys conducted at one point in time), *longitudinal studies* (surveys conducted at different times in which at least the same questions are asked repeatedly), and *panel studies* (surveys conducted at different times in which the same people are interviewed repeatedly).

In a cross-sectional survey, a single sample of respondents is interviewed once and asked a set of questions. All by themselves, cross-sectional surveys do not measure change. Most polls reported in the media involve this kind of survey design.

In a longitudinal design, the same questions or entire questionnaire is administered more than once to a series of independent samples usually consisting of new respondents each time. The estimates produced by each survey are compared to measure gross levels of change in a population. News organizations that invest heavily in pre-election polling utilize these types of surveys, for example, to create trend lines showing aggregate responses to the same question over time. Change here is only assessed at the macro or aggregate level, and changes in different directions within the electorate could cancel each other out, resulting in no net difference. For example, a longitudinal design would allow a news organization to conclude that Candidate A, compared to Candidate B, is now preferred by 5 percentage points more voters than she was a month ago.

In a panel design, the same respondents are interviewed at more than one point in time, and they are usually asked at least some of the same questions each time. Through a panel design, a *pollster* can measure change at the individual or micro level by comparing each respondent's answers to the same question at each point in time. This produces a different (i.e., more precise, detailed, and certain) measure of change than a longitudinal design does, and it allows the pollster to assess how many people may have changed in one direction over time versus how many may have changed in another direction. For example, a panel design would allow a news organization to conclude that Candidate A is now preferred by 10 percent of the voters who previously preferred Candidate B, whereas Candidate B is now preferred by 5 percent of the voters who previously preferred Candidate A—for a net gain of 5 percentage points for Candidate A. Panel designs are not often used by the news media during elections due to special challenges (including costs) involved in re-interviewing the same people repeatedly.

HOW WELL DO POLLS MEASURE PUBLIC OPINION?

Public opinion is a difficult concept to define and has no standard definition. But most people who study public opinion agree that it is an aggregation of the opinions that individuals hold. One of its significant features is that it can be shared through the dissemination of information about what others are thinking.

Differences exist, however, among scholars and others who study public opinion regarding how it can and should be assessed. A small minority of those who study public opinion do not believe that polls and surveys can truly measure public opinion.[2] These people believe that these quantitative techniques only assess what they call "measured opinion" and that true public opinion cannot be captured well by polls and surveys. They believe that it is the "artificiality" of the environment in which survey data are generated (either in *interviewer-assisted* interviewing or through self-administered questions) that makes it impossible for such data to reflect the true opinions of the collective public, which they believe are best measured in settings that promote open discourse among groups of the public. In contrast, most scholars and others interested in public opinion believe that well-conceived and well-executed quantitative polls and surveys can, and do, assess "public opinion" with considerable accuracy.

We believe that polls provide an ideal mechanism for measuring public opinion in a reliable and valid way, if appropriate scientific methods are employed. Such polls have to use *probability samples* so that the measured opinions reflect those in the general population. The questions used must be unbiased, and high-quality recruitment and data collection procedures must be followed to ensure high *response rates* and a faithful recording of the answers. When all of these procedures are used, we believe that polls can give a very accurate measurement of public opinion.

ARE THERE OTHER WAYS TO OBTAIN PEOPLE'S OPINIONS?

People express their opinions in a variety of ways: through demonstrations and picketing, the kinds and amounts of products they buy and display, their membership in specific organizations, or the size of the checks they write to political candidates and special-interest groups. Sales, demonstrations, and memberships are only imperfect indicators of underlying opinions; they do not tell researchers about things like how intensely people hold their opinions or the reasons why they feel the way they do. In contemporary society, some firms are trying to develop ways to use social media communication like Facebook pages or tweets to estimate public opinion. But, none of these methods by themselves are reliable or valid indicators of how many people in the population as a whole might hold the same opinions.

The only way to measure opinions in a reliable and valid way is to combine a scientifically drawn and executed responding sample and a well-designed and well-administered questionnaire. Information collected in this way is used to draw inferences to the distribution of opinion in the entire population and to generalize the results from the sample to the population from which it was drawn. A probability sample provides the way that inferences can be made back to the population with a known degree of confidence. The questions are used to assess what opinions the public holds, on what basis and with what intensity.

WHEN IS A "SURVEY" NOT A SURVEY?

A scientific poll or survey is used to collect information for aggregated statistical purposes. The data are combined for analysis without concern about who individual respondents are or what their answers to the questions were.

A survey is not a legitimate survey when it is used to collect information about individuals for some other purpose than research. For example, some things are called surveys that are really just the compilation of statistics into an index. These appear as surveys of college quality, business climates, or best places to live. In the former case, they involve compiling information on admission rates, test scores, and the cost of tuition in order to rank schools. In the second case, they might involve assessment of skill levels in the workforce, tax rates, the cost of utilities, and the like. In the third case, they compile information on the weather, cost of living, and housing prices. In none of these cases is any sample drawn nor in many cases are data gathered from anyone. In either case, these numbers are combined in some fashion to produce rankings from best to worst.

There are other forms of *pseudo polls*. Sometimes you might receive a solicitation in the mail that contains a questionnaire, often asking a few leading questions and then asking you to join an organization or write a check as part of a fund-raising drive. These activities are known as *SUGing* (Soliciting Under the Guise of survey research) and *FRUGing* (Fund-Raising Under the Guise of survey research). These forms of pseudo polls are discussed in greater detail in chapter 3. Typically, the questionnaires that are completed and returned are never tabulated; but the names and addresses of the individuals who returned them are kept on a list and sometimes even sold to other organizations. The purpose of the mailing was to solicit new members or raise money, not to collect data to be analyzed.

In another case, opinions are solicited through questionnaires placed in newspapers or magazines, by conducting an *800 poll* or *900 poll* by providing a number for people to call, or by providing an e-mail or website address to post comments. These data are usually tabulated and presented as news, but they should not be considered legitimate surveys because they do not involve *scientific samples*. The respondents are *self-selected* and unrepresentative of the population as a whole in several ways. These issues are discussed in detail in chapter 10.

Finally, there are results from statistical modeling that are sometimes called surveys, even though they do not involve any original data collection. These models can be very useful and accurate for many purposes, but they always involve a set of assumptions that relate to how the input data are treated. These assumptions have to be made explicit in order to evaluate the models that produce the estimates, but this is rarely done.

WHY NOT JUST COUNT EVERYONE?

An enumeration, or *census*, of everyone in the population may sometimes be an alternative to a survey, but in the vast majority of cases it will not be as effective as a good survey in producing reliable estimates. A census is usually much more expensive to conduct, and it may be too time-consuming to complete if the population is very large. So, surveys often provide a cost-effective alternative to censuses.

Many people have the impression that a census is more comprehensive than a survey because information is collected from more people. Every enumeration has problems of *coverage*, however, just as surveys do. For example, the decennial census conducted by the US government has consistently undercounted the population, for example, by disproportionally missing minorities, and this is a cause for concern because the undercount is not *random*.

The census is more likely to miss homeless people, those who are very mobile, and individuals of lower socioeconomic status than other citizens. Researchers at the Bureau of the Census recommended adjustment procedures to correct for the undercount in the decennial census, but Congress resisted using such procedures. In 1999, the issue was resolved against using adjustment by the US Supreme Court. But the bureau has begun to use large sample surveys, such as the American Community Survey (ACS), which began in 2005 and collects economic, social, and housing information monthly, rather than merely every ten years, to produce intercensal estimates of the population and its characteristics. The quality of the ACS is currently threatened by continued budget cuts and congressional attempts to make participation voluntary.

Furthermore, if a population is very large, it may take a long time to collect all the data by counting everyone. When a sample is used, information can be collected much more quickly. This is an important consideration if the information is time sensitive, like attitudes toward a new candidate entering the race or reactions to a speech that the president just gave.

WHY IS TIME SUCH AN IMPORTANT FACTOR IN POLLS CONDUCTED FOR MEDIA?

Time is a critical component in *media polls* because the newsworthiness of the information collected is related in part to how quickly it can be collected and reported. There is always the risk that new events in the real world can invalidate poll results.

When candidates participate in a debate, a poll is conducted very shortly afterward to measure the electorate's perceptions of the candidates and to find out what the voters learned. But the information has to be reported quickly before one of the candidates makes a major policy speech or begins a new advertising campaign, either of which can change the way that many voters evaluate the candidates. So, some news organizations conduct a poll that same night and report the results within hours of the debate.

Survey research is a dynamic field of study with continuous research into how methods can be improved. In a period of declining response rates, there are a number of ways that they could be improved. However, most would involve longer *field periods*, and media organizations are not willing to consider them because they are expensive, and it would take more time to collect the data and what is learned may well no longer be newsworthy.

WHO SPONSORS SURVEYS?

Many different individuals and groups sponsor surveys, and people often use sponsorship to make an initial assessment of how much confidence they should have in the results. If the government or an academic organization sponsors a survey, consumers of the data are inclined to believe that the data are neutral and unbiased. This is also generally true for polls sponsored by media organizations.

Poll consumers should be more sensitive to the strategic interests of candidates or special-interest groups who sponsor polls. They should pay careful attention to what kinds of questions they ask or the way in which they report their results in order to evaluate whether any *bias* might be present.

WHO CONDUCTS POLLS?

Polls can be conducted by the same organizations that sponsor them, or the data collection—and even the analysis—can be done under contract. Some polling organizations offer a full range of data collection services, including designing samples and questionnaires; providing data collection services, data entry, and statistical analysis; and writing reports. Some firms specialize in just one aspect of surveys, such as sampling or interviewing. Some research projects may involve subcontracting various services to different companies, but the use of computer networks and high-speed data transmission means that the project managers are never very far from their data.

DO POLLS HAVE AN IMPACT ON THOSE WHO ARE EXPOSED TO THEM?

Polls do have an effect on those who see or hear the results. Sometimes these effects are direct, as people change or adjust their attitudes and opinions based on what they think other people believe. Other times, these effects are indirect, arising because candidates with a low standing in the polls cannot raise enough money to stay in a race, for example, and therefore voters never have a chance to give them serious consideration. The impact of polls on poll consumers is considered in virtually every chapter in this book, and special attention is devoted to this topic in chapters 9 and 10.

NOTES

1. These organizations are Gallup/The Gallup Poll; IPSOS/Knowledge Panel; NORC/America Speak; Pew Research/American Trends Panel; SSRS/Opinion Panel; and University of Southern California/Understanding America Study.

2. Susan Herbst, *Numbered Voices: How Opinion Polling Has Shaped American Politics* (Chicago: University of Chicago Press, 1993).

Chapter 2

What Are Election Polls? How Are They Conducted?

For many citizens, the basic concepts of polling are a mystery. Actually, most polls involve only a limited number of techniques. Election polls are just a special use of survey research techniques, employing procedures developed and refined over most of the twentieth century.

Polls begin with the selection of a sample of people from whom data will be gathered if they agree to cooperate with the pollster. The people who provide data are called the *respondents*. They must be selected in a scientific way if they are to reflect accurately the population they are supposed to represent. In that case, their attitudes and opinions will help to reflect those of the entire population. The respondents are asked a series of questions in a standardized form, called a questionnaire. One common form of polling is conducted on the telephone, although sometimes interviews are conducted face-to-face in people's homes or as they leave their balloting place. In the late 1990s, some researchers began to gather data on the internet, and this trend has grown considerably because of lower costs associated with this mode of data collection and the speed with which data can be gathered. For representativeness, there is a difference between probability-based online panels and nonprobability panels, discussed in detail in chapter 7. The answers to the survey questions are tabulated using computers, and the results are presented in a variety of ways.

An election poll is a survey conducted on topics related to the campaign or conducted during the main campaign period. Some election polls are conducted for candidates to help them develop strategy, organize their campaign, and raise funds. Some are conducted by or for interest groups that have a particular policy or piece of legislation that they support or want to promote. Others are conducted for media organizations to help them produce news stories. Still others are conducted for and by political scientists or other social researchers to understand how campaigns work and to explain the impact of events and news coverage of them on the voters.

The content of election polls is obviously related to politics—asking respondents about the candidates and issues in the campaign. Most election polls are conducted during the campaign period leading up to Election Day; they are called *pre-election polls*. Some polls are conducted on Election Day with voters who are leaving the places where they cast their ballots; these are called *exit polls*. The two kinds of polls share many common characteristics, and each has some unique ones. These similarities and differences are discussed in detail in the answers to the commonly asked questions that follow.

WHAT IS AN ELECTION POLL?

The term election poll refers to a variety of survey types. Some are conducted for media organizations and are designed to provide content for the news. They are different from market research studies used to understand audience characteristics or to indicate what readers or viewers think about the news coverage of the campaign, for example.

Political consultants conduct another kind of election poll. They do these studies for candidates to provide strategic information or feedback to the campaign about alternative strategies to pursue or how successful their strategy has been. Both kinds of election polls are distinct from election surveys conducted by university-based researchers for analysis of the attitudes and behavior of the electorate. Some election polls are conducted early in the campaign when members of the electorate have little information about who the candidates are or what their issue stands are. Other election polls are conducted late in the campaign, just before Election Day, to provide estimates or projections of the outcome of the election. And still other election polls are conducted on Election Day itself, among voters leaving their balloting places, to provide projections of results and analysis of voting trends for the news media.

Campaign or candidate polls employ different questions asked of different samples. Sometimes the candidate wants to know about voter reaction to hypothetical scenarios in the campaign. Sometimes campaign polls are conducted only among people who describe themselves as *"undecided"* about their *candidate preference*. At other times, candidates sponsor polls to demonstrate their popular support so that they can increase their fund-raising, especially in the primaries. Campaign polls usually have very short data collection periods, sometimes involving only one or two days.

University-based surveys of the electorate usually have the lengthiest questionnaires, sometimes involving interviews that take an hour or more.

Their samples may be larger, and the field periods may extend across several weeks. In many cases these surveys are conducted after the election. They provide information for detailed analysis of the electorate but not much content that is immediately newsworthy because they are not timely. But they often provide trend data on partisanship or group voting behavior over time that appears in the news.

HOW MANY KINDS OF ELECTION POLLS ARE THERE?

There are several distinct kinds of election polls. They differ in their purpose, their methodologies, and their timing. Polls are used to assess the voters' issue positions and their knowledge about the candidates. The relative standing of the candidates is evaluated through trial heats. These polls are usually conducted with samples of adults eighteen years of age or older or samples of registered voters.

As Election Day approaches, the samples employed in election polls switch to *likely voters*, that is, those who are most likely to go to vote on Election Day—an important distinction because only slightly more than half of the eligible adults in the United States actually vote in a presidential election, and even fewer in a less salient election. Some media organizations conduct interviews every day within a certain time period with smaller samples of such voters each day and then aggregate the data for several successive days into a larger dataset. These *tracking polls* focus on who is ahead and behind and how these preferences change across relatively brief periods of time in response to campaign events. Prior to 2010, most pre-election and tracking polls were usually conducted on the telephone, although since then most are conducted via the internet.

On Election Day itself, interviewers distribute self-administered questionnaires to voters leaving the balloting locations in their neighborhoods in scientifically selected samples of precincts. These exit polls, consisting of questions that appear on both sides of a single page of paper, are analyzed to produce estimates by early evening of who is going to win each race; they also provide data for post-election analysis of the factors that led voters to support one candidate over another.

HOW HAVE EXIT POLLS CHANGED?

The earliest exit polls, conducted in the 1970s when almost all voting was in person, consisted of paper and pencil interviews administered by interviewers standing outside of sampled polling precincts. However, in the

2020 presidential election contest, almost 60 percent of votes were cast early or by absentee. A partial explanation for this was the COVID pandemic, although legislative attempts to make voting more convenient was a factor as well. Under this behavioral change, exit-polling methods changed as well. Initially the in-person samples were supplemented by telephone samples conducted in the weeks before Election Day. Currently, the use of internet interviews is another supplemental form of data collection. These procedures are discussed in detail in chapter 7.

HOW DO MEDIA ORGANIZATIONS USE ELECTION POLLS?

News organizations use pre-election polls to explore the important issues in the campaign and to explain the dynamics of the campaign and how popular support for the candidates crystallizes or shifts as Election Day approaches. In these ways, pre-election polls provide substantial content for pre-election news coverage. While the range of analytical possibilities is great, most poll-based reporting focuses on who is ahead or behind. Such poll results support the media's natural tendency to engage in *horse race journalism*, which focuses on the relative standing of the candidates and how it changes across the campaign. Both print and broadcast media use these kinds of polls, especially as Election Day approaches.

Exit polls are used to project the outcome of races on election night and to help explain patterns of group voting. Since this is a story best suited to broadcast coverage, television networks and radio stations are most likely to make immediate use of these results, as well as websites for news organizations; these projections and analyses also appear on media websites and blogs on election night. Newspapers also pick up these results to support analysis explaining the meaning of the election. This analysis appears first on their website and then in the newspaper a day or two after the election.

ARE CURRENT PRE-ELECTION POLLS BETTER THAN THOSE CONDUCTED IN THE PAST?

If the meaning of "better" is the application of improved technology and methodology, then the answer is clearly "Yes." Pollsters have learned a lot about sampling, questionnaire design, and data analysis in their ninety years of public polling. There have been periodic crises in public polling, and methodology has improved after each one. The record of the national polls remains strong, but some issues have arisen with some state poll estimates. And in the past decade, a move to estimate Electoral College vote totals based upon state outcomes has complicated public perceptions of the accuracy of the polls.

In 1936, George Gallup got his start in the public polling business by challenging the leading measure of electoral preference of the time, a poll conducted by the magazine *The Literary Digest*. It had been doing its work with a very large *mail survey* sent to telephone subscribers and automobile owners, a highly unrepresentative group of individuals during the Depression of the 1930s. Their survey also had a very low response rate in terms of returned questionnaires. The Republican candidate, Alfred Landon, was projected to be the winner over the incumbent president, Franklin D. Roosevelt, in *The Literary Digest* poll, based on upwards of two million respondents. However, Dr. Gallup applied systematic quota sampling methods to his national survey, using a much smaller sample size of approximately two thousand to make an accurate prediction of Roosevelt as the winner.

In 1948, the public pollsters predicted that Thomas E. Dewey would beat Harry S. Truman, but Truman won handily. A review of the public polls after the election suggested two problems: the use of *quota samples* in which interviewers selected respondents and interviewing that stopped too soon before Election Day. Quota sampling persisted because of its lower costs relative to face-to-face interviews with a probability sample of respondents until the advent of telephone interviewing, but its accuracy was highly dependent on the pollster knowing precise information about the demographic distribution of the voting public.[1] And pollsters began to interview closer to Election Day.

But in 1980, many pollsters underestimated Ronald Reagan's margin over the incumbent president, Jimmy Carter, that apparently came from a very late shift over the last weekend of the campaign after the only presidential debate. In current campaigns, pollsters interview at least through Sunday for their final pre-election polls, and the telephone and internet allow them to gather data even through the Monday before Election Day if they believe the election will be extremely close.

Overall, the accuracy of the national pre-election polls has improved across the last eighty years, but in the last several years there were estimation errors in pre-election polls in several countries around the world and in different kinds of elections. In the United States, there was a problem with the estimates of candidate support in the early 2008 presidential primaries, and there have been issues with accuracy in state-level polls since 2016. But in 2016 and 2020, the national polls were accurate in predicting that Clinton and Biden, respectively, would win the popular vote. Nonetheless, there is no doubt that pre-election polling has become more difficult, for a variety of reasons. They are discussed in greater detail in chapter 4.

ARE THERE SPECIAL PROBLEMS IN CONDUCTING PRE-ELECTION POLLS?

Modern election polls confront four critical problems, although they are more significant for media organizations and candidates, whose work is almost entirely done before Election Day, than they are for social scientists, who often do most of their analysis after the election is over. One is generating a good estimate of who is going to vote. The electorate does not exist until people cast their ballots, so pollsters must estimate the *probable electorate* before it forms. A second is capturing the *volatility* that sometimes appears in the electorate. A third is allocating the preferences of those who say they are "undecided" when they are asked for whom they will vote. Finally, an increasing number of voters are casting their ballots earlier and in other ways than at a polling place on the traditional Election Day, and their preferences must be accounted for in making estimates of the outcome of the election.

In many countries, voting is a two-step process. First you must get registered as a potential voter, and then you must get a ballot and cast it. In most democracies, far less than all the registered voters do vote, so the *likely voters* must be estimated as a first step. Whereas there is a strong scientific and statistical basis for drawing samples and constructing questionnaires, estimating who will go to vote on Election Day is an area where the practitioner's art comes into play. There is no standard, widely accepted way for estimating a person's *likelihood of voting*. Most polling organizations combine the answers to several questions to estimate the likely electorate, and some methods work better than others. When polling organizations experiment with new likely voter estimation techniques, their estimates of candidate support can become more volatile. This happened with the Gallup Poll in the 2000 campaign. And, for example, in the 2013 presidential election in Chile, the country switched from a system of voluntary registration and mandatory voting to one where registration was mandatory and voting was voluntary. Turnout fell substantially, and the Chilean pre-election polls underestimated the winning candidate's margin of victory because the old turnout models did not work.

Identifying those who have already voted and those who have not voted yet but will before Election Day is a problem of growing importance to US pollsters, as more and more of the electorate is choosing to vote early. People can do this by requesting an absentee ballot and mailing it in or delivering it personally, or by going to an *early voting* location to cast a vote on a machine. In the case of some locales, a ballot is mailed to the entire roll of registered voters that they can return, as in Oregon, Colorado, and large portions of the state of Washington. This trend will likely continue as the population ages and more citizens who want to vote try to avoid the demands of standing in line to vote at their local polling place on Election Day. In the 2020 election forty-six states and territories had a provision for early voting. In surveying those who already have voted, it is ideal to use a *secret ballot* approach, such as that used by exit polls on Election Day. But in pre-election polling, early voters are generally surveyed via telephone; this precludes the use of this technique that helps avoid having the respondent report out loud to an interviewer which candidate he or she has already voted for. This is not an issue for information collected by self-administered internet surveys.

It is also important to conduct polls as close to Election Day as possible. Recent presidential elections have been decided by smaller margins, and polls show that growing proportions of the electorate are making up their minds about whom to vote for later in the campaign. Current campaign technology allows candidates to organize and target their advertising campaigns to undecided voters right up to Election Day. The use of telephone interviewing and internet data collection techniques helps pollsters to collect and analyze data closer to Election Day. Data collection now typically takes place at least through the weekend preceding Election Day and sometimes right through the Monday night before if the race is very close.

As mentioned, in the past thirty years, very important changes have taken place in how and when Americans vote, thus complicating pre-election polling. Some states will allow people to vote at various locations for up to three weeks before Election Day, and twenty-two states and the District of Columbia now allow people to register on Election Day itself. Some states are also using *vote-by-mail* procedures, as Oregon first did in 1996 to elect a US senator to replace Bob Packwood. In that same year, the voters of Oregon overwhelmingly passed an initiative to hold all their state elections that way. Now Colorado and Washington are conducting all their elections by mail. Other states have eased the process by which registered voters can request an absentee ballot, even allowing citizens to receive one automatically at every election; thirty-six states now provide "no excuse" absentee ballots. And in some places, voting booths are set up at malls and libraries so citizens can vote at their leisure up to four weeks in advance of Election Day. It is estimated that about one-third of all the votes cast in the 2008 presidential election were cast using one of these early voting procedures, including absentee ballots, and almost two in five votes in the 2012 presidential election were cast "early." By 2020, this proportion increased to 60 percent.

These procedures require that pollsters use new techniques for estimating turnout and the partisan division of the vote, and they are likely to produce some problems for pollsters when they project the outcome of races involving these new procedures, until the new polling techniques are perfected and the public gets used to the new procedures. In early voting states, for example, pollsters are routinely conducting telephone and *internet polls* with early voters or those who might vote early to supplement exit polls on Election Day.

WHAT IS THE APPROPRIATE POPULATION TO SAMPLE FOR PRE-ELECTION POLLS?

Since registration is a minimum requirement for voting, samples for pre-election polls should, in principle, account for this condition. Unfortunately, in most jurisdictions there is no list of registered voters that is both accurate and up-to-date and contains telephone numbers or e-mail addresses. So most pre-election polls usually begin with a sample of *telephone households* and then screen respondents within those households to find out whether they are registered. Survey panels are used to sample those who report being registered to vote. Starting in the 2000 election, some experiments were conducted with samples based upon lists of registered voters, also known as *Registration-Based Sampling (RBS)*, but they did not produce more accurate or less costly estimates of election outcomes than standard sampling techniques; as a result, they have not been widely adopted. More details of sampling procedures are covered in chapter 5.

HOW DO POLLS MEASURE VOTING INTENTION?

Voting intention is a concept that incorporates two different measures. The first is an indication of how likely a person is to go to vote on Election Day, and the second is an indication of which candidate someone prefers; voting intention is a combination of candidate preference and likelihood of voting for that person.

The first concept is usually measured by a *trial-heat question* in the following form:

If the primary election for the Republican presidential nomination were held today, and the names appearing on the ballot were Chris Christie, Ron DeSantis, Nikki Haley, Asa Hutchinson, Mike Pence, Tim Scott, Donald Trump, and Vivek Ramaswamy, whom would you vote for?

Respondents can indicate which candidate they prefer, that they have not decided yet, or that they do not intend to vote. The results from this question are usually reported for all these categories.

The likelihood of voting is usually measured by evaluating the responses to a series of questions. As noted earlier, a minimum condition for voting in the United States is that you are registered, so this item is common to all likelihood scales. Other important components of likelihood include the respondents' interest in the current campaign, their history of voting in similar elections in the past, and their knowledge about where people in their neighborhood go to vote.

By combining measures of preference and likelihood, pollsters can produce an estimate of the outcome based on a formulation of the probable electorate. They can also evaluate whether turnout will have an impact on the outcome—the effects of lower or higher turnout than expected on the distribution of candidate support.

HOW DO POLLS MEASURE CANDIDATE SUPPORT?

Candidate support is measured through a trial-heat question, as described earlier. In many surveys, this question is often asked in two parts. First, people are asked for whom they are going to vote. Those who express an initial preference for one candidate or another (the *core voters*) are then asked how strongly they feel about that choice. Those who say they are undecided are then asked toward whom they are leaning.

The strength of support can be analyzed in several ways. One way is to look at each candidate's "committed" support (those who support him or her strongly), as well as the ratio between these two groups. Another way is to look at the *leaners* and how they divide among the candidates. In either case, it is important for the pollster to indicate to the poll's consumers which base of support is being analyzed and what the differences are.

A strong commitment to a candidate is also a good indicator of intention to vote. So, the strong supporters form the core or base electorate. An analyst can investigate the potential impact of turnout on the election by adding in the leaners and seeing whether the distribution of preferences is different from that of the core voters.

WHAT HAPPENS TO PEOPLE WHO HAVE NOT DECIDED YET?

Every time the trial-heat question is asked in a pre-election poll, a significant proportion of respondents say they are undecided or refuse to say who their preferred candidate is. The proportion of undecideds declines as Election Day approaches and voters get to know the candidates better. Some interviewing techniques can reduce the number of undecideds by allowing people in face-to-face interviews to complete a secret ballot.

There are different ways to report data for the undecideds. Some organizations report the undecideds as a distinct category; other organizations produce estimates of voter preferences based on the percentage of those who named a candidate or party, omitting the undecideds. In the first case, an organization might say that 44 percent of the sample expressed a preference for Donald Trump, 49 percent for Joe Biden, and 7 percent were undecided. If the data were recalculated based on only those who stated a preference (93 percent of the sample), another organization would produce a preference for Biden over Trump of 53 percent to 47 percent.

Many polling organizations use an allocation method to assign the undecideds to one candidate or the other. Different polling organizations allocate the undecideds in different ways. One way is to divide them equally between the two candidates or in proportion to the division of support among those who have already made up their minds. Another way is to allocate them according to party identification, based on the belief that this is the best indicator of how an undecided respondent will vote—an undecided Democrat will eventually vote for the Democratic candidate, for example. In the 1980s and 1990s, party identification had become a weaker predictor of presidential vote, but its importance has increased since then. As a result, this method is of uncertain reliability compared to the past. One theory even suggests the undecideds should be allocated disproportionately to the challenger, in part because they represent people who are reluctant to tell an interviewer that they will vote against an incumbent!

These allocation schemes can make a big difference in the final estimates of an election's outcome. In the 1992 election, the Gallup Organization changed its allocation method; as a result, it severely overestimated support for George H. W. Bush and underestimated support for Bill Clinton. There was a much larger error in the final estimate than Gallup had experienced in the past. In the 1996 election, the problem was in the opposite direction. Clinton's margin over Bob Dole was overestimated by some pollsters after the undecideds were allocated and turnout was considered. And in the 2000 election, although most polls indicated a very tight race, the vast majority showed George W. Bush ahead in the popular vote, although Al Gore actually captured a slight majority. For the 2004 election, spurred by the closeness of the previous election, the major polling firms polled later in the campaign and with increased attention to methodology; and these estimates were some of the most accurate in the modern polling period.

WHAT ARE TRACKING POLLS?

Toward the end of the campaign, some well-funded candidates and news organizations sponsor *tracking polls* to keep a daily record of who is ahead and who is behind. This tracking of the lead complements the preoccupation with horse race journalism that many news organizations have with reporting who is ahead and who is behind. For the financially secure candidate, daily tracking polls are especially useful if the election is close and the strategy fluid.

Tracking polls use different methodological techniques to produce daily estimates for the last two to four weeks of the campaign. For example, smaller samples of respondents can be contacted via telephone or the internet every day and asked a very brief series of questions. On their own, these daily samples of 100 to 300 interviews are too small to provide precise estimates of candidate support or one candidate's lead over the other. Therefore, pollsters use *rolling averages* of three consecutive days' worth of interviewing to produce these estimates. So, interviews conducted on a Monday in October contribute to the production of estimates for three-day periods that cover Saturday–Sunday–Monday, Sunday–Monday–Tuesday, and Monday–Tuesday–Wednesday.

If, for example, each of these estimates was based on 300 interviews per day, then findings would be reported on a combined sample of 900 interviews, aggregated across each of these three-day periods. If candidate A were supported by 49 percent of the sample on Saturday (based on 300 interviews), 45 percent of the sample on Sunday (based on another 300 interviews), and 47 percent of the sample on Monday (based on another 300 interviews), the average support for this period, reported on Tuesday, would be 47 percent (based on a total of 900 interviews).

Candidates also use tracking polls to assess how well their campaign is doing. But these results rarely become public because the campaigns are not interested in divulging this information and they may only collect this data in selected areas where the competition is intense rather than in an entire state or constituency.

ARE THERE SPECIAL PROBLEMS IN CONDUCTING TRACKING POLLS?

Yes, there are, because of the nature of the small daily samples and the way interviews are obtained. Tracking polls are essentially one-night surveys, so they do not employ the same rigorous procedures for sampling and respondent selection that many other polls do. Since interviews are conducted on a single day, typically in the evening, there are rarely any attempts made to *recontact* a household where no one responded to the first *contact attempt*. Furthermore, some polling organizations are less rigorous when they do make contact; instead of selecting a respondent randomly within the household, they may take an interview with anyone in the household. Both shortcuts can produce flawed samples of respondents. Some research has shown that first-contact-attempt respondents are not only more likely to be older and female but also are more likely to be Republican than those who answer the telephone on subsequent attempts to contact them.

Another issue is how to consider the margin of *sampling error* (MOSE). A pollster may collect data from 300 individuals each day and report the results for a three-day aggregate of 900 respondents. However, it is not appropriate to think of the MOSE as close to ±3 percentage points for a sample of that size when any reported change is due to the addition of the most recent daily sample and the elimination of the first day's sample, either of which could have a MOSE of ±6 percentage points.

There are also complications arising from the different methods of early voting and their use, so tracking polls conducted late in the campaign must combine information from a question asking whether the person has voted yet and for whom with questions asking if they intend to vote and for whom. As a result, many firms have stopped conducting tracking polls.

HOW DO TRACKING POLLS COMPARE TO OTHER PRE-ELECTION POLLS?

This depends on how the other pre-election polls were conducted. At the end of a campaign, all the polls are usually based on samples of likely voters rather than registered voters. In the latter case, respondents are screened for registration status, and only those who say they are registered are asked about candidate preference. In addition to being registered, a likely voter is interested in the campaign, has voted in past elections, and indicates she intends to vote in the current one. Research shows that likely voters are more affluent and better educated, factors that make them more likely to be Republicans.

Some news organizations are neither careful nor precise about comparing their tracking polls of likely voters to other polls based on samples of registered voters. A shift from samples of registered voters to likely voters can mistakenly make it look like a race suddenly got closer or farther apart; in reality, it was just the samples that changed. For example, there was a period in October 1992 when this happened, and some news organizations reported that the race between Bill Clinton and George H. W. Bush was getting tighter. The reduction in the size of Clinton's lead was simply a methodological artifact of changing from one kind of sample or reporting base to another.[2] And in the 2000 election, there was more than average volatility in the Gallup tracking polls that was attributed to differences in estimating likely voters.

ARE THERE OTHER TRENDS IN THE REPORTING OF PRE-ELECTION POLLS?

Since the 2000 election, when Al Gore won the popular vote but lost the election in the Electoral College, there has been a renewed emphasis on tracking the likely outcome of the presidential contest in the Electoral College. This happened again when Donald Trump defeated Hillary Clinton in the Electoral College after losing the popular vote. As a result, the use of pre-election polls has shifted somewhat. There is somewhat less emphasis on national tracking polls that show the overall levels of support for the candidates and more on the measurement of the candidates' standing in the most competitive or "battleground" states. These are the "purple states" in flux, rather than the red states that are solidly Republican or the blue states that are safely Democratic. As the candidates focus more of their resources, including their own time and their advertising expenditures there, news organizations focus more of their polling there as well, employing statewide samples of likely voters in the "battleground" states rather than national ones. It can be confusing to compare data from national samples to results from samples in selected states, especially in terms of how support for the candidates is changing.

One important phenomenon in 2020 was that two major polling organizations announced that they would no longer conduct trial-heat polling in the primaries. Gallup and the Pew Research Center report such data during the fall general election, arguing that they can provide important information about how citizens are reacting to the campaign and the candidates, without reporting who is ahead or behind and how that is changing.

HOW DID BIAS APPEAR IN SOME STATE POLLS?

Since the 2020 elections, including the midterm elections, a systematic error occurred in some state polls that underestimated support for Donald Trump or other Republican candidates. This was important because it affected estimates of the Electoral College outcome through the misallocation of state-level victories to Trump or Biden. Different post-election analyses suggested two possible explanations: "shy Trump voters" who gave an interview but would not say they voted/intended to vote for him or Republicans who declined an interview and thus produced biased samples. The evidence for these two explanations tends to discount the "shy Trump voter" explanation and give greater support to the missing Republicans in the samples.[3] This is another issue that pollsters must face in future pre-election surveys, and polling organizations and AAPOR are paying close attention to possible explanations.[4]

CAN THE PUBLICATION OF POLL RESULTS AFFECT WHETHER OR HOW CITIZENS VOTE?

Researchers generally talk about two different impacts of exposure to election projections. One is called the *bandwagon effect*, and it suggests that some people tend to support a candidate they believe is going to win. The other is called the *underdog effect*, which suggests that some people tend to support the candidate they know is trailing. Voters affected in either of these two ways can learn about the relative standing of the candidates—who's ahead and who's behind—from the horse race journalism practiced by most news organizations nowadays. That type of reporting is buttressed by polls used to produce estimates from the trial-heat questions about which candidate is ahead or behind.

Some research suggests that knowing who is ahead or behind and by how much can affect respondents' answers to survey questions about candidate preferences. These findings were explored in a national survey of voters where some of the respondents were told the results of a current poll just before they were asked for whom they were going to vote.[5] These data showed that both bandwagon and underdog effects are present simultaneously in the electorate and that both effects could offset each other in estimating the outcome of the real election.

Recent research suggests that the people who are most likely to be affected by exposure to poll results are those who have weaker preferences for a candidate or weaker affiliations with one of the political parties. The existence of underdog and bandwagon effects in elections (as opposed to research studies) is difficult to demonstrate for a variety of reasons. Measurement is difficult, especially if it is based on respondents' self-reports of how they react to published polls. Analysis of data to demonstrate these effects is complicated, especially if it is based only on surveys taken at one point in time and relatively early in the campaign. But results from several experiments in which people are told about the results of real or hypothetical polls before they are asked their own preference suggest that bandwagon and underdog effects are present simultaneously in the electorate, among different groups of people.

WHAT IS THE CHANCE THAT A PRE-ELECTION POLL WILL PRODUCE AN INCORRECT PROJECTION OF AN ELECTION OUTCOME?

It is not uncommon for pre-election polls to produce estimates of election outcomes that are different from the division of the vote counted on Election

Day. There are several explanations for why this might happen, ranging from chance occurrence to poor methodology. While well-conducted polls are rarely wrong in picking the winner within the margin of sampling error, inadequate funding and methodological shortcuts explain why others are likely to be wrong. Furthermore, in elections since 2000, the growth of cell phone–only households may have led to some inaccuracies in election polling, as explained below.

In any survey, it is possible to draw a bad or unrepresentative sample that does not produce estimates that accurately correspond to candidates' support in the population. Most survey responses, such as the answers given by respondents to the trial-heat question, are reported with a margin of sampling error that suggests an accurate estimate 95 times out of 100. This means that a poor estimate (inaccurate to the degree of sampling error) is likely to be produced 1 in 20 times simply by chance occurrence alone. Essentially, there is nothing that a researcher can do about this type of chance error, but it must be kept in mind when interpreting any poll results. For example, poll consumers can compare results from surveys conducted at about the same time to look for common results and to minimize the impact of possible sampling error.

Many other sources of error are possible in pre-election polls. The most common is an inability to estimate likely voters, or the people who are most likely to go to their balloting places on Election Day. Sometimes the distribution of preferences among all citizens versus those who vote is quite different. Therefore, a bad estimate of turnout can be a serious source of error in pre-election projections. These issues are discussed in greater detail in chapter 5. Recent research has looked at the dynamics of voter preferences as they are affected by the outcomes in prior elections in primaries and caucuses, as well as contextual factors like the racial or gender ratios in the electorate.[6]

In the past thirty years, there has been increasing volatility in the American electorate, with more people making up their minds about whom to vote for later in the campaign. Therefore, if pollsters stop interviewing too early in the campaign (e.g., two weeks before the election rather than the weekend before the election or even stopping on Sunday rather than the Monday before Election Day), they can miss late shifts in voter sentiment or the crystallization of support for one or both candidates. Therefore, their estimates of the outcome could be quite far off.

There also can be question-wording and question-order effects for the trial-heat questions that ask people who they will vote for. Using a secret ballot that respondents mark and drop in a box as part of *in-person interviewing* reduces the proportion of undecideds and is a good way of getting at latent support for a candidate. This is especially important if there is a controversial candidate in a race or if one candidate has a characteristic that might make respondents likely to show support when they really do not intend to support that candidate. Pre-election polls conducted via e-mails or internet surveying can provide respondents with the same experience as using a secret ballot in a face-to-face survey. But this is a technique that cannot be used on the telephone, which is the traditional mode used by many pre-election polls.

One interesting polling phenomenon that occurred during the late 2016 Republican primary period, after he became the presumptive nominee, was the observation that Hillary Clinton's lead over Donald Trump was slightly lower in telephone polls than in those conducted on the internet. Some observers attributed this to a social desirability effect due to the likelihood that Trump supporters would be less likely to express their support for him to live interviewers compared to anonymous responses they could give on a web survey with no interviewer present. It remains to be seen whether this pattern will persist during the 2024 general election campaign.

Furthermore, research has shown that voters are sometimes reluctant to say they prefer a male candidate over a female candidate, or a white candidate over an African American candidate, especially when the interviewer's race and/or gender is different from the respondent's or is similar to the candidate being asked about. These response problems can produce a biased estimate of candidate preference in the electorate, and sometimes they have done so. For example, research conducted during the 2000 presidential election showed that the order and the wording of the trial-heat questions affected the results they produced. Both Bush and Gore did better when either was mentioned first in the question, and the results were also affected by which questions came before the trial-heat question.[7] Additional tests of these results need to be produced. These issues are discussed in greater detail in chapter 6.

Finally, 2008 was the first presidential election in which the accuracy of the projections made by pre-election polls was affected by the cell phone–only population. A study conducted by Scott Keeter of the Pew Research Center using 2006 national exit poll data showed that voters whose only telephone service was with a cell phone voted essentially the same as voters who had a landline. This suggested that the pre-election polls in 2006, which generally were quite accurate, did not suffer because they were almost entirely based on surveys of voters reached via landlines. However, the cell phone–only population in the United States has grown to more than 80 percent; as a result, the demographics and voting proclivities of the group may not change enough to affect the accuracy of pre-election polls if the landline-only voters are excluded from their sampling frames.

WHAT ARE EXIT POLLS, AND WHAT ARE THEY USED FOR?

An exit poll is a survey based on interviews with voters as they leave (or exit) their balloting locations. To estimate the outcome of an election in a particular constituency, a sample of its voting precincts is typically drawn, and at least one interviewer is sent to each sampled precinct. In its early years, exit polls in the general election for presidential years were conducted in every state as well as with a national sample. But when facing budgetary issues, the *National Election Pool (NEP)* undertook data collection in only thirty-one states in 2012, as well as a national exit poll. In 2020, NEP conducted exit polls in twenty-one states along with their national poll. In the past, on a preselected and systematic basis, the interviewer intercepted people who had already voted to obtain an interview, say every fourth or tenth person who came out of the voting place. The interviewer usually hands the voter a questionnaire on a clipboard and asks him or her to fill it out, fold it up, and deposit it in a survey "ballot box." In this sense, an exit poll interviewer uses self-administered questionnaires, one at a time. The questionnaire gathers three types of data. It measures who the respondent voted for in the day's key elections in a particular state (e.g., presidential, senatorial, and gubernatorial), a variety of attitudes held by the voter, and the demographic characteristics of the voter. The latter two sets of information can be used to explain why they voted as they did. In their current form, the NEP exit polls combine pre-election telephone information from early voters with the self-administered questionnaires distributed on Election Day, and some internet data gathered on or close to Election Day.

Election night projections of the outcomes of key races are based, at least in part, on exit polls. Interviewing people as they leave their voting place overcomes a lot of the problems of respondents' misreporting whether they voted or not when they are interviewed on the telephone, for example. These exit poll questionnaires are relatively short (typically less than twenty-five questions) and take less than five minutes to complete because people cannot be kept very long from getting to work or getting home.

Exit polls are important, not so much because they are used to help make the projections reported by the major television networks on election night, but because the information they gather about the voters' demographics and attitudinal predispositions towards the candidates and the campaign issues provides powerful explanations for why people voted the way they did in election postmortems. It is in this way that the so-called "mandate" of the election can be measured (and reported) accurately without relying on the partisan "*spin*" that the candidates, their campaign staff, and political pundits typically put on interpreting the election outcome.

For example, in 1980, Ronald Reagan's strategists described his sound defeat of Jimmy Carter as a "turn to the right" by American voters and an impetus for a conservative legislative agenda for the new Congress. In contrast, the 1980 exit poll data showed there was no ideological shift among American voters. They were primarily concerned about President Carter's inability to influence the economy and settle the Iran hostage crisis, and they wanted a new president who they hoped would do a better job in reducing inflation. As another example, in the 1998 exit polls, voters indicated that they were basing their votes for Congress on evaluations of their local candidates and not on any of their concerns about the allegations regarding President Clinton and Monica Lewinsky contained in Kenneth Starr's report.

In the 2020 election, Fox News used information from their VoteCast data to call Arizona for Joe Biden long before any other network, essentially calling the Electoral College majority for him. This was especially noteworthy because of Fox News's support for Donald Trump. While demonstrating the editorial independence of the election night coverage team and the decision desk, it was the beginning of Donald Trump's claim of a "rigged election" and organizing of the events that led to violence at the US Capitol on January 6, 2021.

WHO CONDUCTS THE EXIT POLLS?

Starting in the late 1960s and until 1990, the three broadcast networks (ABC, CBS, and NBC) conducted their own exit polls. In 1990, these networks and CNN joined together to sponsor a single operation known as *Voter Research and Surveys (VRS)*. In 1994, a further consolidation took place, and this joint operation became the *Voter News Service (VNS)* when the VRS exit-polling operations were merged with the News Election Service, which heretofore had been responsible for gathering actual vote counts at the county level. The three broadcast networks, the Associated Press (AP), which joined the sponsoring group in 1994, and CNN shared the same VNS database on election nights from 1994 through 2002 (Fox News joined the sponsoring group in 1996), although each of the networks used its own methods, models, and expert consultants to produce its projections of winners, while the AP used the VNS projections. VNS was created as a cost-saving arrangement that avoided duplication of effort in data collection at a far lower cost than the sum of what all the major news organizations were spending in previous elections.

VNS provided high-quality data prior to its downfall in the November 2002 election. In 2003, the six major sponsors of VNS formed the *National Election Pool (NEP)* and contracted with Edison Media Research and Warren Mitofsky, the "father" of exit polling, to conduct jointly the 2004 National Election Pool (NEP) service. With Mitofsky's unexpected death in the summer of 2006, Edison Media Research took over sole responsibility for the 2006 exit polls and continues with that responsibility into the 2024 elections.

In the 2016 campaign, Fox News and the Associated Press formed a new data collection and analysis partnership with the NORC (formerly the National Opinion Research Center) at the University of Chicago called *AP VoteCast*. Their research design uses a mixed-mode data collection involving telephone interviews, in-person Election Day exit interviews, and extensive online data collection from individuals who belong to probability and nonprobability research panels. This design is described in detail in chapter 7.

The networks are the primary users of exit poll data in races for president, senators, governors, and select proposals and referenda on election night, although some national newspapers, in addition to the Associated Press, such as the *New York Times*, present important exit poll results in their detailed analysis in the following day or two after the election.

HAVE THERE BEEN ANY SPECIAL PROBLEMS IN CONDUCTING AND INTERPRETING EXIT POLLS TO PROJECT ELECTION WINNERS?

Yes, there have been, and some of these problems became highly visible because of what happened in the 2000 Bush-Gore election, the November 2002 midterm elections, and the 2020 presidential race. In the early evening of Election Day, November 7, 2000, VNS and several of the networks called the Florida presidential race for Al Gore, only to retract that call a few hours later, saying the race instead was too close to call. This premature call was based on exit poll data (from the morning, afternoon, and evening samples) that later in the evening were found not to be representative enough of what the actual voting results were in the *sample precincts* where the Florida exit poll data were gathered. This became clear when the actual vote tallies started becoming available to the exit pollsters shortly after the voting ended in the precincts.

The Florida race then remained too close to call throughout the night of the election and into the following early morning hours.[8] However, at approximately 2:00 a.m. EST on November 8, 2000, Fox News made a premature and highly irresponsible call saying that George W. Bush had won Florida. All the other television networks then called Florida for Bush shortly after that, but VNS and the AP never made a call in that race. Despite this series of unfortunate events, the spin put out by VNS's own media sponsors pointed the blame for the premature call for Bush at VNS rather than at themselves. What followed in the aftermath of the Florida ballot "hanging chads" debacle was a highly politicized series of congressional hearings in 2001 led by Representative Billy Tauzin (Republican, LA) to investigate weaknesses and possible bias in the VNS methodology. These hearings in turn led to a major overhaul of the VNS data-processing system for the 2002 election. However, there was insufficient time for full development and testing of the new software, and it failed miserably in the November elections. Its media sponsors summarily disbanded VNS in early 2003.

Specific challenges faced by exit pollsters are myriad. First, the exit polls that were conducted by VRS, VNS, and NEP on Election Days in the period from 1996 to 2008 each gathered more data than any other survey effort has ever done in one day. More than 100,000 voters were interviewed in each of those exit polls. This is a Herculean task to manage accurately. For starters, this required hiring and training more than 1,000 in-person interviewers (at least one sent to each sampled precinct), each of whom had to shoulder a great deal of responsibility, increasing the potential for introducing errors into the data.

Left alone at the precinct, the interviewer is responsible for both selecting respondents as they exit the voting places and gathering the exit poll data using a questionnaire handed to the sampled voter on a clipboard. When completed, it is placed into the exit poll ballot box. If there are not enough interviewers at a particular voting site, a single interviewer may end up chasing a chosen voter all the way back to his or her car, losing time for an interview with the next designated respondent.

After the data are gathered, they are entered into the central computers of the exit-polling firm, Edison Research. This takes place multiple times during the day of the election (mid-morning, early afternoon, and right after poll closing) with interviewers calling back to the central office to read in their data.

As with any kind of survey, an unusual sample (i.e., one that is inadvertently unrepresentative of the target population) can produce problems in exit polls. In the 1996 New Hampshire senate race, for example, the VNS exit poll estimate showed the Democrat winning in a very close race. In actuality, the Republican won by a very small margin. In this case, subsequent analysis of other races, including the presidential election in the state, indicated a slight bias towards having too many Democrats in the sample. In a very tight race, this can make a difference in who is projected to win.

This is a different problem than the one in New Hampshire in the contest for the 1992 Republican primary. That VRS exit poll estimate showed a closer outcome than the raw vote eventually did. Although the exit poll showed President George H. W. Bush winning, the data from early in the day produced an evening news broadcast that suggested trouble for the incumbent president in his contest with his main rival, Patrick Buchanan. A postmortem analysis of the results from VRS and three other exit polls suggested that Buchanan voters were more likely to participate in exit polls and to indicate support for their candidate than were Bush voters.[9] So intensity of feelings can sometimes affect participation in exit polls, just as it does in other procedures where simple self-selection is possible.

A relatively new issue since the 2000 election was the proportion of the electorate that casts ballots before Election Day through various early voting procedures or voting by mail. With the advent of the new voting methods promoted by some as a convenience and necessary in 2020 because of the COVID epidemic, the exit poll operations were forced to move to complex mixed-mode and hybrid designs. They had to account for early voters by a variety of means, and analysts had to develop models by which data and estimates derived from different subgroups were combined into a single estimate of the election outcome. In the last two presidential elections, distinctive patterns of partisan voting by method became apparent. Democrats were most of the early voters in most states while Republicans provided most Election Day voters, appearing as the "Red Wave" of later returns.

However, the major problem faced by those who make the projections on election night, especially in close races, is to await the actual vote counts that are phoned into the exit pollster's central computer. This process starts shortly after voting ends in the sample precincts but can take several hours to finish. It is only when these actual vote counts for the sample precinct are added to the computer models that an "exit poll bias" can be calculated for a particular race. This bias is the difference between the estimate derived from exit poll interviews in projecting the winning candidate in a particular race in that precinct versus the actual vote in that precinct for that race. Thus, for example, the exit poll data may be found to be right on track with the actual vote, resulting in no bias in that precinct for that race. Or the exit poll data may have shown a 5 percentage point victory for the Republican candidate when in fact the actual vote count showed a 2 percentage point victory for the Republican.

In this case there would be a 3 percentage point "bias" for the Republican. As the exit poll biases at the level of the individual sampled precincts are rolled up to allow for an estimate of the total bias in the exit poll data for a given race, the computer models that are used by the exit pollsters to help call the outcome are constantly adjusted. It then remains for the exit pollsters to decide when the projected outcome is "certain enough" to make a call of the winner. The tradition that Warren Mitofsky and his close colleagues established was to make these decisions very, very conservatively. However, news pressures often conflict with the desire to be conservative and thus premature calls have sometimes been made.

A different problem became rampant in 2004 when there were a series of mysterious leaks of early exit poll data disseminated on internet blogs. The early exit poll data are only meant to be viewed by those monitoring the exit-polling enterprise on Election Day. There is no way of knowing whether these early data are an accurate reflection of how the day's voting will turn out and never should be used to characterize what is happening in an election race. In fact, that is just what the exit poll sponsors do not want to happen, because of their concern that premature and unreliable information from early in the day could affect voters later in the day. To counter this problem in subsequent elections, NEP established a quarantine room in 2006 in which each of the exit polls' sponsors was allowed to send two representatives to view and work with the early exit poll data. These representatives were not allowed any means of communicating with anyone outside the room from the time they arrive until they are allowed to leave (between 11:00 a.m. and 5:00 p.m. EST). Furthermore, there were three independent overseers[10] for the room watching that the news media representatives did not try to send out any messages to anyone about what they were learning from the early exit poll data. The analysts with access to the VoteCast data at Fox News in 2022 followed similar security procedures. As a result, there have not been any leaks of early exit poll data since 2006 and thus there were no concerns that such leaks might affect voting.

WHAT IS THE CHANCE THAT AN EXIT POLL CAN PRODUCE AN INCORRECT PROJECTION OF AN ELECTION OUTCOME?

No media organization wants to be embarrassed by reporting a projected winner only to later find the projection was wrong. As a result, projections based in part on exit poll data are expected to be extremely accurate. However, from a researcher's perspective, the chance is relatively high that a poor exit poll estimate can be made—perhaps 1 in 100 or 1 in 1,000. On a busy general election night, with hundreds of contests across the country, exit poll interviews, used alone, could produce inaccurate estimates in a few races just by chance alone.

In the election analysis operations at NEP, VoteCast, and the networks, the analysts have well-tested complex statistical models to generate the information they use for the projections. This information not only includes who is projected to win a given race but also includes a variety of data about the level of confidence associated with the projection. These models use a lot of additional data beyond that gathered in the exit polls to make their projections, incorporating historical voting data from the sample precincts in which the interviews were taken. This information includes past turnout and the partisan division of the vote. The computer models use this information to evaluate exit poll results as they become available, looking at whether the turnout is much higher (or lower) than usual and whether the vote is more or less Democratic (or Republican) than in the past. In close races, the models also employ raw vote totals, first at the sample precinct level as they become available, and then at the county level for all counties in a state as they become available. However, even under these highly rigorous conditions, mistakes can and have been made, as noted above.

In the 2020 presidential election, Fox News made a call for Joe Biden in Arizona on election night that essentially gave him an Electoral College majority. The AP followed a few hours later. At that moment, Biden had an unusually large lead in the state. However, none of the other networks, relying on the National Election Pool data, made a call for Biden until nine days later. Biden did win certification eventually but by less than 11,000 votes.[11]

ARE PRE-ELECTION POLLS WELL SUITED TO ESTIMATING THE OUTCOME OF THE ELECTORAL COLLEGE VOTE?

To estimate the outcome of the Electoral College vote, an estimate of the winner of each state is necessary. No single polling organization is collecting data in every state, so this is not really an issue for pollsters. There are data aggregators that assemble information from different sources, including polls, to estimate the outcome in each state. The simplest form of aggregation is to take the average of recent state polls to produce such an estimate for each state. This is what a website like RealClearPolitics.com does.[12] These aggregators pay attention to such factors as the pollsters' historical accuracy record as well as how recently their data were collected. Other aggregators like Nate Silver at fivethirtyeight.com employ more sophisticated statistical models. In fact, he produces estimates from three different models: one based on polling data, adjusted for historical accuracy records; another that adds in standard campaign factors like fund-raising and incumbency; and another that adds in the ratings of individual races by outside groups. At their heart, the work of the data aggregators depends upon the quality of state-level polls (and what kind of adjustments they might make to them based on historical accuracy). Historically, the accuracy of these polls has not been as good as the national polls, complicating the task of estimating the outcome of the Electoral

College votes. But the public often cannot distinguish between the accuracy of the national polls and the estimates produced by the data aggregators.

DO ELECTION NIGHT BROADCASTS OF PROJECTIONS AFFECT VOTING?

There is a great deal of public interest in this question, and many Americans believe that the answer is "Yes." For example, a majority (51 percent) of people interviewed in an October 1988 national survey thought that network projections made it less likely for people on the West Coast who had not voted to go to their precincts to vote.[13] It is also worth noting that in subsequent national surveys, researchers found that most people are more concerned about the impact of pre-election polls on others than they are on themselves. This example of a *"third-person effect"* suggests that concerns about the personal impact of polls may be overestimated.

For researchers, however, this is a very complicated and difficult question to answer. No studies have demonstrated an unequivocal relationship between early election night broadcasts and (1) levels of turnout or (2) the margin of vote for a particular candidate later on the day of the election or in the western part of the United States where voting is still going on. But there is a growing body of experimental and quasi-experimental evidence suggesting that some people are affected by election night projections if they are released before voting ends in a particular state. When the presumed outcome of a presidential election is known, some people will tend to stay home rather than go to their local balloting place. This could affect the outcome of races "down ballot" below the presidential contest. And bandwagon and underdog effects may affect other potential voters. This is one of the reasons that the media sponsors of the national exit polls were so concerned about the leaking of early exit poll data on the 2004 Election Day via internet blogs. That, in turn, was a reason they established the "quarantine room" to restrict the ability of any journalist with access to the early exit poll data to communicate with anyone who was not supposed to know anything about those data. The new system has worked perfectly since 2006.

ARE AMERICANS CONCERNED ABOUT THE EFFECTS OF ELECTION POLLS?

Ever since the polling business started, surveys have periodically been conducted to find out what citizens know about polling methods and how they feel about the publication or broadcasting of results during election campaigns. For more than thirty years, surveys have been conducted on various aspects of voters' responses to changes in regulation of the polls.

The results show several interesting things. The typical citizen does not know very much about the methodology of polls, certainly not enough to be able to distinguish between surveys that are well done and those that are not; that is one reason we wrote this book. In general, citizens say they are interested in polling information during most of the campaign, and most believe that poll results contribute positively to the campaign coverage.

While this is generally true for most of the campaign period, at the end of the campaign many voters seem to want to be left alone to make up their minds in peace. They say they do not want to be bombarded with a torrent of poll data showing who is ahead and who is behind. A special case of this concern is voters who are willing to trade information early on election night about who the winner is for a quiet period that would allow voters on the West Coast to cast their ballots without knowing the outcome of the presidential election.

As American politics has become more polarized, researchers have observed another interesting phenomenon called motivated reasoning: In experiments asking respondent to evaluate the accuracy, trustworthiness, and reliability of hypothetical polls, individuals were less likely to give positive ratings when the results showed the majority in the poll disagreed with their own position on an issue or their candidate preference. This raises a question about the public's willingness to expect elected leaders to follow public preferences expressed through polls and their role in a democratic society.

CAN THE US GOVERNMENT REGULATE HOW MEDIA ORGANIZATIONS CONDUCT AND DISSEMINATE THEIR POLL RESULTS?

The answer to this question is clearly "No" under the US Constitution. The Supreme Court has consistently found that the First Amendment prohibits any *prior restraint* on the collection and dissemination of news. Therefore, it is unlikely that Congress could pass any law to eliminate the publication of poll results during the last several days of the campaign or to prohibit election night projections based on exit polls that would survive a court test.

Currently the networks are making projections on the air on election night no sooner than the time at which in-person balloting has stopped in a particular state. Even though the projections may be available earlier, they are not broadcast until the polls close in that state. This is being done under a "gentlemen's agreement" that does not have the force of law, and Congress has considered ways to formalize this arrangement. In continuing discussions, a feasible proposal to eliminate problems for voters on the West Coast would have *uniform poll closings* across the country. This could conceivably be done together with establishment of a uniform number of hours that the polls must be open in each precinct. In this manner, all the votes would be cast before news organizations made a burst of projections. However, such a law would be very disruptive to the current administration of elections in the United States, and it would involve a substantial increase in costs for some jurisdictions. Therefore, such a law is not likely to pass in Congress until solutions are found for these problems.

In many foreign countries without the US Bill of Rights, however, there are laws that forbid the publication of pre-election polls late in the campaign—for the last two weeks in France, for example, or for the weekend before the election in Canada. And other laws prohibit making projections based on exit polls. Organizations like the World Association for Public Opinion Research (WAPOR) and the World Association of Opinion and Marketing Research Professionals (ESOMAR) keep track of these trends in restrictions on the freedom to publish poll results, but these restrictions will not be adopted in the United States.

WHAT OPTIONS ARE AVAILABLE TO LEARN MORE ABOUT HOW POLLS ARE CONDUCTED?

During the fall of 2014, AAPOR announced a Transparency Initiative to make more information available about how polls are conducted on a routine and systematic basis.[14] The purpose of the program is threefold: (1) to make more information available about how a specific poll or survey was conducted, (2) to archive the information for ready public access, and (3) to recognize the firms or survey centers that participate in the initiative. As the program gains wider acceptance, this kind of information will be readily available to anyone with a computer and internet access. AAPOR also produces an assessment of the polls' performance after each election, and these reports are cited in the selected references at the end of this volume.

NOTES

1. In 1948, due to considerable movement of the population after World War II, the 1940 census statistics were no longer sufficient to use as the basis for an accurate quota sample.

2. Some polling observers have disputed these conclusions. See Michael W. Traugott, "A Generally Good Showing, but Much Work Needs to Be Done," *Public*

Perspective (November/December 1992): 14–15; and Larry Hugick, Guy Molyneux, and Jim Norman, "The Performance of the Gallup Tracking Poll: The Myth and the Reality," *Public Perspective* (January/February 1993): 12–14.

3. Geoffrey Skelley at https://fivethirtyeight.com/features/trump-supporters-arent-shy-but-polls-could-still-be-missing-some-of-them/.

4. See, for example, the conversation between Scott Keeter from Pew Research and Josh Clinton, who chaired the AAPOR report on the 2020 election errors, at https://www.pewresearch.org/short-reads/2021/07/21/a-conversation-about-u-s-election-polling-problems-in-2020/.

5. Paul J. Lavrakas, Jack K. Holley, and Peter V. Miller, "Public Reactions to Polling News during the 1988 Presidential Election Campaign," in *Polling and Presidential Election Coverage*, ed. Paul J. Lavrakas and Jack K. Holley (Newbury Park, CA: Sage, 1991), 151–83.

6. Michael W. Traugott and Christopher Wlezien, "The Dynamics of Poll Performance during the 2008 Presidential Nomination Contest," *Public Opinion Quarterly* 73 (2009): 866–94.

7. Monika L. McDermott and Kathleen A. Frankovic, "Horse Race Polling and Survey Method Effects: An Analysis of the 2000 Campaign," *Public Opinion Quarterly* 67 (2003): 244–64.

8. Of note, the second author of this book was on the *election night decision team* for VNS that night with the responsibility to keep tabs on what was happening in Florida as more of the actual voting data were being reported in the exit polls precincts.

9. Warren J. Mitofsky, "What Went Wrong with Exit Polling in New Hampshire," *Public Perspective* (March/April 1992): 17.

10. The second author of this book was one of these observers.

11. https://www.npr.org/2020/11/19/936739072/ap-explains-calling-arizona-for-biden-early-before-it-got-very-close

12. For example, https://www.realclearpolitics.com/epolls/2024/president/us/2024_republican_presidential_nomination-7548.html.

13. Lavrakas, Holley, and Miller, "Public Reactions to Polling News during the 1988 Presidential Election Campaign," in *Polling and Presidential Election Coverage*, ed. Lavrakas and Holley, 171.

14. Detailed information about the AAPOR Transparency Initiative can be found at http://www.aapor.org/transparency.aspx.

Chapter 3

How Do Political Candidates and Organizations Use Poll Data?

The main difference between polls conducted for candidates and media polls is that the former are conducted for private, strategic use, while the latter are used for news content and analysis. Sometimes the results of private polls are leaked to the press because they serve a candidate's interests—either in support of his or her own candidacy, as a way of influencing coverage or perceptions of an opponent, or as a way to influence campaign contributions. Because of their strategic use in the campaign, the results of candidate polls are usually kept confidential.

One problem with making the results of campaign polls public is that they often involve questions designed to evaluate strategic alternatives—"what if" kinds of questions. The campaign may never carry out some (or even most) of these possible strategies, in part because of what the poll results show. Therefore, the responses to these questions are not meaningful or valid for inferring public reactions to the candidates, and they are kept private so that the campaign does not divulge its strategic intent.

Another limitation of campaign polls is that they are often conducted with samples of voters that are unrepresentative of the general population. That is, a campaign may be interested in the attitudes or expected voting behavior of Independent or undecided voters, or people who voted for the candidate the last time he or she ran. These results obviously cannot be generalized to the entire electorate. Sometimes such inferences are made, however, because of deception in the campaign or because reporters are not savvy enough to be able to distinguish the appropriate reference population.

There are even campaign techniques designed to appear as polls that are actually used to raise money or to sway voters. Pollsters' professional associations have condemned some of these simulations of polls because they involve deliberate deception. These types of pseudo polls have contributed to the growing hostility among the citizenry toward receiving unsolicited telephone calls at home, which in October 2003 peaked as part of the Do Not Call List phenomenon.

HOW DO CANDIDATES USE POLLS?

Candidates use polls for many purposes. First, campaigns use polls to learn what the important issues are in the minds of the voters. Such poll results provide a broad picture of the thematic content of the campaign (What issues do I have to discuss?). They are also a way to highlight the relative strengths of the candidate and the opposition in terms of the positions they have taken on these issues (What issues are the strongest for me? Which ones advantage my opponent?).

Candidates also use polls to evaluate the ways in which *elements* of the thematic content of their campaigns are resonating with members of the electorate. Most successful candidates have held elective office, so their policy positions on many issues are well known because they have developed over time. These are typically reflected in a series of votes the candidates cast or speeches they made that indicate where they stand. So candidates do not usually employ polls to decide what positions they should take. This does not mean, however, that candidates do not use polls to evaluate the popularity of different or alternative positions they might take on an issue or to evaluate the impact of different ways of discussing the issues. They may use this information to alter their emphasis or the language they use to discuss issues of particular importance to them or the electorate.

Developing a positive image means that a candidate is both well known and well liked. Therefore, the campaign also needs continuous monitoring of how well recognized the candidate is, whether or not the electorate looks on him or her favorably, and the relative standing of the candidates from opposing parties. By collecting these data over time, the campaign management team can gauge the effectiveness of its efforts and decide whether strategy should be changed or more effort put into advertising, for example.

WHEN DO CANDIDATES USE POLLS?

Research is an important part of every political campaign, and candidates like to have as much information as possible at a reasonable cost. Since polling costs money, the number of polls ultimately conducted during a particular campaign depends on the available resources.

In presidential contests, each candidate will have dozens of polls conducted across the eighteen to twenty-four months of serious campaigning.

In the pre-nomination phase, the campaign needs to obtain information on the current standing and image of its candidate, alone and in relation to the others. This information may also be useful in stimulating contributions to the campaign and dissuading contributors to the opponent's campaign.[1] In a presidential campaign, this information has only limited value at the national level because the real contest takes place on a state-by-state basis through the primaries and caucuses and then in terms of the "battleground states" that could affect the Electoral College outcome.

The presidential primary process is front-loaded so the events in traditionally early states such as New Hampshire and Iowa are unusually important. For each succeeding campaign since 1976, some states have moved up their primary dates so their citizens will have some say in the process of selecting the nominees. In 2008, many states moved their primaries to January and February for this reason, and we had the earliest decision about the nominees ever in an open contest where there is no incumbent president seeking reelection. Since then, the national parties have had mixed success in organizing the calendar for these events, although the calendar has been contested in every presidential election cycle since.

At the point that one of the candidates seems to have the nomination in hand, becoming the presumptive nominee, usually in the early spring, the emphasis may turn temporarily to national polls. These will include assessments of how the candidate will fare against the likely nominee of the other party. In other words, the emphasis will shift temporarily from local to national standing. By the time the general election campaign is well under way, however, just after the nominating conventions, the emphasis will shift back to state-level polls, as success on Election Day depends on winning a majority (270 or more) of the Electoral College votes. During the general election campaign, there will be a lot of national polling available through media organizations at no cost to the candidates.

As Election Day approaches, candidate polls increasingly emphasize the results of the trial-heat question as the campaign strives to do whatever is necessary to carry a state. Because past presidential campaigns were conducted on a fixed budget determined by federal law, the campaigns were continuously faced with resource allocation issues: Should we invest our next $100,000 in television or direct mail? Are we better off increasing our advertising budget in Ohio or Pennsylvania? Should we cut back on our expenditures in Florida and increase our effort in New Mexico? These pressures have been relieved since 2008 through candidates deciding to fund their campaigns independently with as much money as they can raise. In 2012, Barack Obama and Mitt Romney each raised and spent more than one billion dollars on their campaigns, and direct candidate and independent expenditures in presidential campaigns have continued to rise since then. Nevertheless, information obtained through polls helps candidates make such allocation decisions.

Allowing for differences in the procedures by which candidates seek nomination and organize their general election campaigns, all these same processes play themselves out at the state level in the campaigns of local candidates.

ARE POLLS THE ONLY RESEARCH TECHNIQUE FOR COLLECTING INFORMATION DURING A CAMPAIGN?

Polls are an effective way to collect certain kinds of information, but there are other important ways to do campaign research. Some of these include analyzing historical voting patterns in precincts and cities across the constituency and individual voting records available in many jurisdictions, reviewing successful advertising strategies from past campaigns, and keeping track of news coverage of the campaign. Campaigns also use opposition research to learn about opponents—their positions on issues, important votes cast, and even elements of their personal life.

Focus groups are commonly used by campaigns to get a sense of how things are going. Ten to fifteen people are assembled for a group discussion organized around a particular topic. A set of campaign themes might be evaluated for presentation in political ads, for example. Focus groups can provide very useful information to a campaign that is richer in detail than the information obtained in polls.

In a focus group, people are assembled for a wide-ranging discussion about a limited set of topics, but they are encouraged to do this in their own language in response to broad, *open-ended questions*. Campaigns use focus groups to develop an understanding of what kinds of things people are thinking about, but not to estimate how many people hold each kind of view. This is why focus groups are used to evaluate the effectiveness of ads—whether the intended message is being conveyed in the desired way.

In a poll, a *representative sample* of people is drawn from a larger population to which inferences can be drawn. Therefore, a scientific sample of likely voters might be drawn to learn what they are thinking or are likely to do. Each person is asked exactly the same questions to facilitate comparison of responses. If a good sample has been used, the results from the poll—such as the percentage of people who know who the candidate is—can be inferred to the population as a whole.

Starting in the 2012 campaign, many firms used content from social media like X, formerly known as Twitter, to estimate public opinion from interested and engaged groups in the electorate. This is a trend that will continue in the 2024 presidential campaign. Researchers still will not know how representative of the entire electorate the active users of social media are, but their commitment to political discussion and debate through these venues means they are more likely to vote.

DO THE RESULTS OF CAMPAIGN POLLS DEPEND ON WHEN THEY ARE CONDUCTED?

The results of polls do depend on when they are conducted, in a variety of ways. First, polls conducted early in the campaign, during the primaries and before, will often produce results favorable to the best-known candidates. Recognition is a minimum condition for evaluation, which in turn must precede support. So early in the campaign, the best-known candidates will generally have higher *favorability ratings*, and they will do better in the trial-heat questions that evaluate the candidates' relative standing. Later in the campaign, poll results reflect a more reliable measure of how the candidates are doing, when all who remain are relatively well known.

Skillful candidates and their managers can take advantage of such poll results to promote their own candidacies and to try to hurt their opponents. One critical way campaigns do this is to try to stimulate more financial contributions when the polls suggest they are doing well and to dissuade contributors from giving to another candidate when the polls show their opponent doing poorly.

Research has also shown that *candidate viability*, often indicated most clearly by poll standings, has an important effect on how much coverage a candidate gets and whether it is positive or negative. This coverage, in turn, can also affect contributions, volunteer efforts, and eventually the number of votes received. In presidential politics this is a highly effective strategy in the pre-nomination phase when the candidates must raise most of their money on their own. This relationship used to be present in the general election campaign, when the candidates relied on federal funding, but they now raise and spend money on their own. They are not concerned about these effects because they raise all the money they need.

DO THE RESULTS OF CAMPAIGN POLLS DEPEND ON HOW THEY ARE CONDUCTED?

The results of campaign polls, just like those of any other kind of poll, are highly sensitive to the way in which the polls are conducted. Therefore, poll results can be manipulated by altering the data collection methodology.

Because of the relationship between candidate recognition and support, for example, the wording of questions can make a lot of difference in the level of support that a candidate receives. Early in the campaign, an open-ended question in the form of *"Who would you like to see win the Republican (or Democratic) nomination for president?"* will result in quite different (and lower) support levels for a relatively unknown candidate than a question worded this way:

Here is a list of candidates seeking the Republican (Democratic) nomination for president. Which of these would you like to see win the nomination?

Whereas well-known candidates emphasize the results from the first question, lesser-known candidates often use results from the second form of this question to launch their campaigns, by showing voters (and reporters and potential contributors) that they have reasonable levels of support in the electorate. Again, this could represent a case where untrained journalists report opinions suggesting a level of candidate support that is an artifact of question wording. If the question were asked a different way, the results would be different.

DO CANDIDATES USE POLL RESULTS IN STRATEGIC WAYS?

The main purpose of campaign polls is to provide information on what the campaign should do or how effective its actions have been, so campaign polls are always used strategically. The results from campaign polls can be used to evaluate the strengths of one side and the weaknesses of the other; how well an ad campaign is working; or whether a response is needed to an issue raised in the media or by an opponent.

In 1998, during the extended discussion and debate about President Clinton's behavior with Monica Lewinsky and its impact on his ability to govern, it was revealed that he used polls to decide how he should respond to the initial disclosure of the relationship. Immediately after the story hit the news, Clinton summoned a key political adviser, Dick Morris, and discussed the impact that public perceptions might have on his future. Morris reported that he conducted a quick poll and informed Clinton that the public would accept his commission of adultery but not perjury. And this distinction became the basis for Clinton's subsequent strategy with the independent counsel and Congress. In the 2004 campaign, the Republicans were able to exploit the difference between the "war on terrorism" and the war in Iraq, as public opinion polls showed they were advantaged by the first but not by the second.

In the campaign for the 2024 Republican nomination, Donald Trump faces a number of indictments in several jurisdictions. Other candidates seeking the nomination are releasing internal polls showing they have a stronger showing against Joe Biden than Trump in the hopes of attracting some of Trump's base supporters because of their stronger electability. This is also a newsworthy element of the campaign that is pursued through media polls as well.

The release of poll results can also be used strategically to foster a candidacy or to harm an opponent. Press conferences or leaks of poll results might suggest that one candidate is gaining ground or doing better or that an opponent is losing ground or doing worse, in general or especially among an important electoral group such as women or Independents or people who are most likely to vote. An analysis of pre-election polls from statewide races in 2002 showed that on average, those polls that were most different from the election outcome were the ones released by candidates and parties. And the errors were in the direction that favored the candidate who released them![2] This finding has been replicated in subsequent elections and for different levels of office.

CAN CANDIDATE POLLS BE MISLEADING?

Because campaign polls often evaluate strategic alternatives, the release of results, especially in small snippets of information, can be misleading. Candidates sometimes collect data through a form of *push poll* in which they ask a series of hypothetical questions about their opponents. For example, they might ask questions concerning little-known facts about an opponent's personal life or positions on particular issues.

These questions are often asked in a series that takes the following general form:

a. If the election were held today, which candidate would you prefer?

b. Suppose you learned (a statement) about Candidate A. Would you still support her?

c. Suppose you learned (another statement) about Candidate A. Would you still support her?

d. If the election were held today, which candidate would you prefer?

In this sequence, these successive revelations are used to evaluate what kinds of things a campaign might emphasize or disclose in order to move or push support away from an opponent. But the campaign may never actually try such a strategy, some of the revelations may not be exactly true, or the opponent may have a reasonable explanation for the potential charge. The results of this kind of poll should not be straightforwardly extrapolated to the public campaign. These issues are discussed in greater detail in chapter 10.

CAN MEDIA POLL RESULTS HELP A CANDIDATE?

In an election campaign, there is no substitute for good news. Poll results that show a candidate ahead or gaining momentum can stimulate contributions or increase the number of volunteers, energize the staff, or even stimulate voter turnout at the end of the campaign. The candidates and their staffs will try to get the media to repeat these results as often as possible in order to generate a more positive spin that will help their image. So good poll results have clear benefits for a campaign.

CAN MEDIA POLL RESULTS HURT A CANDIDATE?

A good deal of reporting on public affairs involves the use of sporting metaphors: Who is ahead or behind? Who is gaining or falling back? What are the odds that a candidate can win it all on Election Day? Together with this, there is a tendency for people to want to back a winner or to try harder when they think their side has a chance to win, as opposed to being hopelessly behind. Every candidate is interested in demonstrating their viability and a scenario that indicates their prospect of eventual electability.

Election coverage is filled with messages like this. Many of them come from the campaigns themselves, including the candidates, their managers, and party leaders. A good deal comes from political columnists and pundits. Some of them come from polls. When election polls show that one candidate is trailing badly, and the commentary suggests that the outlook is bleak, the campaign can be hurt by poll results. They can have the effect of slowing or completely drying up the flow of funds or reducing the number of volunteers.

In these instances, the campaign staff will try to produce an explanation or spin that minimizes the damage that such polls can produce.

HOW DO POLITICAL PARTIES USE POLLS?

Political parties sometimes conduct their own polls to check their standing with the electorate and to augment the information available to their candidates. A state party may conduct a poll on how the governor's race and the contests for the state legislature are going, and they may also ask about the presidential race. If they supply this information to a presidential campaign, it may have to be counted as a contribution in kind to the candidate.

Late in the campaign, the party is interested in finding out who is likely to vote and which candidates they are likely to support. Polls are used in such efforts as an important part of Get Out the Vote (GOTV) drives. Without ever asking about the presidential contest (because it might be seen as an in-kind contribution under federal campaign laws), the party can ask questions that enable them to classify respondents as likely Democratic or likely Republican voters. They use this information to contact their most likely voters on Election Day to see whether they have voted yet; often they will offer their likely voters a ride to their balloting places if they need one. By delivering a likely partisan to the local balloting location, they have a good idea of how that person will vote for president too.

In the 1996 campaign, there was a novel use of a mail survey by the Reform Party as a way to select its presidential nominee without holding a convention. Unfortunately, this experience highlighted many of the problems of trying to conduct a survey by mail. To begin with, there was no good list of the names and addresses of the party members, so mail ballots were sent to only about two-thirds of the estimated number. Although Ross Perot was preferred by 65 percent of those returning ballots and Richard Lamm by 28 percent, it was estimated that only 5 percent of those receiving a ballot returned it. This raised questions about the legitimacy of the process, especially from the Lamm supporters.

After the 2012 election, the Republican party conducted an extensive internal review, having lost the popular vote in five of the six previous elections. Under the heading of the Growth and Opportunity Project, they used extensive polling that included more than 36,000 online interviews about the future directions the party needed to take. The election of Donald Trump in 2016 was a rejection of the plan, and the party became less inclusive rather than more.

WHY DO SPECIAL-INTEREST GROUPS USE POLLS?

By the very nature of their organization, special-interest groups have a desire to influence legislation, regulation, or public policy concerning matters of interest to their members. Therefore, special-interest groups use polls for a variety of purposes: to maintain contact with their members and to find out where they stand on a particular issue; to collect information from the general public to see where it stands on a particular issue; or to collect and distribute information to public policymakers.

These are all legitimate goals for such an organization to pursue. When a special-interest group collects data for internal management and research purposes, this is no different from a corporation's collecting marketing data for its products. If the data are made public, however, it is appropriate to apply a series of evaluative criteria in order to decide how much weight to give such information. This is especially important when the leaders of the group suggest that the poll results reflect broad public opinion on an issue. For example, it is usually inappropriate to characterize the opinions of the members of the group, who have joined because of their common interests, as a reflection of public opinion or what Americans think on a topic. These assessments are only possible when the group is transparent about its methods of data collection and analysis, which is unfortunately often not the case.

Some special-interest groups also include pseudo polls with highly *biased questions* in their mass mailings. Under the guise of survey research, some organizations send out letters that look like they contain legitimate surveys, for the purpose of soliciting new members (known as Soliciting Under the Guise of survey research, or *SUGing*) or raising money (known as Fund-Raising Under the Guise of survey research, or *FRUGing*). These are inappropriate uses of the survey method, according to the American Association for Public Opinion Research (AAPOR). This organization frequently makes public comments about especially egregious examples of such misuse. Issues of interpretation and evaluation are discussed in greater detail in chapter 10.

ARE THERE PROBLEMS WITH SOME POLLS CONDUCTED BY SPECIAL-INTEREST GROUPS?

There could be a problem because any advocacy group is typically interested in advancing an agenda. This means these groups could be inclined to use nonprobability or otherwise unrepresentative samples and/or biased question wordings to distort data to support their position on an issue.

For these reasons, it is useful if not imperative that consumers of polls always know who sponsored a poll and what questions were asked of whom. Recent research shows that poll consumers discount the accuracy of polls supported by interest groups when the reported results support the announced sponsor's position on an issue. By the same token, they are more likely to believe the results are accurate when they are contrary to the interests of the sponsoring organization. Any responsible group should be willing to identify itself as a sponsor of research and to provide full methodological information on how any polls that it sponsored were conducted. This would include a description of the sample design (who the respondents were and how they were chosen) and a copy of the complete questionnaire that gives full question wordings and the order in which they were presented (what the respondents were asked).

DO ELECTED OFFICIALS PAY ATTENTION TO POLLS?

Many elected officials are so used to employing polls in their campaigns that they are predisposed to pay attention to polls about what citizens think. They have other sources of information that provide cues about public opinion, such as letters from constituents, calls to their offices, faxes, and e-mail that they receive, as well as social media content like Facebook posts or tweets. Given that they are more knowledgeable consumers of poll information than most citizens, they are also better able to understand the sources of such information and know when it should be discounted.

Recent research shows that individuals exposed to poll results will tend to discount them when they disagree with views they already hold, especially when the views are strongly held. This applies to elected officials as well as to regular citizens.

As the Republican-controlled Congress moved to impeach President Clinton in 1998 despite repeated polls that showed public opposition to removing the president from office, Democrats cited the polls as support for a censure motion. Many Republican members, on the other hand, invoked constitutional principles and the need to fulfill their sworn obligation as a reason for ignoring these same polls. Each group was reacting to a clear message from multiple measurements on the same issue, responding in accord with their own partisan conceptions of what needed to be done.

There is also a difference between keeping track of polls conducted by others and sponsoring your own polls. From the perspective of political leaders, the attention they pay to polls and the number of polls they sponsor depends upon their office and their campaign funding. First of all, polls cost a lot of money, so federal officeholders are more likely to sponsor their own polls than state and local officials. Every president since Franklin D. Roosevelt, with the exception of Harry Truman, sponsored a polling operation while he was in office, and this type of activity has expanded over time. Members of Congress, on the other hand, are less likely to do a lot of polling as an institution or much before they have to campaign for reelection.

Another important question is whether elected officials use these polls to choose what position they will take on an issue or to shape their existing positions in a way that will maximize their public acceptance. A substantial stream of research suggests that most politicians don't pander; that is, they do not adopt positions that polls show are the most popular. In thinking about this carefully, this would almost certainly have to be the case. Most elected officials have a long public record of speeches and votes on issues, one that can easily be researched nowadays on the internet. A politician who frequently changed positions because of the latest poll results would be identified quickly and challenged by his or her opponents at every opportunity as a "flip flopper." But it does appear that some elected officials often frame the specifics of their positions in language or concepts that polls—and other forms of research—suggest would make them most acceptable to the largest number of constituents.

It is important to distinguish here between elected officials and civil servants who work in government agencies. Many government agencies are required to take public opinion into account when they embark on new projects or consider new regulations. Polls are again just one of the means that they use to ascertain what opinion is on a particular issue. In many agencies, for example, an environmental impact assessment includes the collection of polling data on what citizens think the consequences of a new project will be, as well as holding public hearings. For their purposes, agencies are often presented with polls sponsored by interest groups who have a stake in a new project, so their evaluation task is often more complicated.

NOTES

1. Diana E. Mutz, "Media, Momentum, and Money: Horse Race Spin in the 1988 Republican Primaries," in *Presidential Polls and the News Media*, ed. Paul J. Lavrakas, Michael W. Traugott, and Peter V. Miller (Boulder, CO: Westview, 1995), 229–54.

2. Elizabeth Martin, Michael W. Traugott, and Courtney Kennedy, "A New Measure for Assessing the Accuracy of Pre-election Polls," *Public Opinion Quarterly* 69 (2005): 342–69.

Chapter 4

How Do News Organizations Collect and Report Poll Data?

Media organizations collectively spend tens of millions of dollars for polls during election campaigns so that they can produce content for news stories. Some news organizations purchase data from market research firms by underwriting the costs of a special survey, while others subscribe to a nationally syndicated service such as the Gallup Poll or the Harris Poll. The largest news organizations in the country—some television networks and major metropolitan daily newspapers—have their own polling units. And newspapers and broadcast outlets operate in partnership with each other when they do not compete directly for the same audience.

Media organizations conduct different kinds of polls at different stages of the campaign. Early in the campaign, the pre-election polls may contain many questions about issues, but the issue content declines as Election Day nears. Then the emphasis in the polls turns toward the trial-heat question measuring candidate preference. In conjunction with news coverage that focuses on who is ahead and by how much, the focus of the polls is on candidate standing. On Election Day itself, major news organizations sponsor exit polls that are used to estimate the actual outcome of the race based in part on interviews with voters leaving their balloting places. These exit polls are also used to analyze and explain why voters cast their ballots the way they did.

Election coverage has always been a good story for news organizations. Elections have high impact on their audience members. They occur on a schedule that facilitates planning the coverage and assigning resources to it. Campaigns involve conflict, and they are filled with willing sources who agree to talk to reporters. And campaigns are almost always resolved on Election Day when winners and losers are declared, with the notable exception of the 2000 and 2020 elections. With the growing use of various kinds of early voting procedures and the delay in counting absentee ballots, this may become the new schedule for declaring winners. Election polls contribute to many of these characteristics of campaign coverage as it has existed for longer than polls have been around. But journalists are happy to use poll data in their stories because they support many of the tendencies and reporting styles they like to use.

One special use happens during primaries when televised debates are involved. The networks are concerned about visual qualities when they televise debates, especially early in the campaign when there may be a large number of candidates before a party's nominee is selected. They do not want too many candidates appearing on the stage because it limits the number of questions that the moderator can ask in order to allow all the candidates a chance to answer. For the sake of limiting participation, many news organizations that sponsor debates establish criteria for inclusion in the event, including fund-raising ability and a minimum level of support in recent polls. This is not a political consideration; it relates to a belief in what produces good news.

Critics of the media argue that polls are used to make news rather than as a tool to strengthen coverage of stories that are inherently newsworthy. They also argue that they produce lazy reporters who substitute poll data for traditional forms of reporting on the street. The issues are not as simple as this. Polls support a different kind of reporting, not necessarily one that is better or worse. But we believe that many news departments need to do more with the data they have to enrich their reporting of campaigns and elections.

WHY DO MEDIA ORGANIZATIONS CONDUCT POLLS?

There are three main reasons that media organizations conduct their own polls. First, they like to have editorial control over the content and timing of the surveys, exercising their own judgment over news decisions and values. Second, they use poll results to inform and structure their subsequent coverage. And third, they enjoy the professional prestige that comes from their peers' acknowledgment of the quality of their polls. This occurs when other news organizations pick up their stories or cite their poll results in stories they produce.

Recent research shows that all major newspapers use polls in reporting, and many sponsor their own polls. Among those that do not sponsor polls, the most frequently cited explanation is that financial resources are not available; otherwise, they would. Television stations are increasingly making use of local polls as well, often in conjunction with a local newspaper; but too often they use questionable research methods that are not likely to produce accurate results.

In the old days of polling that extended from the 1940s to the 1970s, many news organizations subscribed to syndicated services that provided regular signed columns produced by national polling figures such as George Gallup or Louis Harris. The newspapers received one or two prepackaged news stories each week, based on data collected by these organizations, usually through face-to-face interviews. With the arrival of low-cost *telephone surveys* in the 1980s, news organizations realized that they could conduct their own polls at reasonable cost, whenever they wanted and covering whatever topics they wanted. This meant they could exercise independent news judgments about which current events suggested they should field a poll and what questions they should ask. This practice continues today with the rise of web surveys and panels as a low-cost alternative to telephone surveys with their increasing costs.

HOW CAN POLLS CONTRIBUTE TO GOOD JOURNALISM?

Elections are a fundamental part of American democracy because they involve the selection and replacement of our representatives. Most people are not interested in politics most of the time, but the activity of a campaign stimulates periodic bursts of interest, leading right up to Election Day when many voters still go to the polls. Campaigns and elections are an important part of news coverage because of their relevance to American political life. They also occur on a well-known schedule according to a well-understood set of regulations. All of this makes them easy and important to cover. There is conflict between the opposing candidates but then a clear resolution on Election Day. This also makes it easy for news media to organize their coverage.

Good polls contribute to journalism by providing an independent perspective on citizens' views about the candidates and issues involved in election campaigns. Every campaign has willing sources who will discuss their strategy and prospects. But we have come to understand that these political elites (candidates, campaign managers, party chairs, and the like) put their own spin on these assessments. They try to make their own chances of winning look as good as possible and their opponents' as poor as possible.

Well-conducted surveys provide another perspective on the dynamics of the campaign and popular assessments of the candidates, as well as an independent view of the effectiveness of their efforts. A random sample of voters, representative of the electorate at large, can provide an untainted view of what is going on and what is likely to happen on Election Day. Election polls can also provide a perspective on what issues are important to the voters and how these interests relate to what the candidates are discussing.

WHY DO MEDIA ORGANIZATIONS COLLABORATE ON POLLING?

The main reason media organizations collaborate on polls is to share the costs. These partnerships began more than forty-seven years ago when the *New York Times* and CBS News began planning to conduct polls together for the 1976 election. The newspaper had an important resource in the telephone banks in its advertising department that were unused at night, when most of the interviewing was done, while the network had highly skilled methodological and statistical research staff who could design the data collection and analysis of the results. This first arrangement was followed by one between ABC News and the *Washington Post*, which now has multiple polling partners.

Furthermore, these early partnerships involved major metropolitan dailies with morning circulation and networks with evening news broadcasts. Both shared a common news deadline of late afternoon/early evening, though their products appeared on two separate days. This meant that each organization could have access to the data simultaneously. The networks presented the results first but in abbreviated form because a television story is generally shorter than a newspaper story on the same topic. The newspapers presented the story a few hours later but in greater detail. In the first partnership, the television story was described as the product of a CBS News/*New York Times* poll. The next morning's newspaper story was described as the product of a *New York Times*/CBS poll. With the advent of media organization websites, the results are now made available simultaneously online.

Currently, there are partnerships between local newspapers and television stations, and some between weekly news magazines and networks. Formerly, the stories typically appear on a Sunday evening on television and in the magazine on Monday when it hits the newsstand. Again, the advent of websites for news organizations has blurred many of these distinctions. Production of news on a continuous twenty-four-hour cycle means that there is a constant appetite for content among all the partners, and the fact that every news organization has at least one website on which to place content explains this change.

HOW HAVE BUSINESS CONDITIONS AFFECTED MEDIA POLLING?

For some time there has been declining revenue in the news business because of the serious loss of classified advertising in newspapers to web sources like Craigslist.com and competition from news aggregators on the internet. As a result, all media sponsors of polls are operating with reduced or eliminated budgets. Some media organizations have eliminated their own polling operations entirely, while others are conducting fewer polls. Even the *New York Times* and CBS News have reduced their joint effort because of declining revenue and buyouts of key personnel at the newspaper.[1] Several are experimenting with new technology like Interactive Voice Response (IVR) equipment, which uses computers with digitized voices to conduct brief telephone interviews, or are using internet panels for online data collection. Even the exit polls conducted by Edison Research for its media clients have been reduced to fewer surveys in the most competitive races in light of these budgetary restrictions, and a new effort, AP VoteCast, conducted by NORC, Fox News, and the Associated Press is following similar procedures.

ARE THERE SPECIAL PRESSURES THAT AFFECT MEDIA POLLS?

Yes, there are, because the news is now produced on a continuous twenty-four-hour cycle, which is getting even shorter through advanced technology. We can see the continuous production of network television news on the major broadcast networks, CNN, Fox News, and MSNBC as well as local around-the-clock news stations and media websites. So, in order for poll results to be news, they have to be fresh and reflect content that was not made obsolete by events in the real world since the data were collected.

As a result, media polls must be conducted in a relatively short field period. Typically, this means data are collected in forty-eight to seventy-two hours, across two or three nights of interviewing. After televised debates, many news organizations collect data in just a few hours, using the telephone or the internet. One consequence is that response rates in media polls are typically much lower than in surveys conducted across longer field periods. There is less time available to recontact potential respondents who were not home or refused to be interviewed the first time they were contacted. A reduced response rate, which most often means a less accurate representation of a poll's target population, is a clear trade-off that news organizations accept to collect and report timely information. These issues are discussed in greater detail in chapter 5.

WHAT ARE THE STANDARD DATA COLLECTION METHODS USED IN MEDIA POLLING?

From the 1980s until relatively recently, the typical US media poll was based on telephone interviews, usually collected during the evening hours on a weekend across a few days (from Friday to Sunday). The samples of phone numbers were purchased commercially. They consisted either of a combination of telephone numbers taken from listings in directories plus other, randomly selected numbers or entirely of numbers randomly created by computer, not all of which are residential numbers or even working numbers. As explained in chapter 5, this latter approach is used to ensure that the poll samples households regardless of whether their number is listed or published. The major news organizations employ various techniques for selecting a particular respondent within a household where they make contact. Less representative methods involve conducting an interview with whoever first answers the phone.

Media polls usually employ relatively brief interviews, sometimes lasting less than ten minutes and rarely extending for more than twenty minutes. Most of the questions are closed-ended: The respondent is asked to select an answer from a limited number that are offered. Rarely do these surveys employ open-ended questions in which the respondent answers in his or her own words, because they take longer to administer and require additional coding that can slow down the analysis of the data, making them more costly. Details about questionnaires are discussed in chapter 6.

Computer-assisted telephone interviewing (CATI) systems remain a common means of conducting telephone polls. The interviewer reads the questions from a computer monitor and records the answer directly into the computer database. When the interview is completed, the data record for that respondent is immediately ready for analysis. When the last interview is conducted, there is an entire dataset, consisting of the responses from every person interviewed, ready for analysis. A relatively new approach to conducting telephone polls is the Interactive Voice Response (IVR) technique in which a computer-controlled system calls a predesignated sample of households, uses a recorded or machine-simulated voice to recruit a respondent, plays back the questions and answer choices, and then captures respondents' answers that are given either in their own voice or by pushing buttons on their telephone touch-tone pad. Increasingly, many commercial polls involve *mixed-mode designs*, discussed in detail in chapter 7.

Since the 1990s, the use of the internet to gather data and the use of exiting online internet research panels have been growing in use for election polling commissioned by the media. However, too often, especially with nonprobability-based surveys and panels, the respondents in these surveys and panels are not an accurate representation of the voting public. To try to correct for this limitation the pollsters try to adjust (weight) the final sample of respondents to match the makeup of the expected voters in the poll's final sample more closely to the anticipated population of voters in a given election. Unfortunately, there is no guarantee that this works as intended and little if anything is disclosed about the adjustments and their validity. Data in these polls is collected via a questionnaire that respondents access via the internet. This is appealing to the sponsors because this data collection mode is low in cost and quicker in gathering data than the telephone or other polling approaches.

Some news organizations collect data by methodologies that they inappropriately label "polls." These include call-in polls in which readers or viewers are encouraged to call in to 800 numbers (free to the caller) or even 900 numbers (that cost the caller) and mail-in polls in which readers are asked to complete questionnaires inserted in magazines or newspapers. The latest twist in this kind of data collection is a *log-in poll*, in which people can go to a website on the internet and register their views. The major problem with such polls is that they allow respondents to self-select into the sample, thus not affording any controlled sampling scheme or fair representation of the target population.

Another issue with some of the polls is that they involve only one or two questions, excluding information about the personal characteristics of the respondents. The news organization presents just the frequencies for the single question without any further analysis. This presents the reader or viewer with a simple "factoid" without any basis or context for understanding or interpreting it. Results from these kinds of polls should be ignored. These techniques almost always produce biased and completely unrepresentative data because they do not involve scientific samples.

CAN THE METHODOLOGY OF MEDIA POLLS HAVE AN IMPACT ON THE RESULTS?

The methodology of media polls does not necessarily have to have a negative impact on the results, although sometimes it may do so. It is very difficult to assess in quantitative terms what the impact might be, compared to other methods.

On some topics, a short field period that results in a low and unrepresentative response rate can produce biased results because people who are readily available and willing to give an interview often differ from people who are unavailable during that short period. Such respondents usually have higher levels of interest in politics or may be more likely to identify with one party than another. Some news organizations try to collect data in one night or even across a few hours between the early evening news and the eleven o'clock edition. This can be extremely problematic and is likely to introduce substantial bias in the data.

Surveys based entirely on closed-ended questions that do not allow respondents to answer in their own words and with their own frame of reference can sometimes produce biased results. This is especially true if the response categories do not appropriately reflect the types of opinions held by the public.

HOW ARE MEDIA POLLS ANALYZED AND DISSEMINATED?

All polls are analyzed with the use of statistical software written specifically for computers. Typically, the analysis of media polls is not very complicated because it is difficult to produce timely news stories based on complex analysis, but sometimes more extensive reports are prepared and disseminated by the media, including via their websites.

Analysis begins by looking at the *marginals* or simple percentages or counts for each question in the survey. This shows what percentage of men and women are in the sample or what percentage approve or disapprove of Joe Biden's handling of his job as president. These are often called the "topline" results.

The next step is to run cross-tabulations by looking at the joint distribution of the responses to two questions (the *bivariate frequencies*), the most rudimentary form of analysis. This provides such information as the percentage of men who approve of Joe Biden's handling of his job as president compared to the percentage of women who approve. In rare instances, a third question, such as party identification, is added to the analysis. This technique addresses such questions as whether Democratic women approve of Joe Biden's handling of his job at the same level as do Republican women.

Most of the analysis of media polls consists of the presentation of marginals for the entire sample. A small proportion consists of bivariate analysis, and almost no analysis is presented in terms of the effects of third variables. Sometimes data are presented in tabular form, but most often, the results are presented as descriptive statements in printed or spoken text.

Because of space and time limitations, most media polls are woefully under analyzed and do not contribute as much to the news as they could. News organizations are "data rich but analysis poor."[2] Unfortunately, this deprives their readers and viewers of valuable and interesting information available from their polls. However, in the past decade, news organizations have been getting cleverer in their design and use of graphics to illustrate their poll-based stories to make their points about the relationships that appear in their data.

DO REPORTS OF POLL RESULTS DIFFER WHEN PRESENTED ON TELEVISION OR IN NEWSPAPERS?

The typical poll-based story on television consists of a voice-over in which an anchor or commentator is talking about the results as data are presented on the screen. Sometimes the commentator is speaking as file footage is presented to illustrate the main point of the analysis, such as photos or videos of voters going to vote or of the candidates.

Newspaper stories based on polls are longer and involve more detailed analysis. Because they have more space to present results, newspapers often recontact survey respondents and have them amplify the views they expressed in the survey. Sometimes, these stories will also include pictures of the respondents at home or at work, to personalize the findings beyond the aggregated statistics derived from the poll.

With the advent of news organizations' websites, there is the opportunity for the presentation of longer and more complex analyses. Some organizations, such as Pew Research, provide a full report for each survey that includes a complete description of their methodology, the full questionnaire, and the topline results. They also may provide a full dataset for downloading for secondary analysis.

CAN MEDIA POLLS CONDUCTED BY DIFFERENT NEWS ORGANIZATIONS PRODUCE DIFFERENT RESULTS?

Yes, they can and often do. The simplest explanation for these differences is that the two polls used different samples or questions or that they were conducted at different times. During the campaign, some polls are based on interviews with samples of adults age eighteen and older, while others are based on interviews only with adults registered to vote. Since only about two out of three adults are registered, these different populations can produce different results, even when all other things are equal.

Even if the samples are similar, the questions may be different enough to produce seemingly different results. One survey may ask about approval of how Joe Biden is handling his job as president; another may ask about approval of his handling of the economy. Different polls might offer different response categories to these questions, which also affects the comparability of the results and can present a problem for comparative interpretation. Newspaper stories prepared from these polls could have quite different headlines referring to Biden *approval ratings*.

The order in which the questions are asked can also have an effect on the results. Gallup, which "invented" the *presidential approval* question, always asks this question first in its surveys so no other question can affect the answers. Research has shown that asking questions about the economy first, for example, produces different responses to the presidential approval question than not asking such questions first, depending on whether the nation's economy is in good condition or poor shape. Issues of question wording and question order are discussed in greater detail in chapter 6.

Obviously public opinion can change over time because of intervening events. So, two news organizations could report polls conducted a few weeks apart in a period when a major international event took place. Whether this event reflected positively or negatively on the president could explain differences in his approval ratings, all other things being equal. For example, immediately after the capture of Saddam Hussein in December 2003, George W. Bush's approval rating shot up. The same phenomenon occurred for Barack Obama after the killing of Osama bin Laden in 2011. However, polls in 2022 did not show the same public reaction to Joe Biden's support for Ukraine after Russia invaded, in part because inflation remained high in the United States after the pandemic, which resulted in Biden's approval on the lower side. Another example regularly occurs during the pre-nomination campaign, when primaries are scheduled almost every week in the first few months of the year; how well a candidate did in last week's primaries can affect his evaluations in the next week's polls.

Sometimes polls conducted by the media appear to show different results because the wordings of the questions or the response categories were different. For example, there were many polls fielded right after Russia invaded Ukraine in February 2022. In May, the Associated Press asked the question "Would you say you have: a great deal of confidence, only some confidence or hardly any confidence in Joe Biden's ability to handle the situation in Ukraine?" And they reported that 21 percent said they had a great deal of confidence while 39 percent said they had only some confidence. Fox News fielded a poll at about the same time asking the question "Do you approve or disapprove of Joe Biden's response to Russia's invasion of Ukraine?" and reported that 44 percent approved while 50 percent disapproved. This Fox News poll suggested greater support for Joe Biden's response, but a direct comparison is confounded by the difference in the measurement of support for him with two different question wordings.

On rare occasions, media organizations that share polls make different news judgments about how to use the results. In February 1998, several news organizations conducted polls to measure support for what seemed to be the imminent bombing of Iraq because of its failure to comply with United Nations resolutions. CNN and *USA Today* shared a poll conducted by the Gallup Organization, but they made different news judgments about what the most important findings were. CNN led its story by suggesting that support for military strikes had declined compared to two weeks earlier (54 percent opposing military action compared to 46 percent at the start of the month). The headline on the front page of *USA Today* was "Public Solidly Behind U.S. Attack on Iraq," based on the results from another question showing that 76 percent of those surveyed would approve of air strikes if they occurred. These data also appeared in the CNN story, but they did not receive the same prominence.

Another instance occurs when multiple news organizations conduct polls on the same topic but ask somewhat different questions. In May of 2023, during the negotiations over the US national debt ceiling, several organizations tried to measure public support for a variety of arrangements to raise it.[3] A CNN poll of adults reported that 60 percent said the debt ceiling should increase along with spending cuts. A Fox News poll showed 57 percent of registered voters had a similar preference. These last two polls asked a similar question with three response options, including one not to raise the debt ceiling at all. Two organizations (NPR/PBS/Marist and Monmouth University) asked a question with only two response options: raise the debt ceiling with spending cuts or raise the debt first and then address spending cuts. They each reported that half of the respondents wanted the two policies dealt with separately. The Monmouth University poll reported that twice as many preferred a clean debt deal to one with spending cuts, 51 percent to 25 percent, but this question had an explicit "No opinion" category. In the NPR/PBS/Marist poll, only 6 percent volunteered the same response. These results were not contradictory of course, but differences in the specific questions asked can explain the differences in the conclusions.

WHY ARE THERE SO MANY POLLS REPORTED IN THE MEDIA?

Because election polls provide such interesting and useful information for journalists, news organizations are inclined to use their results when they are available. The news is often about conflict and is filled with sports metaphors about who is ahead or behind and why. The reporting of poll results, especially for the trial-heat question about who is ahead, naturally lends itself to this emphasis on horse race journalism.

Many news organizations produce or sponsor the collection of their own survey data, and often these results enter the general news stream through the wire services or syndicated columns. But there are other sources of polling data during a campaign. The candidates are always conducting surveys, and they frequently provide results to reporters, sometimes through carefully orchestrated leaks. Of course, they are more likely to do this when they think they have information to bolster their candidacy.

American politics is increasingly characterized by the activity of organized special-interest groups, and these groups often sponsor polls on topics of particular interest to them. These groups then prepare press releases or hold press conferences to present their poll results. Since a good deal of the news comes from coverage of such events, this is another avenue for polls to get into the news.

Finally, there is some research suggesting that the focus of campaign coverage has changed over time, with a growing emphasis on the strategy and dynamics of the campaign.[4] Many candidates and their managers attribute their own or their opponent's behavior to movements in reaction to poll results. At the same time, reporters describe actions candidates take or visits they make as necessary because the polls show they needed to strengthen their position among a particular group of voters.

Research shows that these generic references to polls or public opinion, without any citation of source or actual data, are a growing element in campaign coverage. This can be a special problem for voters interested in substantive issues in the campaign who can find coverage only of the dynamics and strategy of the campaign. Some critics argue that a preponderance of news preoccupied with candidates behaving in a strategic fashion with regard to each other and not responding to the voters' interests in issues has led to a growing cynicism about government and declining turnout.

NOTES

1. See http://www.politico.com/blogs/on-media/2016/08/future-of-cbs-new-york-times-poll-is-up-in-the-air-227372.

2. Richard Morin, "The 1992 Election and the Polls: Neither Politics nor Polling as Usual," in *Presidential Polls and the News Media*, ed. Paul J. Lavrakas, Michael W. Traugott, and Peter V. Miller (Boulder, CO: Westview Press, 1995), 124.

3. For a fuller discussion and comparison of these results, see https://www.washingtonpost.com/politics/2023/05/25/what-polls-tell-us-about-debt-limit-fight/.

4. Thomas Patterson, *Out of Order* (New York: Knopf, 1993).

Chapter 5

Why Do Pollsters Use Samples?

One of the most important decisions that every pollster has to make is how to best allocate the finite money that will be available for conducting a poll. There are two critical components to a poll that have real cost implications: (1) the number of people to interview and (2) the number of questions to ask. On the one hand, for any given budget, the longer the questionnaire takes to complete (the more questions asked), the fewer the number of respondents (the people who can be interviewed). On the other hand, the larger the sample of the completed questionnaires is, the less information that can be obtained from each respondent. The mode of interviewing also affects cost. *Telephone surveys* cost less than face-to-face surveys involving interviewers, and self-administered web surveys cost even less.

This is a critical trade-off for pollsters to make because a larger sample size provides a more precise estimate of how many people prefer one candidate over the other or support or oppose a particular policy, for example, deporting all residents who entered the United States illegally. But being able to ask more questions can provide important explanatory information about why some respondents prefer Candidate A to Candidate B or which kinds of people are likely to favor or oppose the deportation of all illegal immigrants.

Sampling is one of the most important tools that pollsters have to help them conduct representative surveys. A well-drawn, scientific sample allows a pollster to gather data from only a very small fraction of a population, but to draw inferences with a known degree of confidence back to the attitudes or behavior of the entire population of interest (such as the voting eligible population). But this can be done reliably and with confidence only if the sample is drawn according to certain laws of probability. When these procedures are followed, pollsters can accurately estimate the opinions of the more that 160 million American adults who will be registered to vote in the United States in 2024 with a sample of only a few thousand of them.

Many of the concepts underlying sampling are straightforward and easily understood. But some sampling concepts are almost counterintuitive, and many people find them confusing. One of the most important—and confusing—concepts is that the same-sized random sample will produce essentially as accurate an estimate of opinions in a city (e.g., Dallas), as it will for an entire state (e.g., Texas), as it will for an entire region of the country (e.g., the Southwest), or as it will for the entire United States. That is, the *precision* of an estimate derived from a sample is a function of the size of the final sample itself—almost entirely independent of the size of the population it originally is drawn from, except in the case of very small populations (those less than three thousand). This concept and other basic principles of sampling are discussed in the answers to the following questions.

WHAT IS SAMPLING?

Sampling is a technique for selecting a subset of *units* (such as people) from a population to produce an estimate of some attribute or characteristic of the entire population at a reasonable cost. In election polls, the typical units are individuals, usually adult citizens of the United States. The use of scientific sampling procedures allows a representative subset of citizens to be selected for interviewing. The information collected from people in a sample—such as their preferences for president of the United States—can be used to estimate the division of the vote in the entire population on Election Day.

The practice of sampling actually involves two steps. The first is the design of a scientific sample, and the second is the implementation of the sample in a valid and reliable way. In the first step, the statistical procedures of probability theory are used to decide how units will be selected. In the second step, administrative procedures are used to ensure good selection so that the sample has a representative response rate, and good *coverage* is achieved.

WHAT IS INVOLVED IN A SAMPLE DESIGN?

Three steps are involved in designing a sample. The first is to define the target population, the group of people for which the estimate will be made. The second is to select an appropriate sampling frame, which essentially is a list that contains all the members of the population that one wants to represent. It is important to have a clear and precise definition of the target population because it guides the search for an appropriate sampling frame. The third step is to choose an appropriate probability method of selecting the units from the frame from which data will hopefully be gathered.

The target population could be people who are likely to vote on Election Day. The sampling frame contains a list of all the units, or elements as they are sometimes called, in the population, in this case all of the eligible voters. A probability method of selection is one in which every element in the target population has a known, nonzero chance of selection. Sometimes all the units have the same chance of selection; other times, they have unequal (but nonzero) chances of selection.

Many election pollsters rely on *sample designs* that are not based on probability selection methods. Instead, they survey people who voluntarily make themselves available to be surveyed, but as a group these volunteers most often do not closely reflect the target populations of interest for election polls. These polls normally do not use sampling frames, and they do not produce results that have a known degree of confidence associated with them. The sampling approaches for election polls which use *nonprobability samples* are discussed in more detail later in this chapter.

WHAT IS THE TARGET POPULATION FOR AN ELECTION POLL?

In the 2024 pre-election surveys, pollsters typically will be interested in measuring the opinions and voting intentions of those Americans who actually will vote in the November 2024 general election, that is, the group of likely voters, or sometimes called the *probable electorate*. This group of Americans represents the target population for many of the 2024 election polls.

This definition will differ slightly by the phase of the campaign, however. In the beginning, most pollsters will be interested in interviewing US citizens who are eighteen years of age or older. They will not be too concerned about registration status because many of these people still have time to register before the general election. After the primaries, pollsters will be interested in the "voting-eligible population," in particular because (a) eligible citizens in most states can register to vote late into an election campaign and effective Get Out the Vote (GOTV) drives will motivate many to do that; and (b) campaigns that stimulate voter interest can change turnout on Election Day. As such, the attitudes and behavioral dispositions of this target population can be of strategic interest to politicians in close races and to journalists covering close races.

During the summer and into the general election campaign, starting around Labor Day in 2024, the population of interest becomes registered voters. And as Election Day nears, the target population becomes likely voters, or those who have a high probability of voting in the November 2024 election.

Some data from the last presidential election illustrate how these target populations differ. In 2022, an estimated 48 percent of Americans age eighteen and older voted in the general election in November. The approximately

122 million voters in 2022 represented about 76 percent of those registered to vote that year. Thus, an important challenge for pollsters is to accurately identify those who are registered and then among that cohort to accurately identify those who are likely to vote. And this is especially difficult for pollsters because many people who are not registered, and many of those who are registered but are not likely to vote, fail to report that accurately when they are contacted for an election poll.

In past years, the issue of defining the target population has been much more straightforward for the researchers who conduct exit polls for the primaries and general election. For exit polls, the target population traditionally was all people who turned out to vote at voting places on Election Day. Since these people were interviewed leaving their balloting places, the definitional problem was reduced substantially. However, the trend in the last two decades has been towards more and more voters choosing to vote early; in the 2020 November election, during COVID, 101 million Americans voted before Election Day. Thus, exit pollsters have had to expand their definition of their full target population to also include these "early voters." This has meant that they must utilize additional means of sampling, such as telephone surveys of these early voters, to supplement the sampling they do at select voting precincts on Election Day. In contacting people via telephone in an early voter survey, pollsters face the challenge of those who erroneously report they have voted when in fact they have not.

Furthermore, the effective population of interest for most 2024 election polls will be somewhat narrower in scope. For example, many national polls are limited to residents of the continental United States (the forty-eight contiguous states), and residents of Alaska and Hawaii are excluded from the target population and thus the sampling frame. A major reason for excluding Alaskans and Hawaiians is that the proportion of the US population residing in those two states is very small (less than 1 percent of the total population of the nation), and their exclusion has little effect on the estimates of opinions and voting intentions that the 2024 national polls will measure. Furthermore, the majority of Alaskans traditionally support the Republican candidate in presidential elections (in 2020, only 43 percent voted for Biden), whereas the majority of Hawaiians support the Democratic candidate (in 2020, 64 percent voted for Biden); thus, the voting trends in these two states tend to balance each other out. As a result, pollsters make a conscious cost-benefit calculation to accept a very small bit of inaccuracy caused by omitting Alaskans and Hawaiians from their election surveys in exchange for reducing expenses by not gathering data for national samples in those states.

Furthermore, anyone who does not speak a language in which the poll questionnaire has been written cannot be interviewed and is also technically omitted from the target population. For example, approximately 8 to

10 percent of the American population are only able to complete a survey if the questionnaire is presented to them in Spanish. However, only a small proportion of residents in the United States who only or mostly speak Spanish will vote. Some 2024 election polls will include the capacity to gather data from those who need to be interviewed in Spanish, such as some of those conducted in California, but because of the expense most polls will only interview in English. In the past, pollsters have believed correctly that in almost all instances, restricting the population of interest to a more practical definition of the effective population—and thus, for example, excluding Hispanic citizens of the United States who are likely to vote but who need to be interviewed in Spanish—would not make any appreciable difference in the accuracy of their polls' projections of a likely winner or in their determinations of the opinions of the American electorate. However, with the new population trends in the United States showing an increasing percentage of the adult citizenry not speaking English as their first language, more pollsters may need to consider adding the capacity to gather election poll data in languages other than English. Some of Donald Trump's comments about immigrants in the United States may also have spurred their turnout in the 2016 and 2020 elections. This likely will also be especially important in polls that focus on local elections in certain areas of the United States.

WHAT IS A SAMPLING FRAME?

Simply put, the *sampling frame* is a listing of the target population from which an initial sample is drawn. There is no standard list of all the registered voters in the United States that can be used by pollsters as a sampling frame for election polls, at least not one that is accurate and up-to-date and contains the telephone numbers at their residences or their e-mail addresses. In some cases, such a listing exists for subsets of the population, somewhere physically on paper or in a computer file. Some commercial firms have created lists for substantial number of registered voters[1] or politically relevant groups in the population such as Democrats.[2] Most election administrations make a list of their registered voters available (containing no information about their vote choices, of course), and this information is combined with other commercially available information to construct their lists.

When such a frame does exist, it can be used to draw a sample by selecting a portion of the voters or households from the list. For example, pollsters interested in doing a statewide poll in a state with a small population, such as North Dakota or Rhode Island, might be able to assemble an entire listing of registered voters in the state to use as a sampling frame. Then they would have to associate the correct telephone numbers with the names of the registered voters if they were conducting a telephone poll. With currently available technology, this task would not be feasible in a large state or for the nation as a whole because of the prohibitive cost.

DO TELEPHONE DIRECTORIES MAKE A GOOD SAMPLING FRAME FOR ELECTION POLLS?

No, they do not, and rarely have in the history of election polls. In fact, the 1936 election polling debacle when *The Literary Digest* magazine predicted that the Republican, Alf Landon, would beat the Democratic incumbent president, Franklin D. Roosevelt, it was partially because telephone directories had been used as a major sampling frame for that election poll.

Telephone directories are rarely used as the sampling frame in modern election polls because many people are not represented in any telephone book. This is because they do not have a published (or listed) number or they do not have a telephone in their home. By 2024, it is projected that more than 80 percent of American households will not have a telephone number that is listed in a directory—either landline or cell—and 3 percent will have no telephone service at all. Those, as a group, who do not have a number listed will be demographically very different from those, as a group, who do have a number listed, in that they will be much older, less educated, and of lower income. Since each of these demographics is correlated with traditional voting preferences, election polls based on a telephone directory sampling frame will underrepresent the candidate preferences of members of these demographic cohorts (e.g., the candidate preference of African Americans who traditionally have given strong support to Democratic candidates).

DO LISTS OF E-MAIL ADDRESSES MAKE A GOOD SAMPLING FRAME FOR ELECTION POLLS?

No, they do not. There is no existing list of e-mail addresses that comes anywhere close to representing the population of US citizens who will vote in the 2024 elections. And it is unlikely that such a comprehensive list will exist in the coming decades. Even if such a list of voters with e-mail addresses could be compiled in 2024, it would vastly underrepresent older voters who are the demographic cohort least likely to have and use an e-mail address, but who as a group, tend to vote differently from younger adults.

WHAT IS THE SAMPLING FRAME FOR A TYPICAL PRE-ELECTION INTERNET POLL?

The sampling frame for a typical pre-election internet poll will vary depending on whether the poll is gathering data from a sample that was selected solely to participate in the election poll or whether data will be gathered from a sample that is part of a preexisting research panel, such as a group of people who have agreed to participate in a series of ongoing surveys being conducted by a survey organization, of which the pre-election poll turns out to be one. If the sample for the election polls is chosen from a frame comprised of a preexisting research panel, then the question really is what frame(s) were used to create that panel. There is no standard approach for choosing a frame or frames for creating internet panels and thus no standard answer to this question. Suffice it to say that there is considerable variation in the representational quality of the frames that are used to create research panels, with some being woefully unrepresentative of any knowable target population and others being reasonably representative of the US adult population.

The quality of the sampling frame used to create internet research panels also will vary depending on whether a probability or a nonprobability approach to sampling is being used. There are a limited number of probability-based internet panels in the United States (fewer than twenty), whereas there are hundreds of nonprobability panels. The probability-based panels, such as the AmeriSpeak panel at NORC (at the University of Chicago), use a national address frame that is as high in quality as the best US government frames. However, many of the nonprobability internet panels do not use any formally devised frame but simply recruit volunteers; as a result, they cannot accurately describe where their panels' members originally came from. Thus, these panels often cannot legitimately claim to represent a known target population such as the general population of the United States.

In the case of a pre-election poll that is not connected with an internet research panel but does gather data via the internet, the sampling frame may be one of addresses or of randomly generated telephone numbers (both cell phone and landline numbers). Households and thus people are sampled and contacted from the chosen frame and requested to go to a website to complete the pre-election questionnaire for the poll.

In the case of a pre-election poll that is conducted with members of an internet research panel, the panel may have been formed in various ways. The much more scientific of those ways include using a frame of addresses to originally establish the panel. In the far less scientific approach, the panel is originally formed without using any formal frame, and thus it cannot claim to represent a knowable target population. Instead, "invitations" to join such panels go out via various means (including pop-up invitations when people are visiting various websites), and some extremely small proportion (fewer than 1 percent) of the people exposed to these invitations self-select to join the panel. In the case where no formal frame is used, the researchers have no control over who is invited to join and thus who does join.

WHAT IS REGISTRATION-BASED SAMPLING (RBS)?

Registration-Based Sampling (RBS) is a sampling approach for conducting election polls that has been used with growing frequency in the past three decades. RBS frames for a given geopolitical area can be created by pollsters from public records for a political jurisdiction, or they can be purchased from vendors who already have created the frame. But the creation of an RBS frame by a pollster can be a very laborious and costly endeavor, so it is likely to happen only for relatively small political jurisdictions.

An advantage of RBS is that the name of the sampled voter is available for use in gaining that respondent's cooperation at the time of their recruitment. Another major advantage of the RBS frame over a telephone number frame is that the RBS frame often comes with other valuable variables to help plan the sampling design for an election poll. A major disadvantage of the RBS frame is that the quality of RBS frames varies considerably across different jurisdictions, and in some cases coverage of the probable electorate can be so poor as to render the RBS frame invalid. Because RBS frames have addresses, and often telephone numbers, and some have e-mail addresses for each registered voter, the mode of data collection can be mail, telephone, in-person, internet, or any combination of these.

The use of RBS will increase in 2024 compared to its frequency of use in 2020 and 2022, but many pollsters still do not have the time or will not take the time, which can be considerable, that is required to switch their sampling designs to include RBS. However, the potential advantages of RBS for election polling are such that it will nevertheless grow in usage, especially as the accessibility and quality of registered voter databases increases in the coming years.

WHAT IS THE SAMPLING FRAME FOR THE TYPICAL EXIT POLL?

Exit polls are conducted via in-person interviewers with citizens immediately after they have voted and are leaving their balloting places. Collecting quality exit poll data requires a major logistical and extremely expensive effort, especially at the national level, but the sample design traditionally has been quite straightforward. It involves multiple stages at which different units are selected. The initial sampling frame is a theoretical listing of all possible voting places within the geographic region of interest. For a national exit poll to estimate the outcome of the presidential race, which consists of a series of state-level exit polls, the sampling frame starts with all 3,043 counties in the United States. Within a state, the counties are assigned to different strata (i.e., geographic subgroups) that are usually, but not always, contiguous whole counties. In the next stage, a systematic selection of voting precincts is drawn from a list of all precincts in each stratum, ordered by their typical vote for one of the two major political parties. In the third and final stage, a random sample of voters in each sample precinct is continuously drawn for interviews throughout the day and evening of the election, until the balloting stops.

For the 2020 general election, Election Day exit polls were conducted at 746 precincts. There was a national exit poll and 24 state exit polls. All the national and state exit poll cross-tabulations also included mail and early voters interviewed by either a telephone sample (RDD sampling) or Registration-Based Sampling (RBS) with a live interviewer. In addition, eight states with a high proportion of early voters also included data collected using exit polls of early voters at early voting locations. The total number of interviews for the national exit poll cross-tabulations was 15,590. The total number of interviews for the 24 state exit poll cross-tabulations was 68,857.

For the 2022 general election, Election Day exit polls were conducted at 488 precincts. There was a national exit poll and 11 state exit polls. All the national and state exit poll analyses also included data from mail and other early voters interviewed by an RBS survey. The RBS surveys in 2022 were conducted using live interviewers, as well as online with contact made via text to cell phones and by e-mail. In addition, 7 states with a high proportion of early voters also included data collected using exit polls of early voters at early voting locations. The total number of interviews for the 2022 national exit poll analyses was 18,571. The total number of interviews for the 11 state exit poll cross-tabulations was 35,520.

HOW LARGE DOES A SAMPLE NEED TO BE?

Two important principles are associated with the size of a sample. The first is that the larger the sample size, the more precise the estimate of an election outcome that can be made from it, especially when using a probability sample. And the estimate can be made with greater confidence. People who design samples use the term *margin of sampling error (MOSE)* to describe the precision of a sample estimate if using a probability sample. This is a well-respected statistical measure that provides an estimate of the likely difference between a finding from a sample compared to the actual or true value in the population due solely to chance deviations, without considering any other form of survey error. However, the MOSE concept is inappropriately used by many who conduct nonprobability election polls.

All other things being equal, final sample sizes should be as large as necessary to provide the degree of sampling precision (and confidence) that the pollster requires to produce a good estimate of the election measure (e.g., which candidate is likely to win). This consideration comes into play because the money saved by interviewing fewer people can often be used to increase the length of the questionnaire itself or to improve quality control during recruitment and data collection. But a general rule of thumb is that in a horse race poll that is trying to determine which of the candidates is leading, the closer the election is thought to be the larger the final sample size of completed questionnaires is required for the poll. That is because a pollster needs the greater precision and confidence that a larger sample size produces when an election is very close.

The second important principle is that the precision of a sample is typically not related to the size of the population from which it is drawn unless the population is very small (less than 3,000). In order to produce an estimate with a given MOSE, the same-sized sample would have to be drawn from a city of 100,000 adults, or a state with a population of 15 million adults, or the entire United States, with its population of more than 300 million adults.

WHAT IS THE MARGIN OF SAMPLING ERROR (MOSE) FOR A PARTICULAR SAMPLE?

The larger a sample, the more precise are the estimates it produces, and the more confident one can be about the poll results, providing a probability sampling approach was used. If a nonprobability sampling approach was used for the poll, then the MOSE cannot be calculated, and users of the poll will remain uncertain about how much confidence they can place in the poll's findings. Unfortunately, this reality is often ignored by those who conduct election polls using nonprobability sampling approaches. So let the consumer of such polls beware.

A larger sample produces a better estimate than a smaller sample, all other things being equal. The precision of a sample is described by its sampling error, or the margin of sampling error (MOSE) around the estimate that it produces. The margin of sampling error is a way of describing an interval of uncertainty within which the true value of the statistic (e.g., what proportion of voters are going to support the Republican candidate) for the entire population is likely to fall.

There are standard statistical formulae, originally developed for application to agricultural research in the first half of the twentieth century, that can be used to determine how confident the pollster should be that a finding in the sample (e.g., the percentage who say they will vote for Candidate X) reflects the target population's opinions or intentions on that measure. The *New York Times*, for example, traditionally has printed a methodological sidebar when reporting the results of its election polls. This sidebar explains the size of the poll's MOSE in language like the following:

> *In theory, in nineteen cases out of twenty, the results based on such samples will differ by no more than 3 percentage points in either direction from what would have been obtained by seeking out all American adults. For smaller subgroups, the margin of error is larger.*

Here, the newspaper is explaining that there is a degree of confidence (nineteen in twenty, or 95 percent confidence)—not a certainty—that an estimate derived from the entire sample will approximate the same figure in the target population, within ± 3 percentage points.

Suppose a pollster conducts a survey to measure President Biden's approval rating. In response to a specific survey question, 29 percent of those interviewed say they approve of the way Joe Biden is handling his job as president. A sample of 1,500 respondents has an approximate margin of error of 2.5 percentage points associated with it, at the 95 percent *confidence level*. That means that one can be reasonably confident (one can expect that 95 times out of 100) that another similar survey would find that President Biden's approval rating lies between 26.5 percent (29 percent minus 2.5 percent) and 31.5 percent (29 percent plus 2.5 percent) of the population.

It is important to note that the MOSE does not get smaller in a direct fashion as the sample size increases. For example, if one sample is twice as large as another, it will produce a MOSE that is only about one-third smaller, not half smaller.

Using a nonprobability approach to sampling does not allow one to estimate the confidence that is associated with a poll finding using the MOSE. This is a distinct disadvantage in interpreting findings from nonprobability election polls.

HOW DOES SAMPLE SIZE AFFECT THE PRECISION OF A POLL'S ESTIMATES?

That depends on how precise an estimate the pollster needs, in relation to how much money the organization or sponsor of the poll wants to spend for a probability sample. It also depends on how the pollster wants to break down the findings across demographic subgroups (females vs. male voters), as each of those subgroups are smaller than the entire sample and thus measurements based on those subgroups will be less precise than measurements based on the entire sample.

For most measures of public opinion, such as attitudes or intended voting behavior, a MOSE of between 3 and 5 percentage points normally proves to be tolerable. That is, most political issues do not produce opinions that are evenly divided (50–50) and therefore analysts are confident they can report that a majority favors one side or the other. Even in election analysis, most elections are not decided by margins of less than 52 to 48 percent, so a winner can safely be called in most cases with a MOSE of ± 3 percentage points.

On the other hand, if there were reason to believe that an election would be very close or that opinions were evenly divided on an issue, a polling organization might decide that a larger sample was needed to produce a more accurate estimate of the division of opinion or to indicate which side of an issue really had a majority of people supporting it. Table 5.1 shows the MOSE associated with estimates produced from simple random probability samples of different sizes and for different confidence intervals. As an aid in interpreting the table, the entries for samples of size 1,500 indicate that the amount of error due to chance alone would be ± 2.5 percentage points for 95 out of 100 samples drawn. For a greater level of confidence (say, knowing that the sample estimate was within sampling error of the population value in 99 samples out of 100), the MOSE for the same-size sample would of course be larger and thus less precise—approximately ± 3.3 percentage points. If

Table 5.1 Margins of Sampling Error for Simple Random Probability Samples

Sample size	Tolerance at the 95 percent confidence level	Tolerance at the 99 percent confidence level
100	± 9.8 percentage points	± 12.9 percentage points
200	± 6.9 percentage points	± 9.1 percentage points
400	± 4.9 percentage points	± 6.5 percentage points
750	± 3.6 percentage points	± 4.7 percentage points
1,000	± 3.1 percentage points	± 4.1 percentage points
1,500	± 2.5 percentage points	± 3.3 percentage points
3,000	± 1.8 percentage points	± 2.4 percentage points
5,000	± 1.4 percentage points	± 1.8 percentage points

the sample size is doubled to 3,000 (that is, about twice as much money was spent collecting the data), the MOSE at the 95 percent level of confidence reduces to only ± 1.8 percentage points versus ± 2.5 for the sample of 1,500.

If a pre-election poll using a probability sample of about 1,100 voters finds that 45 percent intend to vote for Candidate X, then the poll actually has found that somewhere between 42 and 48 percent of the target population can be expected to vote for Candidate X. When using a probability sample, this range of 42 to 48 percent is technically referred to as a *confidence interval* around the population value; and the statistical procedures for calculating this MOSE (± 3 percentage points in this example) will lead to a correct finding 95 percent of the time.

The table shows that there are very substantial reductions in the MOSE up to sample sizes of about 1,000. Beyond that, however, the improvements are less than 1 percentage point for reasonable increments in the sample size. For this reason, the typical media election poll has a sample size between 1,000 and 1,500 respondents and rarely exceeds that because the cost of gathering additional completed questionnaires does not reduce the MOSE enough to justify the appreciable increment to costs.

A final point is that most probability samples used for election polling are not *simple random samples*, and instead are much more complex than that simple sampling design. When more complex sampling designs are used, they tend to increase the imprecision that is associated with a given final sample size of completed questionnaires compared to the MOSE that a simple random sample would provide. This increase in the MOSE is quantified by a statistic known as the design effect or deff. With a simple random sample, the deff is 1.0. But with the most complex sampling designs, it exceeds 1.0 in value. Most media polls use sampling designs that have a deff of 1.3 or larger. When the deff of a sample exceeds 1.0, it lowers the size of what is termed the "effective sample size" and thus lowers the precision of the poll because it increases the poll's MOSE. For example, with a deff of 1.5, a poll using a probability sample with 1,000 completed questionnaires would have an effective sample size of 667 (1000/1.5), and the MOSE for that poll would be ± 3.7 percentage points, not ± 3.1 percentage points.

Of note, there are other sources of potential errors in surveys that do not come from sampling, and they are discussed in chapters 6 and 7.

WHY ARE SOME SAMPLE DESIGNS PREFERABLE TO OTHERS?

Sample designs differ in three major ways. First, they need to be based on the laws of probability to take advantage of such concepts as the margin of sampling error (MOSE). Second, they also vary in terms of the precision of the estimates they produce. And third, they vary in the ease with which they can be implemented.

A probability design is one in which every unit in the population has a known, nonzero chance of being selected for a poll's initial sample. If some units (e.g., people registered to vote) have no chance of being selected, or they can select themselves into the initial sample, then this is not a probability design. Some designs are less efficient than others; that is, they produce estimates with larger MOSEs. Simple random samples generally have the smallest sampling errors associated with them, but they are rarely used in election polls because there is no single list of registered voters that pollsters can use to select names at random. Pollsters must find or construct a frame by using, for example, *dual-frame random-digit dialing* (DFRDD) techniques to select telephone households and then to select a respondent from among the eligible adults who reside there. There are different ways of going through this procedure, some of which are preferable to others.

Generally, DFRDD samples have slightly larger sampling errors than simple random samples. Some polls are not meant to gather findings to describe the larger population with a known degree of accuracy. For example, in the early stages of the election season, a candidate's private pollster may want to study the opinions of a relatively rare group within the larger population—such as African American Republicans. The pollster (and the candidate) may not need to estimate how all African American Republican likely voters think about certain issues but may simply want to get a general sense of what issues appear to be of most concern to this cohort. The challenge here is to sample, recruit, and gather data from enough African American Republicans to meet this need.

One approach would be to use a nonprobability *snowball sample*, one in which each African American Republican interviewed is subsequently asked to nominate other African American Republican family members, friends, or other acquaintances who will subsequently be contacted for an interview. This process continues until the sample "snowballs" to its final desired sample size. There is no MOSE for this "poll," but that will not matter for the needs of those funding and carrying out this particular study.

WHAT IS A PROBABILITY SAMPLE?

If a pollster selects voters from a sampling frame that contains the members of the target population and two additional conditions are met, then the poll has employed a form of probability sampling. These two necessary conditions are that (1) everyone in the sampling frame has a nonzero chance of being selected, and (2) the pollster can determine the actual probability of each person being selected. The value of probability samples is that they allow pollsters to use well-known statistical formulas to determine how likely it is that the findings from the poll's sample accurately reflect the opinions and intentions of the target population with a known level of confidence.

Some pre-primary and pre-election polls in 2024 will be conducted via telephone interviews. These polls are likely to use dual-frame random-digit dialing (DFRDD) techniques to reach households that contain the likely voters to be interviewed. Here, the target population is voters residing in households with a telephone, be it a cell phone and/or a landline; the sampling frame consists of all possible telephone numbers within the geographic area covered by the poll. But the issue of calling into a known geographic area has become increasingly more complex for pollsters to negotiate as (1) people are constantly moving in and out of geographic areas and taking or bringing their cell phone number with them and (2) as the prevalence of number portability grows. This undermines knowledge of the geographical location in which the owner of the phone number resides. In order for a DFRDD sample to be a true probability sample, the pollster must know the probability of each household (or in the case of a cell phone sample, each person) being reached and the probability that a given adult within the household was selected from all adults residing in that household. These are characteristics of households that change over time, reflecting changes in American lifestyles. Polling organizations must track these changes carefully and consistently so they can account for them in their sampling procedures.

For example, a person who can be reached at home on three cell phones has three times the chance of being in the DFRDD sample compared to someone with only one cell phone. Furthermore, people with a landline who live with several other adults (such as a husband and wife and their two adult live-in children) each has a smaller probability of being selected within their own household as the designated respondent to be interviewed than do those who live with no one else or just one other adult. Thus, pollsters have to ask respondents to telephone surveys how many separate residential/personal telephone numbers (landline and cell phone) they have and how many other adults can be reached via these numbers in order to know how to calculate the probability of selection for each person who is interviewed. If pollsters cannot calculate these probabilities of selection, they cannot make proper use of the statistical formulas for calculating the survey's margin of sampling error (MOSE).

WHY AND HOW DO POLLSTERS CHOOSE ONLY ONE PERSON WITHIN A HOUSEHOLD TO INTERVIEW?

When a pre-election telephone poll is conducted with someone in a household sampled via its landline or with a mail survey, researchers need to decide which person in the household should be interviewed. If the poll reaches a household with only one adult, then that person is the "designated respondent." However, most American households (more than 75 percent) have two or more adults in residence. In these households it would not be valid if interviewers simply were allowed to interview the first person to answer the phone or to open the mail, because there is a tendency for women and older adults to be the ones most likely to answer a ringing landline telephone or open the mail in multiple-adult households; and this would result in a sample with unrepresentative demographic characteristics. Instead, the researchers normally will deploy a systematic selection approach to guide the interviewer in choosing one and only one person to interview among all potentially eligible adults who reside in the household. There are many ways this systematic selection can be accomplished, but a common method used by election pollsters using the phone is to have the interviewer simply ask to speak with "the adult in the household who has had the last (most recent) birthday" or to ask for the one who has the "next" birthday. In theory this will select a random person among all eligible adults in the household. In practice, it does not always exactly work as it is intended, but it nevertheless avoids the biasing problems caused if the first person answering the phone or opening the mail was always the one interviewed.

When a cell phone number reaches someone in a geographically eligible household, interviewers can assume that in most cases there will be only one person who answers the cell phone. However, in a minority of cases—exactly how many in the US is uncertain, but estimates range up to 20 percent—the cell phone is used by more than one person. In these cases, interviewers should be directed to use a systematic selection technique to choose one of them to interview (e.g., the "last birthday" or "next birthday" method) rather than simply conducting the poll with the person who initially answers the cell phone.

With surveys that recruit people via addresses, including when a research panel is originally created in this fashion, the same issue of selecting one and only one eligible person per household to complete the questionnaire comes into play. That is, it generally is not prudent to allow anyone in the household to complete the questionnaire if the poll wants to legitimately claim that a probability sample of persons has been conducted.

Thus, it is not enough for a poll to be valid merely to have a representative sample of households sampled. In addition, a systematic method must be deployed to choose a representative sample of eligible people within the households.

WHAT IS A NONPROBABILITY SAMPLE?

Any group of people can be polled and treated as a sample. Unless pollsters use certain well-known and well-established probability sampling techniques, however, the pollster will have no way of estimating, with a known degree of confidence, the extent to which the respondents' answers represent any definable larger population. Whenever a sample of voters is selected without a clear specification of the target population they are supposed to represent, or the probabilities of selection are unknown, or respondents are allowed to self-select into, or otherwise volunteer to be part of, the poll's sample, the pollster has employed some form of nonprobability sampling. And, when a nonprobability sample is used, the pollsters cannot legitimately claim to know the poll's margin of sampling error (MOSE).

Strictly speaking, unless the pollster uses some selection rule that represents the target population well and then uses some selection rule that gives everyone in the frame a nonzero chance of being selected, the pollster is using a nonprobability sample. If the pollster gives everyone in the sampling frame a chance of being selected but does not know the exact probability of selecting each person in the sampling frame, then once again the pollster is left with a nonprobability sample.

For example, market researchers often use a surveying technique referred to as *mall intercept interviews*: interviewers in a shopping mall stop several people and try to interview them. The findings from this type of nonprobability sample cannot be generalized to a target population because the researchers can accurately define neither what population is represented by the *intercept sample* nor the probability that each person in this unknown population had of being selected. Election *straw polls*, another form of nonprobability sampling, often use sampling techniques that resemble mall intercept sampling. There is no way to determine with any confidence the accuracy of an estimate of candidate preference derived from such straw polls in relation to the target population of persons who are likely to vote in the election.

In the past decade, some pollsters using nonprobability samples to predict election outcomes have started to report a statistic that they believe provides somewhat similar information as the margin of sampling error and confidence intervals do for a probability sample. This statistic is sometimes called a "credibility interval." There is a belief among some pollsters that the credibility interval that can be reported for a nonprobability pre-election poll provides valuable information about the confidence that should be placed on the poll's findings. However, this statistic is controversial because of the assumptions that must be made about what is being studied and how it is being studied. Sometimes the implications of these assumptions are ignored, and other times they are not even considered. Therefore, election poll followers are well advised to be cautious in interpreting any election poll using a nonprobability sample that reports a credibility interval with the same sense of assurance that pollsters using a probability sample have when they report their poll's margin of sample error and its confidence intervals.

ARE NONPROBABILITY SAMPLES EVER COMBINED WITH PROBABILITY SAMPLES?

Yes, they are, and this approach to election polling is growing in usage. The impetus for doing this is that much larger samples can be generated at a much lower total cost than if just probability sampling were being used for all the data collection. This is especially appealing to pollsters who want to do national election polling but also want to get ample subsample sizes for all the state elections of interest.

The justification underlying this hybrid approach to sampling is that the findings from the nonprobability sample can be calibrated (i.e., adjusted) by the findings of the probability sample. The rationale here is that there can be much greater confidence that the findings of the probability sample are accurate than the confidence that can be placed on the accuracy of the noncalibrated nonprobability sample. This hybrid approach is still in its infancy and much more testing is needed in the coming years before its ultimate value is known. But currently some of the major survey organizations in the United States have begun using such hybrid approaches for election polling. For example, in 2020, the NORC at the University of Chicago used their TrueNorth surveying modeling with their AP/NORC VoteCast election survey by combining data from a relatively small sample from its probability-based AmeriSpeak panel (4,101 respondents) and a larger probability sample from a registered voter file (41,776 respondents) to help to calibrate the data that came from a much larger nonprobability sample (87,186 respondents) to measure voting intentions nationally and at the state level in 2020. This hybrid approach correctly projected the winner in 90 percent of US Senate and governor elections and the Biden-Trump presidential elections, including forty-five of fifty states before final vote adjustments were made as part of the *weighting* process.

WHAT IS A RANDOM SAMPLE?

A sample can be drawn from a sampling frame in many ways. One common technique is called a *random sample* because the elements contained in the sampling frame are chosen for the sample at random. "At random" means that the choice of any one individual in the sampling frame is completely arbitrary and based only on chance. Sometimes a random sample is drawn with every person in the frame having an equal chance of being chosen. This is called an equal probability of selection method, or an *EPSEM sample*.

The main advantage of a random selection procedure is that it avoids any conscious or subconscious human bias from entering the selection process. A simple random sample uses a set of random numbers that, nowadays, are typically generated directly by a computer program; formerly, they were selected from random numbers tables that were printed in statistics books (also generated at one time from a computer before they were typeset). The series of numbers consisting of 3, 47, 428, and 1,752 is a random series of numbers that, if applied to a sampling frame, would lead to the selection of the 3rd, 47th, 428th, and 1,752nd persons listed on the sampling frame.

Although it is unlikely to happen, a set of random numbers may yield an unrepresentative sample from the sampling frame. By representative, we mean a sample that matches quite well the various demographic, behavioral, and attitudinal characteristics of the population of interest as articulated by the sampling frame. For example, although it would be highly unlikely, it is possible just by chance that a random set of selections could fall almost entirely within the first half of the sampling frame. In this example, if there were any order within the sampling frame, such as place of residence within the survey area, then these choices might be random but not necessarily representative at all and may well bias the results of the poll.

WHAT IS A SYSTEMATIC SAMPLE?

A *systematic sample* is a special form of *random sampling*. A systematic sample forms a sample that is more likely than a simple random sample to represent the sampling frame. It does this by forcing the random selection to take place over the entire sampling frame, from the beginning through the end. The way that this occurs is straightforward. First, a *sampling interval* is determined. The sampling interval is simply the total number of persons in the sampling frame divided by the number of persons to be initially sampled. If there were 1,000,000 persons in the sampling frame and the number to be sampled was 2,000, then the sampling interval would be 1,000,000/2,000, or 500. In this example, the next step in the systematic sampling process involves choosing a "random start" between 1 and 500, say 322. Then the 322nd person on the sampling frame would be the first one selected. After that, every 500th person (822nd; 1,322nd; 1,822nd; 2,322nd; etc.) would be selected from the sampling frame. The last person to be chosen for the sample would be the 999,822nd person on the frame. A systematic random sample has the advantages of being both random and more likely to be representative of the sampling frame, if the width of the sampling interval is in no way correlated with any peculiar pattern or order in the sampling frame itself.

WHAT IS A STRATIFIED SAMPLE?

A *stratified sample* is another form of random sampling that strives to ensure that the sample is also representative. Stratified sampling occurs when the sampling frame can be grouped into meaningful subcategories (strata), such as by age or race or place of residence or even party affiliation. Then either simple random sampling or systematic sampling procedures can be applied within each subgroup (i.e., each *stratum*) on the frame, ensuring that a proportional number from each group gets chosen—something that will not necessarily occur with simple random sampling or even with systematic sampling. For example, assume that a pollster is sampling from registered voter lists that show whether someone has voted in a Republican or Democratic primary in the recent past. If Republican voters are expected to constitute 55 percent of election turnout, then a sampling frame of registered voters could be stratified by likely party affiliation, and then 55 percent of the sample could be chosen randomly or systematically from the Republican stratum.

Despite the advantages that stratified sampling affords pollsters who want to ensure a random and representative sample, stratified sampling is often not feasible because not all lists can be grouped or organized according to meaningful strata.

DO YOU NEED A LARGER SAMPLE SIZE WITH A NATIONAL POLL THAN YOU DO IN A STATEWIDE OR CITYWIDE POLL?

It comes as a big surprise to many people to learn that a sample size of 1,000 voters is no more accurate, from a sampling error standpoint, in measuring the voting intentions in a citywide election (in which the turnout will be several hundred thousand voters) than a sample of 1,000 voters will be in a national election that will have 160 million citizens voting. In this example, each poll's margin of error (MOSE) would be essentially ± 3.1 percentage points, with 95 percent confidence. In most instances, polls intended to measure voting intentions among the electorate within an MOSE of ± 3 percentage points will need a final sample in the range of approximately 1,100 voters, regardless of how many citizens will actually vote in the election. This rule begins to break down when the actual number of voters (the size of the target population) is very small. In statistical terms, "small" applies to target populations that are less than 10,000 in size. So, if an election in a small town will have a turnout of 2,000 voters, the MOSE for a pre-election poll of 1,000 of those voters—half the voters—is in fact smaller than ± 3 percentage points, as intuition might suggest. Even in this example, however, the MOSE would decrease by only 1 percentage point to ± 2 percentage points in a poll in which half the population of interest would be measured.

This may defy logic, but nevertheless it is statistically accurate. Ultimately, it all hinges on the role of chance and the less-than-total certainty a pollster has with anything other than a complete census. Sometimes pollsters increase their sample sizes as Election Day approaches. For most national pre-election polls taken late in the campaign, the traditional sample size will be approximately 2,200 voters. This number is chosen because pollsters want to be able to predict the election outcome within ± 2 percentage points. If pollsters for a statewide gubernatorial or senatorial election wanted the same level of accuracy, they too would need to survey about 2,200 voters across that state. This level of accuracy allows pollsters to predict winners of races as close as 52 percent to 48 percent with considerable confidence.

WHAT IS THE RESPONSE RATE TO A SURVEY?

Every election poll faces real fiscal limits and practical time constraints. To be useful to their varied sponsors, including being newsworthy for their media sponsors, election polls must measure voters' opinions and intentions within a known and meaningful time frame. These limitations almost always lead to some people being sampled for a poll but never being interviewed. The difference between the number of people initially being sampled for a poll and the actual number interviewed is reflected in the poll's response rate.

In its simplest form the response rate is the proportion of sampled voters from whom data are eventually gathered. It essentially compares the proportion of respondents who provide the data being sought versus the proportion of nonrespondents who were sampled but did not provide data.

For example, if 1,200 households were sampled for an internet questionnaire poll but only 800 completed the questionnaire (one per household) during the poll's field period—the number of days, or even hours, that elapse from start to finish during which time data are being collected—then the poll's response rate would be 800/1,200, or 67 percent. In this simple example, the size of the poll's nonresponse rate would be 33 percent, since one in three sampled households did not provide data.

In most election polls, the pollster has a predetermined final sample size that needs to be achieved. If using a telephone poll, the pollster then has interviewers try to contact enough sampled voters to reach the desired sample size. This process occurs because it is both the sample size and the response rate that drive the process. That is, the more sampled voters who refuse to participate or who are never contacted during the field period, the more phone numbers interviewers have to process to achieve the desired sample size. If a poll is conducted over a weekend, then the response rate will likely be much lower than if it were conducted over a longer period, such as a week. This will happen because sampled people are harder to reach within a short field period (e.g., two days or less) than in a longer field period (e.g., a week).

There are many causes of nonresponse in polls, and thus for low response rates, but the primary problems that pollsters encounter are *noncontacts* and *refusals*. A noncontact occurs whenever a sampled household or person is never reached to be interviewed during the poll's field period. The busy lifestyles of members of the electorate and technologies such as internet spam filters, Caller ID, privacy managers, and the like have made it much harder across the last thirty years to contact sampled voters in polls that have a short field period. Refusals too have become more frequent as many members of the public have come to feel hounded by telemarketers and other fund-raisers, market researchers, and pollsters—some of whom are unscrupulous in their methods and intents.

In 2024, the response rates for most of the media-sponsored pre-election telephone polls will be less than 10 percent. That means that in these polls 9 out of 10 of those who were sampled will not provide any data. And for many internet polls the response rates will be lower than 1 percent, with fewer than 99 out of 100 people invited to participate in the poll failing to provide any data. Yet, remarkably, many otherwise good quality election polls will generate predictions that are very close to the outcome of the elections the polls are meant to predict. For this to happen, these polls must not be suffering from any appreciable *nonresponse error* or bias despite having very low response rates.

Furthermore, for those internet polls that use a probability-based internet panel, the original research panel very likely had less than a 10 percent response rate when it was being formed. Then when its panel members are sampled to participate in a specific pre-election poll, a typical response rate within the panel sample is likely to be in the 50 to 70 percent range. In contrast, for *opt-in internet panels* that did not use probability selection methods to form the panel, it is impossible to calculate an original response rate at the time the panel was formed. But it is highly likely that the rate was far less than one percent. When these panels are used for pre-election polling, the sampled members of these types of panels are likely to respond at a rate of 20 to 40 percent. Some opt-in nonprobability-based internet panel election polls are very accurate whereas others are not.

HOW DOES NONRESPONSE AFFECT SURVEY ACCURACY?

There are many possible threats to the accuracy of a survey. One is associated with sampling error, i.e., the MOSE. Another important source of *nonsampling error* is nonresponse error, which can occur in a poll if the sampled group from whom data are gathered holds considerably different opinions and intentions from the sampled group from whom no data are gathered. Nonresponse error is one of the major reasons that a sample of voters who completed the questionnaire for a poll may not accurately reflect the attitudes and behavioral intentions of the entire target population.

To illustrate how this works, imagine a primary election in which a younger female challenger is running against an older male incumbent, and both have similar positions on the issues that matter to voters. Suppose further that the male incumbent had been in office for several decades and that the female challenger is running on the theme that "change is long overdue." Also, assume this theme is more attractive to younger voters. However, younger voters are notoriously hard to reach for survey data collection. As such, nonresponse by people of a particular age range (e.g., those registered to vote who are 18 to 34 years of age) in a pre-election poll could predictably lead to considerable nonresponse error. Suppose further that a two-day internet poll of 500 likely voters, with a margin of sampling error of ± 4 percentage points, showed the male incumbent was preferred by 54 percent of those surveyed, with 46 percent supporting the female challenger. Applying the poll's margin of sampling error would lead to the conclusion that the male incumbent would receive between 50 and 58 percent support and the female challenger between 42 and 50 percent support. This looks like a close race, but with the male incumbent expected to win. If this poll were conducted over the weekend before the election, it would not be unusual for the poll to achieve a response rate of 20 percent or less. Years of experience show that most polls of voters find it much harder to reach younger adults, especially on weekends, than older adults. In this example, suppose the response rate was 14 percent, and 60 percent of the nonrespondents were likely voters who supported the female challenger.

Here, the size of the nonresponse error would be calculated as follows. Among likely voters, 46 percent of the 14 percent of all those sampled who did respond to the poll favored the female challenger, and they represent 6.5 percent (0.46 x 0.214 = 0.0644 or 6.44 percent) of the total electorate. To this would be added the 60 percent of the 84 percent who did not respond to the poll but who favor the female challenger; this equals another 52 percent (0.60 x 0.86 = 0.516 or 51.60 percent) of the total electorate. Thus, the female challenger would be expected to win this election with a clear majority of the vote (6.5 percent plus 51.6 percent = 58 percent). In other words, the analysis suggests that the first estimate that the challenger would receive only 46 percent support had a nonresponse error of 12 percentage points (58 percent minus 46 percent)!

The reader may wonder "But how is anything known about nonrespondents?" Surprisingly, in the past two decades several statistically sound methods have been devised to estimate the direction and size of the nonresponse error in polls and surveys. So, there are reliable techniques to learn useful information about nonrespondents. But these methods are expensive to carry out, and thus they have not been reported in pre-election polling.

DO THE NEWS MEDIA ACKNOWLEDGE THE ISSUE OF NONRESPONSE IN POLL ACCURACY?

The previous technical treatise on nonresponse and poll accuracy aside, it has been highly unusual for news stories to report anything about the response rate and nonresponse for a political poll, let alone say anything about the poll's possible nonresponse error. But it is not surprising that this information traditionally went unreported, as there never has been a public clamor for such information to be released by the media. However, since the late 1990s, response rates have occasionally become an issue in the reporting of political polls.

In the fall of 1998, when the Republican-led US House of Representatives was considering the implications of independent counsel Kenneth Starr's allegations about President Bill Clinton, the American public continued to show fairly strong majority approval of how Clinton was doing in his job as president. In the ensuing struggle to win political and public support for the Republican efforts to impeach Clinton, then conservative political columnist Arianna Huffington wrote a column trying to discredit the myriad public media polls showing solid public support for Clinton. She did this, in part, by implying that they were inaccurate because of low response rates. Huffington also noted that her efforts to learn about the response rates of these public polls were met with many evasive replies by the polls' media spokespersons.

What Huffington appeared either not to understand or not to acknowledge is that media pollsters had not usually been questioned about the response rates of their polls. Thus, it was not necessarily surprising that they were unable to immediately provide her with the information she sought.

Why should this be so—that media pollsters themselves may not have immediately known the response rates of their latest polls? Public pollsters collect data under deadlines, and they will almost always report the results they have obtained under those conditions. In the 1990s, disclosure standards of organizations such as the American Association for Public Opinion Research (AAPOR) and the National Council of Public Polls were ambiguous on the need to supply response rates. However, in the late 1990s AAPOR began to take a much stronger stand about disclosing response rates by publishing a manual on how standard response rates should be calculated.[3] And then in 2010, AAPOR took an even stronger stand with its Transparency Initiative on the need for public pollsters to readily disclose considerable details about their polling methods, including their response rates and the possible nonresponse bias that may have resulted in a poll.[4]

Pollsters and other survey researchers do not yet have very good theories to explain or predict under what circumstances a low response rate will produce errors and when it will not. A low response rate, in and of itself, does not automatically mean that a survey is inaccurate. In fact, research by the Voter News Service, the organization that conducted the national exit polls for the major networks and the Associated Press until 2002, showed that response rates to exit polls at the sample precinct level were unrelated to the accuracy of the exit poll data in predicting the actual election outcome in the precinct. Similarly, other recent research suggests that a low response rate to an otherwise well-conducted pre-election poll may sometimes be correlated with an improvement in the accuracy of the poll in predicting an election outcome because it appears that those most likely to participate in these polls are also those most likely to vote in the election.

The important lesson here is that a survey's response rate does not necessarily mean that the poll is accurate. Pollsters often try to reduce the potential for nonresponse error by making statistical corrections to their data to "adjust" (weight) for differences in their sample compared to their target population. These adjustments do not always work well, however. Unfortunately for pollsters and their clients, the only way to know how well these adjustments worked is to wait until after the election.

WHAT DOES IT MEAN WHEN POLL DATA ARE WEIGHTED?

Weighting refers to certain statistical adjustments that often are made to the raw data that the sampled respondents provide. These adjustments take place before the data are analyzed, in order to try to improve the accuracy with which the data from the respondents reflect those of the target population, such as their voting intentions and opinions.

Poll and survey data are typically adjusted statistically (i.e., weighted) to try to reduce various biases that may exist in the *unweighted data* that are gathered. Weighting is generally done for three specific reasons. First, whenever a probability sample is used and the respondents have had an unequal chance of being sampled, weighting should be used to balance the probabilities of selection so they reflect what would have happened had there been an equal chance of selection for each respondent. For example, in election polls conducted via telephone, this is done by adjusting for the number of different telephone numbers (landline and cell) in the household and for the number of voting-age residents in the household who might have answered the phone number used to sample the household. For example, each person who has two telephone numbers that can reach them at home might receive a weight of 0.5 (1/2) to compensate for the fact that he or she was twice as likely to be selected as someone with only one phone number.

A second purpose of weighting is to try to correct for any noncoverage in the sampling frame that was used for the pollster's target population. Election pollsters often weight their data if they have not drawn their sample from a sampling frame that well represents those voters who are likely to vote in the upcoming election. For example, opt-in online polls by definition do not cover the portion of the voting public who does not have access to or chooses not to use the internet. This group on average is much older than the rest of the voting public and as a group often votes in ways that are different from their younger counterparts. Therefore, pollsters that use opt-in online samples recognize that they need to adjust for this under coverage of older voters in their samples because if they did not do that their poll findings would be biased.

A third purpose of weighting is to try to correct for the nonresponse that is present in every election poll, no matter how it is conducted. Media polling organizations often weight their data because of low response rates that result in unrepresentative samples for polls with a very short interviewing period. For example, women have been traditionally more readily reached in polls that last only a few days than are men, and thus most polls will interview proportionately more women than their actual percentage of the population.

Whereas women make up about 52 percent of the adult population in the United States, it is not unusual for a pre-election poll to end up with a sample that is 60 percent or more female. If women, as a group, are more likely than men to vote for a certain candidate—such as the Democrat—then unweighted poll data that reflect proportionally too many women will misrepresent the target population's actual voting intention for that candidate. In this example, women would receive a weight of 0.867 (their population percentage/their sample percentage, or 52/60 = 0.867) and men would receive a weight of 1.200 (48/40) before the pollster began to analyze the data.

One difficulty with weighting to adjust for nonresponse is that the pollster cannot be completely certain that it will have the intended consequence of improving the survey's accuracy. In fact, some research has suggested that pre-election poll accuracy is improved if the data are not adjusted for certain demographic discrepancies between the sample of interviewed respondents and the target population. This is another area in which the art of polling, as opposed to only the science, comes into play in the use of election poll data.

Unfortunately, when pollsters weight their data to reduce potential bias, they end up lowering the precision of their estimates for a given sample size by inflating their margin of sampling error. This is a trade-off that pollsters accept, but many pollsters do not adequately take this into account when they report their final margin of sampling error. In turn, many journalists fail to take this into account when they interpret the meaning and implications of election poll results that come from weighted data.

WHY HAVEN'T I EVER BEEN INTERVIEWED IN AN ELECTION POLL?

There are more than 300 million adults in the United States who could conceivably be eligible to be sampled and interviewed for an election poll. A rough estimate suggests that more than 5,000 but fewer than 10,000 elections polls were conducted during the 2020 election season. Private pollsters who did not publicly release their results did many of these. If each of these polls contacted an average of 600 voters—most polls do not use sample sizes as large as 1,100 or 2,200—then in 2020 something like 3 to 4 million adults may have been interviewed or contacted by an election-polling firm. Thus, the chance that any one of the 260 million residents would have been contacted would only be approximately 1 in 99 (i.e., a 1.013 percent probability).

Over the years, the probability of any one voter being contacted by an election poll would increase, but rather slowly, especially since it has only been in the past thirty-five years that we have experienced an explosion of election polling. So, it really is not surprising that most Americans would say they have never been interviewed for an election poll.

However, many more Americans have been sampled for an election poll than those who have been contacted, when nonresponse is considered. In fact, it is likely that at least five times as many Americans have been sampled for election polls compared to the number actually interviewed. Many of these voters are not aware that they were sampled because they were never reached at the time the polling tried to contact them. A final consideration is that as more pollsters are using internet panels for their election polls, it is likely that fewer of the public are being sampled for election polling purposes than in past years.

NOTES

1. See, for example, https://www.mailing-lists-direct.com/consumer-mailing-lists/registered-voters/.
2. See https://catalist.us/data/.
3. The second author of this book was an original author of this manual: https://aapor.org/standards-and-ethics/standard-definitions/?_zs=S2m2W1&_zl=NlFx8
4. https://aapor.org/standards-and-ethics/transparency-initiative/

Chapter 6

How Are Questionnaires Put Together?

The questionnaire is the main data collection device in a poll or survey. You can think of it as the vehicle or tool for gathering information from survey respondents. It serves the same function that an electron microscope does for a biochemist or a powerful telescope for an astronomer. For this reason, many survey researchers refer to the questionnaire as the *instrument*.

Each questionnaire consists of several questions. These are the specific tools that pollsters use to take their measurements. Regardless of whether people are surveyed via mail, telephone, the internet, or in person, it is the individual survey question that is the source of the data that pollsters later analyze.

Pollsters often refer to a question as an *item* in the questionnaire. Election poll questionnaires typically include items that measure people's opinions; knowledge of the candidates and issues; voting intentions in forthcoming primaries or elections; whether and how they voted in past elections; and background demographics and other characteristics such as gender, age, education, and party identification.

The quality of the data collected in a poll is related to which questions are asked, how the individual questions are worded, how the respondent is allowed to answer the questions, and even the order in which the items are asked. The details of these issues and the results of some research on their effects are summarized in the answers to the following questions.

DOES A QUESTIONNAIRE FOLLOW A PARTICULAR ORDER AND FORMAT?

At a certain level, it does. You can think of a questionnaire as a script for a structured, albeit indirect, "conversation" between the researchers and each respondent. The conversation is sometimes administered for the researchers via human interviewers (e.g., as with telephone or in-person, or video interviewing), sometimes via nonhuman forms of technology (e.g., as via an internet-connected smartphone or other computer devices, or via an Interactive Voice Response system), and sometimes even via written documents (e.g., as with mailed paper materials). The questionnaire generally begins with a set of opening items that are friendly and not too taxing for the respondent. This occurs so that the respondent can be put at ease and some rapport can be established between the researchers and the respondent, indirect as that might be. As a result, the respondent will be less likely to terminate the interview prematurely. The substantive questions about the survey's topic(s) are then gathered. Finally, personal *demographic questions* and other possibly sensitive topics are generally placed later or at the end of the questionnaire.

Other than that, good pollsters consciously think about the ordering of each question within the questionnaire to minimize problems that may occur by asking certain questions first that subsequently may bias the answers to later questions.

DO DIFFERENT SURVEY QUESTIONS SERVE DIFFERENT PURPOSES?

Yes, there are many different purposes for various kinds of survey questions, and their use depends on the information the pollster wants to collect. Some questions might serve a single purpose, while other questions might serve multiple purposes.

Some survey questions are formulated so the pollster can simply describe what is occurring in the electorate at the time the poll is taken. For example, asking the question "Do you approve or disapprove of the way Joe Biden is handling the economy?" allows the pollster to report, in a descriptive fashion, the percentage of the public that approves, the percentage that disapproves, and the percentage that is undecided at the time the poll was conducted.

Other questions are used because they allow the pollster both to describe and predict specific opinions or behaviors in the electorate. For example, a pollster might survey citizens in one state and measure their opinions about a political issue such as the rights of transgendered Americans. The pollster will look for correlations between the respondents' demographic characteristics and their attitudes toward the issue. If there are statistically significant correlations, the pollster can develop a model (formula) to predict attitudes toward the transgendered using the demographics. As a result, the pollster might then be able to reliably predict the transgendered attitudes of unsampled citizens in another state, just by knowing the demographic characteristics of the population in that state.

Still other questions are asked because they allow the pollster to describe, predict, and explain why something might happen or might have happened. Take the case of a pollster working for a political candidate who conducts a survey to help the candidate's campaign staff plan their future advertising. All the respondents are asked to evaluate the candidates near the beginning of the questionnaire. Then the sample is randomly divided into two halves.

A random half of the respondents are prompted with some positive information about the candidate, and the pollster again measures the respondents' opinions of the candidate and the opponent. The other random half of respondents are prompted with negative information about the candidate's opponent, and then their opinions of the candidate and the opponent are measured again. If the favorability ratings of the candidate and the opponent change under the two different prompts, the pollster has found something to explain the positive/negative differences, at least to a certain degree. This type of cause-and-effect (i.e., experimental) research can be very useful in planning the campaign's future ads.

Some questions serve an entirely different purpose for pollsters. These include demographic questions such as a respondent's sex, age, race, and education that are used to weight (i.e., adjust) the data before it is analyzed to account for differences in the characteristics of the sample versus the same characteristics in the target population. In addition, some other questions, such as asking telephone survey respondents about the number of phone lines on which they can be called at home, are used to weight the data before it is analyzed to adjust for unequal probabilities of selection.

IS THERE MORE THAN ONE KIND OF FORMAT FOR SURVEY QUESTIONS?

Yes, there are many kinds of formats for survey questions. A basic distinction among question types is whether or not the item provides a respondent with a fixed set of answers—what pollsters call *response alternatives*—to choose from or whether the respondent is allowed to answer using her or his own words and phrases.

When respondents are allowed to answer a question in their own words, the survey item is called an *open-ended question*. An example of a common political open-ended question is:

What do you think is the most important problem facing the country today?

In contrast, when respondents are presented with a group of answers to choose from, the item is called a *closed-ended question*. An example of a closed-ended question is:

Do you strongly agree, agree, neither agree nor disagree, disagree, or strongly disagree that the United States should support Ukraine until they regain their territory taken by Russia after its invasion?

Other times, respondents might be asked a question, given several response choices, and then asked to pick all that apply. This is a special form of closed-ended question that provides for multiple responses. For example, from the 2020 election:

Which of the following, if any, is a reason why you intend to vote for Joe Biden? Strong Character; Good Policies; He Is a Democrat; Don't Like Donald Trump? Please tell me all of the reasons, if any, that apply to you.

Since open-ended questions allow respondents to use their own words to express a complex answer, the resulting data are usually thought to be a more valid reflection of the respondents' attitudes than when restrictions are placed on the range of possible answers by forcing a choice among a predetermined set of alternatives.

Formerly, a difficulty with open-ended questions was that their answers had to be coded (i.e., classified) by humans into meaningful categories before the pollster could make analytic sense of them. This coding process was labor intensive, and therefore time-consuming and expensive. Now it is possible to code each response quickly with computer software that can identify topics and sentiment.

Closed-ended questions provide a range of responses that can make some respondents feel constrained in their ability to answer. Closed-ended questions sometimes create difficulties for pollsters because they offer a somewhat artificial and simplistic range of choices for an item. Some respondents find it frustrating to have to answer a question in the pollster's terms rather than in their own words. A set of closed-ended response categories for an item must be both *exhaustive* (i.e., each possible answer should fit into one of the response categories) and *mutually exclusive* (i.e., each possible answer should fit into only one of the response categories).

In the 2004 exit poll, the National Election Pool added a category to the question that it usually asked about the main reason that a voter chose the presidential candidate whom they reported voting for. About one-fifth of the respondents (22 percent) selected "moral values" as the main reason out of the seven reasons that they were offered. This response became an important media point to explain why George Bush won reelection and by a larger margin than expected, partly because Bush voters were more likely to give this response than Kerry voters. This finding was replicated in a split-half design experiment conducted by the Pew Research Center. In a random half of their sample, they asked the same question, and 27 percent selected "moral values" as the main reason. In the other half, they asked the question using an open-ended format and then coded the resulting responses for any that reflected "moral values." In this administration, only 14 percent gave answers that could be construed as falling in that category.

These results suggest that while "moral values" meant different and more important things to Bush voters than Kerry voters, the assessment of their role in voters' choices could be construed partially as an artifact of question format.

ARE THERE OTHER DIFFERENCES BETWEEN OPEN-ENDED AND CLOSED-ENDED QUESTIONS?

In the main text of many closed-ended questions, the respondent is often offered only two alternative positions with which to "agree" or "disagree" or "favor" or "oppose." In an open-ended question, they can express their opinion in an unstructured way in their own words.

In addition to the response alternatives offered, the process by which the answers (the data) are taken from respondents differs by the format of each of these types of questions. For polls conducted over the telephone or in person, closed-ended questions are easier for interviewers to administer. They simply read the item and its response alternatives, and then they record the choice corresponding to the respondent's answer. If the respondent is unclear or seems unable to give an immediate answer, the well-trained interviewer simply repeats the closed-ended item and its choices, reading exactly what the pollster has written. If the respondent still is unable or unwilling to answer, the researcher typically has provided the interviewer with choices that are not read to a respondent but indicate that the respondent was "uncertain" or "refused." Research shows that on the telephone, respondents tend to select the last choice offered. For web surveys, respondents tend to favor the first category in a list. This explains why response options should often be offered in a randomized order.

In open-ended items, interviewers often must prompt respondents to get them to answer more fully. Here the challenge is for the interviewer to do this in a *"nondirective"* fashion, that is, by using words that will not bias the answer the respondent will provide. Often, this is not very easily done. Furthermore, the *verbatim responses* (i.e., exactly what a respondent says in answering the questions) recorded by interviewers sometimes are very difficult to read if they are handwritten and/or contain poor spelling or abbreviations. This problem is reduced in online questionnaires when respondents type in their own answers.

In self-administered questionnaires, such as those used in mail and internet surveys, respondents must work harder to answer open-ended items than closed-ended items. For the latter, the respondent simply must mark a choice. For the former, the respondent must write out the answer either by printing it or in longhand. To some extent, this *respondent burden* can reduce the frequency and length of responses to open-ended questions, so the poll is likely to suffer from incomplete or at least abbreviated answers to self-administered questions—answers that would have been prompted for greater detail if an interviewer had been administering the item. Legibility of handwriting can also be a serious problem when open-ended items are gathered in self-administered mailback paper and pencil questionnaires.

WHAT IS AN UNBALANCED QUESTION?

Poll questions also can vary in terms of whether they are *balanced* or *unbalanced*. This attribute generally refers to the continuum of the response alternatives that are offered in closed-ended items.

A balanced question is constructed so that it equally represents both sides of an issue and provides the respondent with a scaled set of response alternatives that has an offered true conceptual midpoint and an equal number of possible response categories on each side or the midpoint. Balanced questions are worded to make explicit two (or more) sides of an issue. For example from a 2022 poll, *"Some people think that the United States should supply more aid to Ukraine to help them defeat the Russians, while other people think the United States has supplied enough aid to Ukraine"* would be balanced wording for use at the start of a poll item measuring a respondent's own opinion about providing aid to Ukraine. If the item had been worded with only the first part of this phrasing, *"Some people think that the United States should supply more aid to Ukraine to help them defeat the Russians,"* leaving out the explicit phrasing that there are others who disagree, this would be unbalanced wording. Questions with unbalanced wording often bias the answers that respondents give.

As an example of an unbalanced set of response alternatives, consider the prospect of a respondent's agreement with a candidate's position on an issue when offered, "strongly agree, agree somewhat, and disagree" as choices. These alternatives are unbalanced because there is no conceptual midpoint within the set of responses. A balanced version of the response alternatives would include something like "strongly agree, agree somewhat, disagree somewhat, and strongly disagree." Here the conceptual midpoint is located between the two "somewhat" responses, and the response alternatives are balanced on both sides of the conceptual midpoint.

The reader should note that the midpoint in this last example is not represented by an offered response choice. Some questions would offer a true midpoint, such as "neither agree nor disagree." Whether a set of responses is balanced or unbalanced does not necessarily guarantee that it will bias respondents' answers. Nevertheless, a balanced question offers a respondent a set of symmetrical response alternatives from which to choose and does not suggest that there is a preferred answer to the question.

DOES THE WORDING OF A QUESTION MAKE A DIFFERENCE IN THE RESPONSES A RESPONDENT PROVIDES?

It most assuredly does! Even small variations in wording and grammar may represent completely different questions to some respondents. Although slight wording differences do not necessarily represent different concepts, small variations can lead to significant differences in the responses elicited. Unfortunately, the pollster will never know what differences alternative wordings make unless the different wordings have been carefully and systematically pretested—a laborious and costly process that many pollsters choose to avoid.

Survey methodologists have identified a general set of question wording problems, and the problems that they represent for respondents have been studied extensively and are generally well understood. They include questions that use complicated language or have a complex structure; use a *double negative*; contain more than one question (*double-barreled question*); use leading phrases; or pose threats to respondents because they concern sensitive topics. Examples of each of these wording problems are discussed in more detail later in this chapter.

The impact of small changes in question wording can produce dramatic shifts in responses. For example, on August 17, 1998, after giving video testimony before Kenneth Starr's grand jury, President Bill Clinton gave a brief televised address to the nation. Gallup was one of several polling firms that measured popular reaction to the president's speech. The next day, Gallup reported a 20 percentage point drop in the president's favorability rating compared to one week earlier (40 percent compared to 60 percent). This finding was at odds with other polls conducted after the president's speech.

Gallup reviewed the details of its poll and realized that the phrase "as a person" had inadvertently been added to its standard question:

Now thinking about Bill Clinton as a person, do you have a favorable or unfavorable opinion of him?

Gallup fielded another poll in which both forms of the question were administered to two random split-halves of the sample, as well as two equivalent forms asking about Hillary Clinton's favorability. The poll showed markedly different results for the two questions about Bill Clinton, but there was no difference in the responses to the two questions about Mrs. Clinton. Gallup concluded that the public had become attuned to the difference between evaluating Bill Clinton as the president and as a person.

WHAT IS THE PROBLEM OF COMPLEX LANGUAGE IN A POLL QUESTION?

Many respondents cannot well understand a poll question when it is phrased in terms of special language or it uses a complex structure. Poll questions should be well understood by every person from whom data are gathered, including those with the lowest levels of education (who may not be fully fluent in the languages a self-administered questionnaire is being provided in) and those who have little worldly experience.

The following is an example of a poll question that would be difficult for some respondents because of technical or complex language:

Do you think it would be better for the government to fund more research on fuel cells to reduce pollution from automobiles?

This question refers to an advanced technology for reducing automotive pollutants, but a respondent would practically have to be an automotive engineer to understand what a fuel cell is and how it works, as well as whether this program merits additional government investment. So, most people asked this question would have no idea how to answer it.

Here is another example of complex language:

Do you think Congress should pass legislation to facilitate single-payer cost reimbursement health plans for indigent patients?

A respondent probably would have to be employed in some area of the healthcare industry to have a chance of understanding that this question refers to a proposed change in Medicaid. So, many of the responses to such a poll question would not be very informative because they would be based on a faulty knowledge base or, in some cases, a respondent's pure guess about what the question means.

When pollsters are trying to measure opinions on important national issues whose details may be unfamiliar to many citizens, the researchers sometimes use an introduction to the question to present background information on the issue. If these descriptions become too long or too complex in structure, respondents may lose track of the original intent of the question or important details of the issue they are being asked to express an opinion about. Here is an example of the wording of a question introduction from the 1990s:

The United States is negotiating a treaty with its neighbors, Canada and Mexico, called the North American Free Trade Agreement, or NAFTA. The purpose of the treaty is to reduce duties and tariffs on goods manufactured in one country and exported to the others. Do you favor or oppose passage of NAFTA in the US Congress?

The NAFTA treaty involved many complex issues, which is one reason that it took such a long time to negotiate and for the Congress to debate its benefits. It was difficult for pollsters to create simple, understandable questions to measure public opinion concerning NAFTA; it is sometimes hard to imagine what kinds of opinions could be measured with complex question wordings like this one.

WHAT IS A DOUBLE NEGATIVE IN A QUESTION?

A question that involves a double negative poses a concept in such a confusing way that the pollster cannot be sure which meaning of the question the respondent is answering. As a simple example, suppose a pollster asked respondents whether they agree or disagree with the following statement:

Sometimes my life seems so uncomplicated that I cannot figure it out.

The respondents must decide (1) whether their lives are "complicated" or not and (2) whether or not they can or cannot figure it out, before they (3) can decide whether they agree or disagree with the statement.

This may seem like an easy problem to avoid in wording questions, but one of the most interesting controversies in polling involved a question with an added negative in it. In 1993, the Roper Organization released data on Americans' beliefs about the Holocaust in which they suggested that almost one-quarter of Americans doubted that the Holocaust had occurred. This level was much higher than equivalent proportions of from 1 to 5 percent of various European samples that were asked a similar question about the same topic.[1] This conclusion was drawn from responses to the following question asked of a representative national sample in the United States:

Does it seem possible or does it seem impossible to you that the Nazi extermination of the Jews never happened?

In translating this question from its original French wording, the US pollster added another negative to the question, and it clearly confused respondents and altered their answers. A series of question-wording experiments subsequently conducted by the Roper Organization, Gallup, and CBS News clearly showed that the difference in US response patterns could be linked to the double negative. When the exact same wording of the question was asked in the United States that was asked in the other countries, the distribution of responses was essentially the same.

WHAT IS A DOUBLE-BARRELED QUESTION?

As readers may recognize, wording poll questions so that they yield unbiased and reliable data can be a considerable challenge for even the most skilled pollsters. But the mistake of writing a double-barreled question is a potential pitfall to which only a careless pollster is likely to fall victim.

A double-barreled item contains a *question stem* that poses more than one concept to the respondent, and that complexity is not clearly related to the alternatives offered in the response categories. Typically, a double-barreled question should be rephrased as two separate questions because it really is asking respondents about two separate concepts. These concepts might be related, but in order to gather valid data, each must be asked about in a separate question.

Take the case of asking about a president's approval level with an item that combines two aspects of the president's job. As an example, think of the following question:

Do you approve or disapprove of the way President Biden is handling the country's foreign and domestic affairs?

Answers to this item are almost meaningless for pollsters because they cannot know whether respondents who said approve really meant they approved of the president's handling of *both* foreign and domestic affairs or approved of his handling of *only one* of these aspects of his job and disregarded the other in their answer. The same confusion would exist in trying to interpret the meaning of a "disapprove" response. Does "disapprove" mean disapproval of the president's handling of only foreign affairs, only domestic affairs, or both? Both pollsters and consumers of poll results cannot interpret answers to double-barreled questions with any confidence.

Instead of linking two concepts in a double-barreled question, careful pollsters avoid the mistake by splitting the two concepts into two separate questions. Then the attitudes about each element of the president's handling of his job can be assessed independently and unambiguously.

A general rule of thumb that readers can apply to evaluating poll questions for this problem is to look closely at items that contain the word "and." This is not to suggest that all items with an "and" are double-barreled, or that all double-barreled items contain "and." Nevertheless, many double-barreled items do contain "and" or "or"; thus those words can be a useful tip-off in detecting this problematic question form.

WHAT IS THE EFFECT OF A LEADING PHRASE IN A QUESTION?

A leading phrase in a poll question can frame the question in such a way that some respondents may be more influenced to agree or support a proposition that it contains or, in a different case, to disagree or oppose a proposition that it contains.

An example of how this works is a question that begins with a phrase indicating that the president supports a particular policy or that it is his policy. When questions are asked this way, especially in a period of an international crisis or conflict, experiments show that respondents are more likely to express support for the policy than if the question did not include that phrase. These differences would be found in responses to the following two alternative forms of asking similar questions about support for new legislation on gun control:

Are you in favor of or opposed to legislation limiting Americans' ability to purchase assault weapons?

as opposed to

If President Biden proposes legislation to Congress to limit Americans' ability to purchase assault weapons, would you favor or oppose such legislation?

In another version of this framing issue, a leading phrase might indicate that many Americans support a particular side of an issue as a prelude to asking respondents for their opinions. Suggesting that many people hold a particular position can also produce more responses in support of that position:

Many Americans favor legislation limiting the sale of assault weapons. How about you? Do you favor or oppose legislation limiting the sale of assault weapons?

ARE RESPONSES TO QUESTIONS ON SENSITIVE TOPICS AFFECTED BY HOW THEY ARE WORDED?

They most certainly can be. Sometimes a single word or phrase can produce more responses in support of or in opposition to a public policy.

In many areas of controversial public policy, measurements of public opinion are highly susceptible to question wording. For example, a pollster who is measuring the electorate's attitudes toward the abortion issue will gather different attitudinal responses depending on whether the word "legal" is included in the item wording, as in the difference between the following questions:

Do you agree or disagree that a woman should be able to get a legal abortion for any reason of her choice in her first three months of pregnancy?
versus
Do you agree or disagree that a woman should be able to get an abortion for any reason of her choice in her first three months of pregnancy?

Another important phrase in questions designed to measure opinions about government actions or proposed legislation involves the use of terms such as "forbid" and "allow." In general, Americans are much less likely to agree that the government should "forbid" certain forms of behavior than to agree that the same behavior should "not be allowed." Pairs of alternative questions posed in the following way will produce different patterns of response:[2]

Do you think the United States should forbid public speeches in favor of communism?

as opposed to

Do you think the United States should allow public speeches in favor of communism?

In response to the first question, 39 percent of the sample indicated "Yes," such speeches should be forbidden. In the second case, 56 percent of a sample indicated "No," such speeches should not be allowed (i.e., should be forbidden).

Another factor affecting the public's response to public policy questions is the degree of specificity contained in the descriptions of the policies. For example, different questions asked in the fall of 1995 about US involvement in Bosnia suggested different levels of support for President Clinton's actions. When ABC News posed the following question, 57 percent said they opposed the president's plan, while 39 percent supported it:

Clinton said now that a Bosnia peace treaty has been signed, he's sending 20,000 US troops there as part of an international peacekeeping force. Do you support or oppose sending 20,000 US troops to Bosnia as part of an international peacekeeping force?

But Gallup, in a survey conducted for *USA Today* and CNN, found that only 40 percent expressed opposition, while 46 percent of the public supported the administration's plan when the question was asked in the following way:

Now that a peace agreement has been reached by all the groups currently fighting in Bosnia, the Clinton administration plans to contribute US troops to an international peacekeeping force. Do you favor or oppose that?

The use of the term "contribute," as well as the absence of the number of troops expected to go to Bosnia, was cited as the explanation for higher levels of support in the Gallup survey than in the ABC News poll.[3]

CAN THE WORDING OF A QUESTION BE MANIPULATED TO PRODUCE A CERTAIN RESULT?

An unethical pollster can purposely manipulate (bias) the wording of a question to push respondents' choices in a direction the pollster desires. As a result, consumers of polls should evaluate descriptions of public opinion on an issue in terms of the exact questions that were asked.

Take the example of a pollster working for a candidate who advocates a certain environmental protection policy. The unethical pollster could strongly distort the proportion of the public who appears to support the candidate's policy if the question wording contained an unfounded or exaggerated listing of the damages that the environment might suffer if the policy were not put into effect. Such opinions could also be affected by a phrase indicating that the policy could be implemented without any significant increase in taxes.

Whenever possible, the careful consumer of poll results should look at the wording of the items used in the poll. We believe that this is especially important for journalists, who too often use and disseminate poll findings without critically scrutinizing whether or not the item wording might have biased the findings.

DO THE RESPONSE ALTERNATIVES IN A CLOSED-ENDED QUESTION MAKE A DIFFERENCE IN THE RESPONSES THEY ELICIT?

Yes, they can. The words or phrases used for response alternatives can make as much difference in the pattern of answers that respondents provide as the wording of the question itself.

It is important to recognize that the set of response alternatives offered for closed-ended poll questions provide the context within which the pollster allows the respondent a choice. Although different polls might measure a concept with a question stem that uses the same words—*"How would you rate the president's performance on economic affairs? Would you say . . . ?"*—the items are technically and operationally different and may yield quite different data unless the available response alternatives offered to respondents are also identical.

For example, an item assessing the president's job performance could use a variety of response alternatives, such as the following:

- Very good, Good, Fair, Poor, or Very poor
- Good, Fair, or Poor

- A, B, C, D, or F
- Acceptable or Unacceptable
- Satisfactory, Somewhat Satisfactory, Somewhat Unsatisfactory, or Not at all Satisfactory

Varied response alternatives provide different contexts, so they easily can lead to different answers. Unless items that measure the same concept with the same wording also use the same response alternatives, then any observed differences in the pattern of answers between the items could merely reflect the different answer categories from which respondents picked. Does "good" mean the same thing when it is bounded by "very good, fair, or poor" as it does when it is grouped with "excellent, fair, or poor"? In this example, its meaning is probably not the same, but most likely it is quite close.

But what if "good" were used within the set of response alternatives "good, fair, or poor"? In this case, all respondents who thought the performance being rated was better than good are limited to "good" as their most positive choice. In contrast, the two earlier sets of responses provide the respondent a better-than-good category to choose, if that is the opinion the respondent holds.

So once again, let the poll consumer beware: Comparisons across poll items that purportedly measure the same concept, even when their question stem is worded the same, are ambiguous unless the wording used in the response alternatives of the items also is exactly the same.

WHAT IF A RESPONDENT IS UNDECIDED, UNCERTAIN, OR DOESN'T HAVE AN OPINION ON A QUESTION?

Another special problem with sets of response alternatives is whether they explicitly include a category for respondents who are uncertain of their opinions or likely behavior. Survey questions that do not provide an explicit option for "Don't know" or "Undecided" are called forced-choice questions.

Considerable past research has shown that having an interviewer read an explicit "don't know" or "uncertain" response choice—as in, *"Do you agree, disagree, or are you uncertain?"*—will elicit many more uncertain responses than if the respondent is not explicitly offered such a choice. Thus, pollsters must constantly decide which approach is more valid: adding or omitting "uncertain" in the set of response choices that are offered explicitly to the respondent.

Sometimes with an interviewer-administered questionnaire, the "Don't know" or "Uncertain" option is not explicitly offered in the question wording itself, but the interviewer has instructions to accept such an answer if it is volunteered by the respondent and to move on to the next question. This issue is further complicated by the different data collection modes in which polls are conducted. In a self-administered exit poll questionnaire, if "uncertain" is listed within the set of responses, then the respondent will see it. In a telephone survey, however, an "uncertain" option is likely to be listed only for the interviewer to mark and only when respondents volunteer that they feel that way; that is, the respondent will not be read the option by the interviewer. Thus, by explicitly providing the "Uncertain" or "Don't know" choice to the respondent in a self-administered data collection mode, that response alternative will be used more often than if the respondent is not read that response alternative with an interviewer-administered questionnaire.

WHAT IF A RESPONDENT GIVES A "DON'T KNOW" RESPONSE TO A QUESTION?

Pollsters have done a considerable amount of thinking over the years about what to do with a respondent who says "Don't know" (or its equivalent) when asked a poll question. They have considered two major yet separate issues: (1) How should an interviewer react to such a response? and (2) How should such a response be analyzed?

As a rule of thumb, the problems caused by "Don't know" responses can be markedly reduced if the wording of the question makes respondents comfortable with just responding that they do not have an opinion about something that the poll is trying to measure.

In some cases, a respondent may simply be uncertain of which answer to choose. Here, it is not that the respondent does not have opinions about the issue but that the opinions are not fully formulated or the response alternatives being offered do not reflect the respondent's uncertainty. Take the example of a respondent who has both favorable and unfavorable opinions about a political candidate. If these positive and negative opinions completely balance out each other in the respondent's mind, then this respondent will be hard put to pick an answer from a response set of "very favorable, somewhat favorable, somewhat unfavorable, or very unfavorable." In this instance, many pollsters will establish a system by which their interviewers are trained to detect this uncertainty and treat it as an "undecided" response. The interviewer is given the discretion to record it as such.

In other cases, the pollster may have devised a series of follow-up questions that can be used to extract additional information from the respondent to determine whether the respondent is truly undecided or is leaning in one direction or the other on the issue. In 2024 *pre-primary polls*, a common form of the trial-heat question was:

If the primary election for the Democratic presidential nomination were held today, and the names appearing on the ballot were Joseph Biden and Joseph Kennedy, whom would you vote for?

Early in the general election campaign, relatively large proportions of respondents indicated they were undecided. Those respondents who said they were undecided were often asked a follow-up question of the form:

If you had to choose, would you say you were leaning toward Joseph Biden or Joseph Kennedy?

Then, candidate preferences can be tabulated with the "leaners" added in or left out, and the results can be reported in the same fashion as well.

In other instances, a respondent might be truly uninformed about an issue and not at all reticent about reporting that. In this case, the respondent's honesty should be both valued and respected by the pollster because the validity of the data is improved by recording such candor. Unfortunately, *social desirability* causes many respondents to give an answer from the response choices offered, especially if being spoken to by an interviewer, rather than admit they do not have an opinion or do not know about a public policy issue and thereby appear ignorant.

Some pollsters choose to report data that exclude the "Don't know" responses, effectively reducing the sample size for that question. Others include these responses as an indication of how informed the sample is about the issue under question.

In the first case, the pollster should make clear that some respondents have been excluded from the analysis. The second case probably presents a more accurate representation of the general public's opinion on the issue.

DOES THE ORDER IN WHICH QUESTIONS ARE ASKED MAKE A DIFFERENCE IN THE RESPONSES ELICITED?

Again, the answer is a definite yes! In addition to the words and the grammar used in a poll item, the placement of an item within the questionnaire can make a considerable difference in the answers that respondents give. Pollsters refer to this phenomenon as a *context effect* because the placement represents part of the context within which the measurement is taken.

The questions must be asked in a certain order so that meaningful information can be collected. For example, there are two standard ways in which pollsters ascertain how familiar respondents are with the candidates. One concept is unaided *candidate recall*, and it measures the ability of the respondents to extract the names of the candidates from their memory. It is usually asked in the following form:

Do you remember the names of the candidates who are running for governor in this November's election?

A second concept is aided *candidate recognition*. It is a less rigorous test of familiarity because it measures the ability of respondents to recognize the names of the candidates from a list they are given. It is usually asked in the following form:

I am going to read you a list of the names of candidates running for office in this November's election. Please tell me if you recognize the name I read and for which office they are running.

If a pollster is interested in both concepts, recall and recognition, then the unaided question (recall) must be asked before the aided one (recognition) and not vice versa. There are other examples of the importance of structure, such as asking respondents to tell the interviewer what they know about an issue before beginning a series of questions that ascertain whether respondents agree or disagree with specific aspects of alternative policy proposals for dealing with the issue.

One classic example of order effects in election polls is associated with the set of items that ask the public to provide approval ratings of the incumbent president. Some polls simply measure overall approval of how well the president has been doing his job and always place this item at the very start of the poll. The Gallup Organization invented this question and has always placed it first in its political/election questionnaires. Other polling organizations ask a series of questions about how well the president is doing on specific aspects of his job, such as in foreign and domestic affairs or with the economy, in addition to an overall approval item. In the latter case, some pollsters place the overall approval item at the start of the sequence, before asking about specific aspects of the job. But some other pollsters place it at the end, after first asking about the specific job aspects. Past research on these context effects has consistently shown that asking the overall approval rating before the more specific ratings tends to elicit higher approval scores on the overall measure than when it is asked after a list of specific job approval items.

Order effects within questionnaires are one of the most well-documented problems with polls and surveys. Knowing this, many pollsters strive for accuracy by constantly testing their questionnaires for such effects. Unfortunately, there is not always a practical solution to eliminate an order effect. However, concerned pollsters who find themselves in such a predicament can randomly assign different question orders to different poll respondents and then see what difference, if any, the ordering makes in the responses they get. For example, half a sample might be asked the overall approval rating before the specific ratings, and the other half will be asked the overall rating after the specific ones. In this way, the pollster can measure whether there are any differences caused by the different item orders and then can try to adjust for the effects after the data are analyzed, but before they are reported.

ARE SOME QUESTIONS TYPICALLY ASKED EARLY IN A QUESTIONNAIRE AND OTHERS LATER?

Yes, there is a general pattern used to order the sections of question items within most election poll questionnaires. Although there is some variation across the questionnaires used by different polling organizations, in many cases this is the basic pattern: (1) attitudes, (2) intentions and past behaviors, and (3) demographics and other background information.

There are two primary reasons that this general pattern is used. First, it makes for good rapport between the interviewer or the researcher (in the case of a self-administered questionnaire) and the respondent. Second, this pattern is generally the one that is least likely to affect or distort the answers to subsequent questions.

Respondents become most easily engaged in a poll when they are asked interesting, nonthreatening, and not overly intrusive questions right at the start of the questionnaire. In fact, sometimes pollsters will design their questionnaire so that it begins with a question or two whose purpose is simply to help establish rapport. It has been found that asking people about their easy-to-answer attitudes and opinions toward various political issues at the beginning of a questionnaire serves these purposes very well—such items are generally nonthreatening and are interesting for respondents to answer. A common question used to begin a political poll is "What do you think is the most important problem facing the country today?" This question has no right answer and indicates that the researchers are interested in the respondent's assessments of current affairs.

After asking about some of their opinions, it works well for the questionnaire to move on to items that measure a respondent's likelihood of voting and candidate preferences (such as *"If the election were held today, would you vote for . . . "*) and/or past voting behavior (*"In the 2020 presidential election, did you vote for Donald Trump or Joseph Biden?"*). Finally, the respondents are informed that the questionnaire is coming close to ending and that there are a few more questions about the respondent's background that can be used in analysis of the respondent's substantive responses to the previous questions.

Many pollsters believe that the demographics and some background questions fit better at the end because the respondents have been warmed up by the previous questioning and are more ready to provide personal information after knowing what else they were asked about. If a poll begins with demographic questions, respondents might feel threatened by personal questions about approximate annual income, for example, without having any sense of what other information this response will be used to analyze. One question that has a high *refusal rate* is income; in many surveys, more than 20 percent of respondents refuse to give an answer.

The second main reason that pollsters use this pattern is that they think it has less potential for distortion (error) due to question *order effects*. Questions about opinions and attitudes are generally most sensitive to the context within the questionnaire in which they are asked. Behavioral report items are less so, and demographic questions the least. Therefore, placing the opinion items first instills greater confidence in the validity of the responses they elicit than if they were placed after behavior items and background questions.

WHAT IS THE PROBLEM OF A "SOCIALLY DESIRABLE" RESPONSE TO A SURVEY QUESTION?

Sometimes survey questions address a topic on which there is a clearly preferred or expected response, referred to as a "socially desirable" response. When large numbers of respondents give such a response, there may be a bias present in the data as one type of response is under- or overreported in relation to what the "true" value would be in the population. For example, people who are asked whether they voted in the last election are more likely to report that they did when in fact they did not, producing biased overestimates of turnout. This finding has been reproduced over time and across countries, and research on the nature of this socially desirable response has been evaluated in validation studies where the respondents' actual voting records are checked against the survey responses. Almost all the errors are in one direction as essentially no one reports that they did not vote when they did.

Social desirability can also appear when respondents are asked about sensitive or illegal behaviors such as drug use or sexual activity. People are less likely to report drug use or drunk driving convictions, for example, than is the case for them. This has been demonstrated in studies that start with samples of people with drug convictions or arrests for drunk driving to see how they respond to questions about this behavior in a survey questionnaire.

Finally, there are socially desirable responses to questions about attitudes on such topics as race relations or affirmative action. For widely discussed and debated issues, individuals can develop a sense of which views are more socially acceptable and which are not. So, responses to survey questions on these subjects suggest that the population is more racially tolerant or more supportive of affirmative action than they are. These discrepancies can occur when pre-election polls are conducted during campaigns involving biracial contests where the surveys indicate greater support for the African American candidate than is typically reflected in the voting that subsequently takes place. The same phenomenon occurs in pre-election polls asking about support for affirmative action, for example, in relation to referenda results on these topics.

HOW DO RESEARCHERS KNOW WHETHER QUESTIONS ARE BIASED?

Bias in a poll question refers to the *systematic error* that can be caused by its wording or its placement within a questionnaire. By systematic error, we mean inaccuracies that lead to a measurement that is consistently higher or consistently lower than what the true value is. For example, a bathroom scale that always overweighs people by an extra five pounds in relation to their actual weight is a biased measurement tool. The scale produces a faulty weight that is consistently but systematically incorrect. Survey items can have the same kind of inaccuracy problem.

The best way to test for potential bias is to pretest questions. A *pretest* involves conducting a few interviews (e.g., twenty to thirty), not necessarily even from a probability sample of respondents, in order to learn whether the questions are being understood, the response categories are appropriate, and information is being collected that corresponds to other known or reasonable distributions of opinion on the same issue. Some survey items are so blatantly biased that this is obvious once pointed out; in other cases, a pretest is required to demonstrate the problems that are present. (Chapter 10 explains how unscrupulous pollsters may purposely introduce biased question wordings to influence poll results.)

There are many times when it is not at all obvious that a question may have a bias associated with it. Given the availability of resources (time and money), methodological checks can be incorporated into either a questionnaire or additional data analyses that can be performed after a poll is conducted—or both. Unfortunately, not many pollsters have the necessary resources or the interest to do this.

One of the best techniques to investigate possible question bias is the so-called *split-half design*. In this design, there is a *random assignment* of various question wordings or question orders to different subgroups in the sample.[4] Random assignment can occur whenever there are at least two versions of a poll item or ordering of items that need to be investigated; the randomization process is used to determine which respondents are asked which version. In the analysis, the response patterns to the two or more versions of the question(s) are compared to see if differences appear.

The split-half design is what other social scientists typically refer to as a *true experiment* to measure cause-and-effect relationships. If the analysis shows that a meaningful difference is associated with the different question wordings or orderings, then the pollster can confidently conclude that at least one of the wording or ordering versions is in some way biasing the data. But often it is not obvious what the pollster can or should do about this.

ARE THERE OTHER WAYS TO TEST FOR BIAS IN A QUESTIONNAIRE?

Another basic approach to detecting bias is to conduct additional data analysis to explore any patterns of correlations that would not be expected to occur if the questions were unbiased. This approach sometimes requires a difficult judgment call on the part of the pollster about whether a pattern of bias has been discovered. But, all things considered, it is better for pollsters to do such analyses and consider these issues than to ignore them.

For example, a pollster might find that answers to a particular question varied by the race of the respondents. This could be a signal that the wording or the topic of the question produced biased responses to the item. Sometimes this can occur for reasons such as social desirability, whereby respondents offer answers they think the researcher expects them to give.

Many elections in the United States involve contests between African American candidates and White candidates, and the number of these elections is increasing. In the past, research such as in the 1982 contest in California for governor (which gave the phenomenon the name of the "Bradley effect" because of the Black Democratic candidate's name) and in Virginia for governor and New York City for mayor in 1989 showed that polls conducted during such biracial campaigns result in White respondents, as a group, overreporting their support for African American candidates.[5] Whites are even more likely to do this when they are interviewed by African American interviewers than by White interviewers.

More recent research suggested that this relationship had mostly disappeared as the level of racial rhetoric in American campaigns became muted, and the conclusion was also that there never was an equivalent "Whitman effect" (named for a Republican governor of New Jersey) that involved overreporting of support for female candidates.[6] What has happened in the past decade as political and racial rhetoric has become much more polarized is not known. Pollsters could address these possibilities with experiments within interviewer-administered data collection polls that match, or do not match, by random assignment the race or gender of their interviewing staff with the race or gender of their respondents. However, it is not always possible, feasible, or even desirable to match the race of the respondents and the interviewers in pre-election polls in those campaigns. Knowing that these relationships exist, however, suggests that any data collected in such polls should be analyzed by race of respondent and race of interviewer to see whether differences in response patterns are observed. However, this is rarely reported to have been carried out.

In the 2016 and 2020 elections, support for Donald Trump was underestimated in many polls, and a question arose as to whether some respondents were reluctant to tell interviewers that they were going to vote for him ("shy Trump voters") or they were less likely to agree to be survey respondents (*differential nonresponse*). Secondary analysis of existing surveys as well as some experimental work suggest that differential nonresponse is the most likely explanation.

In sum, there are many ways that researchers can try to learn if poll items are biased. Some are very straightforward, such as simply thinking logically about a blatant and atrocious item and correcting its deficiencies. In most cases, though, pollsters do not make obvious and colossal mistakes in writing biased questions. Instead, they must be willing and able to plan careful investigations of possible bias in their polls and to estimate the direction and magnitude of its effects.

NOTES

1. See Tom W. Smith, "Poll Review: The Holocaust Denial Controversy," *Public Opinion Quarterly* 59 (Summer 1995): 269–95.

2. This classic example can be found in Howard Schuman and Stanley Presser, *Questions and Answers in Attitude Surveys* (New York: Academic Press, 1981), 281.

3. Richard Morin, "How Do People Really Feel about Bosnia? It Depends on How and When You Ask the Question," *Washington Post National Weekly Edition*, December 4–10, 1995.

4. The process of random assignment is used to manipulate the questions that are asked or the order in which they are asked. It should not be confused with random sampling, which is a process for selecting survey respondents so that they represent the target population. See Lavrakas et al., *Experimental Methods in Survey Research* for a fuller description of these techniques.

5. For research on these issues, see Michael W. Traugott and Vincent Price, "Exit Polls in the 1989 Virginia Gubernatorial Race: Where Did They Go Wrong?" *Public Opinion Quarterly* 56 (Summer 1992): 245–53; and Steven E. Finkel, Thomas M. Guterbock, and Marian J. Borg, "Race of Interviewer Effects in a Pre-election Poll," *Public Opinion Quarterly* 55 (Fall 1991): 313–30.

6. See Daniel J. Hopkins, "No More Wilder Effect, Never a Whitman Effect: When and Why Polls Mislead about Black and Female Candidates," *Journal of Politics* 71 (July 2009): 769–81.

Chapter 7

How Are Data Gathered for Election Polls?

After an eligible respondent, typically someone eighteen years of age or older, has been designated (selected) as the one person in a household to provide answers to questions in an election poll, the actual process of data collection begins. In most interviewer-administered polls, this happens through what could be thought of as a "scripted conversation" whereby a trained interviewer asks the respondent a series of closed-ended and/or open-ended questions. There are several different ways in which this conversation can take place—on the telephone, face-to-face, and/or with the aid of a computer when video interviewing is done. In the case of in-person exit polls, interviewers traditionally hand the respondents a questionnaire and have them immediately fill it out themselves. The voters then drop the questionnaire into a "ballot box" that the interviewer is carrying. In mail surveys and when using internet data collection and Interactive Voice Response (IVR), which are data collection methods where no interviewer is involved, the "scripted conversation" with the respondent takes place with the respondent reading the letter or e-mail or listening to the IVR phone call that has been sent/made to invite her/him to participate in the poll. If the respondent decides to cooperate, then s/he follows the instructions that have been sent or spoken and proceeds to complete the self-administered internet, mail, or IVR questionnaire at her/his own pace.

Any of these modes of data collection can be used to gather data in scientific election polls. From the 1930s to the 1970s, the traditional mode for gathering election poll data was to use interviewers who asked people questions face-to-face. Interviewing people in-person has also been used in the unscientific straw polls that were conducted by journalists, political campaign workers, and interested citizens in the United States as early as the mid-1800s. Face-to-face questioning was the preferred interviewing method for many years because it was both practical and timely. It was practical in the sense that voters were often sampled and interviewed at their home addresses. Unlike nowadays, these were times when most Americans were comfortable letting a virtual stranger (the interviewer) who had just rung their doorbell or knocked on their door enter their home to conduct an interview. And it was timely because until the last fifty years, prior to the revolution in news production brought about by modern computing technology, the media did not require immediate access to their poll findings in order to make news.

From the early 1980s through the late 1990s, almost all election polling was done via telephone surveying. In the past twenty-five years, a growing portion of election polling data collection has been done each year via the internet. Many of the internet polls use respondents who are self-selected members of internet research panels. A growing portion of election polling data also started being gathered in the 1990s via IVR systems using recorded or machine-simulated "interviewer" voices to read questions to respondents. Increasingly, pre-election polls are being conducted with mixed-mode collection.

WHAT IS THE MOST COMMON FORM OF DATA COLLECTION IN ELECTION POLLS?

Before the 1980s, in-person data collection was the predominant mode used for election polls. But starting in the late 1970s, there was a shift to telephone interviewing as the preferred mode of survey data collection. By the early 1980s, virtually every pre-election poll was conducted via landline telephone. This shift came about as residential penetration of telephones in the United States exceeded 90 percent of all households, which convinced pollsters and other survey researchers that the telephone was a viable and cost-effective method for sampling and thereby reaching a representative sample of Americans for polling purposes. At the same time, *random-digit dialing (RDD)* procedures were being perfected as a sampling technique, allowing pollsters to reach households regardless of whether their landline numbers were listed or published. In combination, these factors affected the cost, timing, and quality of data that could be gathered via telephone in a way that they became as good as, and often more attractive than, what could be collected via face-to-face interviewing.

However, in the early 2000s, an avalanche-like movement began with people abandoning their landline phones and choosing to rely only on a cell phone. By 2024, more than four-fifths of all adults in the United States will only use a cell phone for their telephone service. Because of this, and other reasons, pollsters who want to collect election poll data via the telephone may entirely stop using landline numbers in their sampling. However, a cost-related downside of using cell phone numbers in the United States for data collection is that the Telephone Consumer Protection Act of 1994 has been interpreted by the US Federal Communications Commission and the Federal Trade Commission to prohibit the use of any mechanical means (e.g., a modem or an auto-dialer) to place a call to a cell phone number for whom the party doing the dialing has not received prior permission to call that number. Anyone who violates this federal regulation is subject to at least a $500 fine for each violation. So, when cell phone numbers are used in election polls and other surveys in the United States, they must be dialed manually by interviewers. As a result, cell phone interviews are now more expensive than interviews conducted on landline phones.

In the past two decades, there has been an explosion in internet research panels, including those that are used to gather election-related data. Starting in the late 1990s, some pre-election polling data began to be gathered via the internet, for example by Harris/Black. The 2000 election cycle was the first time that internet surveys were used extensively for data collection. However, due to the pattern of access to the internet among the American electorate, it is extremely difficult and costly to select an internet sample that is truly representative of the American electorate. Even as of 2024, access to and usage of the internet in the United States will skew towards middle-aged and younger males, in particular those with higher incomes and higher education. These demographic characteristics often correlate with both voting behavior and political attitudes. As such, many internet samples do not reflect the entire electorate's voting preferences or attitudes.

Most of these internet panels use relatively inexpensive methods that allow the panel companies to be able to gather data for their clients very quickly and at a low cost, especially compared to the cost of other polling modes of sampling and data collection. Therefore, each year since the late 1990s, more and more election polls are based on data that have been gathered via the internet, and the internet very likely will be the data collection mode for most election polling data that will be gathered in 2024.

It also is important to note that a small number of internet research panels in the United States (fewer than thirty) are formed using high-quality scientific sampling techniques, and these panels often produce election poll findings that are as accurate as the best of polls that are conducted via other sampling and data collection means. But there are only a few of these panels and they will account for only a very small portion of the election polling data gathered via the internet in 2024.

WHAT OTHER FORMS OF DATA COLLECTION ARE THERE?

Scientific election polls can also be gathered via a mail survey, although in most cases this is not feasible to do on a timely enough basis for the purposes that the data are meant to serve, be it for news or a political campaign's needs. The costs of data collection by mail are relatively low, but a typical mail survey requires upwards of at least a month of elapsed time and multiple follow-up mailings in order to achieve a high-quality and representative responding sample.

This notwithstanding, for many decades, one of the most accurate pre-election polls in the United States was conducted by mail by the *Columbus Dispatch* newspaper; its record of accuracy since the early 1980s until 2016, when it stopped being conducted equaled or bettered pre-election polls conducted on the telephone or via the internet in Ohio.

Another data collection mode, Interactive Voice Response (IVR), has been used since the 1990s as part of election polling, and some of these polls have provided very accurate pre-election estimates of election outcomes. This mode of data collection, which will be used in 2024, employs a recorded human voice, or a machine-simulated human voice, to read the questionnaire to a respondent who has been sampled via a telephone number. The IVR system first speaks a poll question followed by speaking the response choices for the question, each of which is associated with a number on the phone's keypad; for example, "If Yes, press 1. If No, press 2." In this way, no human interviewing costs are incurred and a large number (more than 1,000) of completed poll questionnaires can be generated within a few days. However, as explained later in this chapter, there are challenges with some aspects of IVR data quality that have yet to be satisfactorily solved.

Since the late 1990s there also has been an important data collection development in exit polling, related to the increasing numbers of Americans who are voting before the day of the election (so-called "early voters") and thus cannot be sampled and measured at voting places throughout the United States on Election Day. These voters must be sampled, and data must be gathered from them either via a telephone, an IVR system, the mail, or the internet. This must be carried out in advance of Election Day for the exit polls to be accurate in a growing number of states that have significant numbers of early voters. Thus, in the United States the national exit poll and many state exit polls have become mixed-mode surveys in which more than one form of data collection is gathered.

WHAT ARE THE ADVANTAGES AND DISADVANTAGES OF FACE-TO-FACE DATA COLLECTION?

Face-to-face interviewing evolved as the dominant mode of quality survey data collection at a time when there was little or no telephone service to most US households. It is no longer the predominant mode of data collection for election and other public polls because of its great cost. But it has some distinct advantages over the telephone, mail, IVR, and internet for data collection.

The main advantages of in-person interviewing are linked to the social realities of having the interviewer in the physical presence of the respondent. First, questionnaires can be much longer with face-to-face interviews than with other data collection modes because neither the interviewer nor the respondent gets fatigued as quickly. It is not unusual for face-to-face interviews to take an hour or more, without seeming a burden to the respondent. Second, more complicated question formats can be used in face-to-face interviews, especially those conducted via *computer-assisted personal interviewing* (CAPI) software, including ones that employ visual aids as part of the questioning. Third, if a question requires respondents to look up an answer in their household records, they can be more easily persuaded to do this during a face-to-face interview in their home. Finally, an in-person interviewer can unobtrusively and directly code information about the person, the home, and the neighborhood while visiting the location in which the interview takes place. This can be done without asking the respondent questions, as would be necessary for other data collection modes.

Apart from its relatively high cost, face-to-face interviewing has other disadvantages. Most importantly, there is the lack of constant interviewer supervision that is possible in a centralized telephone facility. Second, it is becoming increasingly difficult to find interviewers who are willing to go into certain neighborhoods and areas to conduct interviews because they are concerned about their personal safety. At the same time, respondents also are becoming less willing to let a stranger into their homes, even when the interviewer has ample identification and prior notification has been given that the interviewer will be arriving at a specific time on a specific day.

In addition, during the past three decades, more concern has arisen about the possible biases that may affect sensitive data (e.g., candidate preferences) that are gathered directly by an interviewer, especially one who is working in person. An example of this occurs in election polls when the demographic characteristics (e.g., gender, age, or race) of the interviewer (who can be seen by the respondent in a face-to-face survey) or a live online video interview and of the respondent interact with these same characteristics of the candidates who are running against each other in a particular election. That is, a male interviewer may well get a different answer from a male respondent than from a female respondent about candidate preferences when the candidates are not the same gender than (1) when the candidates are the same gender and/or (2) the interviewer is a female. In addition, the presence of an in-person interviewer is often thought more likely to lead to socially desirable biased answers to a sensitive question (e.g., *"Are you currently registered to vote?"*) than when the same question is asked by a telephone interviewer or especially when asked in a self-administered survey with no interviewer present.

WHAT ARE THE ADVANTAGES AND DISADVANTAGES OF VIDEO-ASSISTED DATA COLLECTION?

This is a new form of data collection that pollsters and survey researchers began to use during the COVID pandemic, when face-to-face interviewing was curtailed due to the danger it posed to respondents and interviewers. It uses an internet connection such as Teams or Zoom to have a live interviewer interview a respondent. It requires respondents to agree to schedule a specific time to have an interviewer recontact them for the interview.

This form of data collection was not used for the 2020 or 2022 election polls, but it likely will be used for a very small proportion of the election polling in 2024. The best ways to carry it out are still being developed and tested, so it remains a work in progress. But, as a data collection mode, it shares many of the advantages and disadvantages of in-person data collection. However, it is significantly less expensive than in-person interviewing to carry out.

WHAT ARE THE ADVANTAGES AND DISADVANTAGES OF TELEPHONE DATA COLLECTION?

The main advantages of the telephone as a data collection mode compared to in-person interviewing traditionally have been (a) speed in obtaining data, (b) ease of sampling target populations, and (c) the opportunity to institute quality control over recruitment and interviewing. However, changes in the use of cell phones among the public in the past twenty years have made it more difficult for election pollsters to know with confidence how to draw representative samples of the electorate for interviewing via telephone. In terms of speed, a telephone poll can be conducted much more quickly than a face-to-face survey because it is much easier to contact respondents at a time convenient for them and for interviewers to recontact hard-to-reach respondents. It is much easier (and less costly) to redial a telephone number, for example, than have an in-person interviewer make a second trip to a home.

Furthermore, the widespread use of computer-assisted telephone interviewing (CATI) procedures means that the data can be recorded simultaneously in a computer file as the interviews take place. In contrast, mail surveys suffer greater time delays in gathering and processing the data, while internet data collection is typically the fastest mode for data collection. Furthermore, while an address-based sampling frame for face-to-face, mail, or internet data collection leads to uncertainties about whether housing units are occupied, a researcher using a telephone sampling frame immediately learns if a telephone number is no longer in service. The researcher does not have to wait to learn that an interviewer went to a home only to find out that the residents had moved or that a mailed questionnaire has come back marked "return to sender" because the intended respondent no longer lives there.

Another set of concerns with telephone surveying in the US that has arisen in the cell phone era has to do with the legal and ethical issues. Due to US federal regulations about dialing cell phone numbers, pollsters cannot use automatic dialing technologies to place calls to cell phones. Instead, surveys need to have interviewers who hand-dial the numbers or else they would be in violation of FCC/FTC regulations. This raises the cost of conducting *cell phone surveys* appreciably. In addition, people are reached on their cell phone in all types of locations. Some of these locations are not conducive to conducting good quality telephone interviews either because they are unsafe for the respondent to do so and/or the quality of the data the respondents provide will not be as good as if they were interviewed at their home. Part of this problem is due to the myriad multitasking behaviors in which many respondents engage while being interviewed via a telephone (watching TV, using the internet, reading a book, paying bills, cooking, going to their place of employment, walking in their neighborhoods, and the like), especially when using their cell phone. In contrast, with in-person and video-assisted data collection, multitasking on the part of the respondent will almost never occur since an interviewer is present.

A third advantage concerns the safety of telephone interviewers who do not need to travel anywhere. Sometimes this also works as an advantage for respondents who do not want to allow an interviewer into their homes.

WHAT ARE THE ADVANTAGES AND DISADVANTAGES OF SELF-ADMINISTERED MAIL AND INTERNET QUESTIONNAIRES?

An election poll that uses a self-administered questionnaire can achieve a good response rate and have some significant advantages over surveys with personal and telephone interviewing. The most important feature is the privacy with which respondents can provide their data. This leads to less (fewer and smaller) social desirability biases in certain types of data gathered via these modes, because there is no human interviewer present to affect a respondent's answers to sensitive questions, including common election poll questions such as those asking about which candidate(s) a respondent intends to vote.

With mail and internet data collection, many respondents also find it more convenient to be able to self-schedule the time when they will complete the questionnaire. This is especially attractive to respondents who have a busy lifestyle. The internet especially appeals to younger-aged respondents who are used to using their smartphone to communicate via texting. These data collection modes also give respondents more opportunity to think about their answers to the questions. And pollsters have the possibility of including visual aids as a supplement to complicated question formats. Respondents also find it easier to look up information without feeling rushed by the presence of an interviewer.

Another advantage of self-administered data collection is the relatively low cost. However, it actually costs much more to conduct a high-quality mail survey of the public than most people realize, because of the need to do several follow-up mailings to achieve a representative response rate. The same is true for internet data collection when a survey is using a probability sample to recruit sampled voters to complete the poll's questionnaire via *computer-assisted web interviewing*, or CAWI. But these costs are still substantially lower than face-to-face and video-assisted interviews and are generally lower than telephone interviews. When data collection for an election poll takes place among sampled members of an existing internet panel, the cost per completed questionnaire is generally the lowest of all survey data collection modes, except for via the Interactive Voice Response (IVR) mode.

Mail surveys, but not most internet surveys, also afford respondents the opportunity to retain their *anonymity* (whereby the researchers do not have any way of knowing anything about the identity of the person or household that provided the data), instead of merely receiving a pledge of *confidentiality*. But this is a complex issue because devising a mail survey that provides true anonymity precludes the use of many techniques that are usually needed to increase otherwise low response rates that result in unrepresentative samples and raises recruitment costs.

There are also many disadvantages associated with self-administered questionnaires. Whenever sample recruitment procedures allow respondents to make the decision about whether or not they will participate in a poll without the persuasive influence of an interviewer, then self-selection biases can result. This always is what happens with opt-in internet surveys, including research panels that are formed via that nonprobability sampling approach. Although low response rates can be overcome if a mail or internet survey is well designed and well implemented, differential nonresponse—where different types of people are more or less likely to participate in the poll—remains the bane of many internet opt-in polls. And, in part because of the added time required for follow-up mailings and other means of recruitment, many pollsters forgo using additional strategies to achieve a more balanced representation of their target population because their clients' deadlines do not allow for the time that is required.

Another significant disadvantage of mail surveys, but not internet surveys, is the length of time required to conduct them. This is the most common reason for ruling out an election-related mail poll with a self-administered questionnaire as the data collection mode. It simply takes much too long to conduct a valid mail poll for most of the needs of the news media and for most private poll sponsors, such as candidates.

Furthermore, from the perspective of the resulting data themselves, self-administered questionnaires sometimes produce incomplete or ambiguous answers for open-ended questions that cannot be clarified in the way they could if an interviewer were administering the questions. Therefore, there is often more missing and unusable data in a mail survey than one that is conducted by interviewers. In contrast, with internet CAWI questionnaires, pollsters often program these in a way that does not allow a respondent to skip a question or to add an idiosyncratic response that is not part of the response choices the pollster has provided for a question. The trade-off in doing this, however, is that these restrictions frustrate some internet poll respondents, thereby causing them to quit filling out the questionnaire, and thus become only partial respondents or essentially nonrespondents to the poll.

WHAT ARE THE ADVANTAGES AND DISADVANTAGES OF SELF-ADMINISTERED IVR QUESTIONNAIRES?

Data that are gathered via the IVR mode are among the lowest in cost of any type of survey data collection. They also are among the fastest to collect. This is the appeal for election and other political polls using this mode of data collection for the news media, political candidates, and their sponsors.

However, since a recorded or a machine-simulated voice administers the questionnaire in the IVR data collection mode, one would think that there is no human being involved who could be affecting the data that are gathered. But, not enough is known about what goes on in respondents' minds when they are providing data via an IVR mode. Do some respondents tend to forget that they are being "interviewed" by a machine? This may be happening on occasion, but the research on IVR-gathered data does indicate lower levels of biased answers to sensitive questions due to social desirability compared to when a human interviewer is actually gathering the data. Thus, some researchers temporarily switch the data collection mode within a questionnaire to IVR for administering sensitive questions in questionnaires that otherwise are interviewer-administered.

IVR also has known disadvantages as a data collection mode. One of the two most important to pollsters is that the length of an IVR-administered questionnaire needs to be kept relatively short—likely twenty questions or less. That is because experience shows that with IVR data collection the proportion of the respondents who answered the first question in the questionnaire then begins to decrease, question by question, as the interview goes on, and it is not unusual to have less than half those who started the questionnaire actually answer the last question.

The second main disadvantage with IVR is what is termed a *primacy effect*. These data biasing effects occur when respondents exhibit a tendency to choose answers that are presented first or early in a list of response alternatives. Primacy effects with IVR occur when people tend to choose an answer before all the response alternatives to a question have been spoken to them. This is especially a problem with *attitudinal questions* that have four or more response alternatives, such as "Strongly Disagree, Somewhat Disagree, Neither Disagree nor Agree, Somewhat Agree, or Strongly Agree." Thus, the answers that come later in a list are not heard by the respondent, and thus are not chosen as often as they would have been had the respondent heard all the responses to choose from. Those pollsters who use IVR for election poll data collection can reduce these primacy effects in their data by having more than one version of their questionnaire deployed for data collection, so that a random half of respondents hear one order of response alternatives and the other random half hear the opposite (a reverse) order of the answer choices. To our knowledge, nothing has been reported about the proportion of IVR data collection polls used in 2020 and 2022 that deployed such an ameliorative approach to address the problem of primacy effects in their election polls.

In summary, the reader should note that it is not that all polls that use IVR data collection are suspect, but rather that those that use the technology without any effort to reach a representative sample cannot know anything about coverage and sampling error or the likely accuracy of the findings. And those that fail to try to correct for primacy effects often are working with biased data. These caveats notwithstanding, the IVR-polling organization SurveyUSA, for example, using much more sophisticated methods than most IVR polls, was very accurate (89 percent) in predicting election outcomes in 2022.[1]

WHAT IS MIXED-MODE DATA COLLECTION?

Whenever more than one mode of data collection is used in the same poll, then it can be said that the poll has had mixed-mode data collection. This type of mixing of modes has become more common for many high-quality surveys in the past decade, for many reasons, but it is rarely reported to have been used for election polling studies. It takes extra time and costs more to plan and implement a poll that uses more than one data collection mode. So those are reasons for mixed-mode data collection to be rarely used in pre-election polling. Furthermore, different data collection modes have different effects on the data that they generate. For example, interviewer-administered modes have more social desirability biases in their data than do self-administered modes. Interviewer-administer modes of data collection are much more susceptible to primacy-effect biases (where respondents are more likely to choose answers that come early in a list of choices), whereas as self-administered modes of data collection are more susceptible to *recency-effect* biases (where respondents are more likely to choose answers that come towards the end of a list of choices). Because of these and other differences in data that come from different modes, it often is uncertain where it is valid to combine data from more than one mode without additional statistical adjustments that pollsters will generally shy away from. However, mixed-mode designs are increasingly used in exit polls.

WHAT DO POLLSTERS DO ABOUT "MISSING DATA"?

Missing data in a poll refers to questionnaire items for which a respondent does not provide a substantive answer. The respondent may simply skip answering the question (on purpose or carelessly), report that s/he does not know an answer, or refuse to answer. This is also known as *item nonresponse*. This can be a problem for pollsters because it often is the case that certain types of respondents, for example those with lower educational attainment, are more likely to have missing data in their questionnaires than other types of respondents. When these different types of respondents also hold different political attitudes and preferences, then their missing data may bias the findings of an election poll if certain statistical adjustments are not successfully made.

The one question in election polls that consistently has the greatest proportion of missing data asks for the respondent's income. It is not unusual for upwards of 30 percent of the public to fail to provide a substantive answer about their personal or household income. Since a person's income often correlates with her/his political attitudes and preferences, this can bias the data that a poll gathers about how those attitudes and preferences correlate with income.

To try to reduce or even eliminate the biasing effects of missing data, researchers can try to impute (create) plausible substantive answers for the data a respondent failed to provide. This is done via sophisticated statistical procedures that consider a lot of the substantive answers to other questions in the poll that the respondent did provide. However, there is no guarantee that this will in fact reduce any bias that the missing data might be causing, and it is a time-consuming and expensive procedure to use. Thus, it is rarely reported that election polls have used such techniques to try to improve the data quality in their polls.

ARE THERE OTHER NON-SURVEY METHODS FOR PRODUCING ESTIMATES OF WHAT PUBLIC OPINION IS ON A PARTICULAR TOPIC?

Many social researchers, including some pollsters, have turned to large quantities of social media data that are available on the internet to estimate public opinion on particular topics that might produce a lot of commentary or on evaluations of political candidates. Two common sources are tweets available on X, formerly known as Twitter, and searches employing Google, such as Google Trends data. The frequency of the mentions or use of particular words and phrases are often analyzed as well as the valence of the messages using something called sentiment analysis of the message content. An election-related usage of social media data was illustrated by multiple studies of internet searches for Trump and Biden yard signs and bumper stickers during the five months prior to the November 2020 election, using Google Trends data.[2] Those data showed that the searches closely tracked the horse race poll findings in this period after about a one-week lag.

However, there are several limitations associated with this use of social media data. The first is representation, in that researchers usually do not know the characteristics of those who are sending the messages and making searches, such as their age, race, or gender. Furthermore, there are questions of who has access to the software or applications used to transmit such messages or conduct the searches. It obviously requires access to technology and often a service agreement on technology like a cell phone or computer with internet access, which introduces a socioeconomic bias among those who have such access. Finally, the estimation of the level of support or opposition to a particular policy or candidate often involves assumptions made by the researcher that are typically not made explicit when reporting the results.

An additional point is that these "Big Data" do not usually come from random samples of all available content, so traditional confidence intervals around the estimates that researchers produce cannot be calculated. While tweets were the most common form of social media used by social scientists and political consultants in their work, new policies at X, formerly known as Twitter, and changing algorithms have limited access to tweets, and it is expected that use of this platform will decrease significantly or disappear. Some researchers produce other types of metrics that they believe are analogous to confidence intervals, but their calculation of these metrics also involves assumptions that typically are not disclosed.

WHO GETS TO BE AN INTERVIEWER?

When they conduct face-to-face, telephone, and live video surveys, polling organizations employ interviewers to gather the data from respondents. In order to collect reliable and valid data, these interviewers must be skilled, well trained, and well supervised. Quality polling operations recruit and train adult interviewers of all ages, genders, and ethnic and racial backgrounds. During the recruitment process, polling organizations look for interviewers who have a pleasant voice with ample volume. Interviewers should speak neither too quickly nor too slowly, and they should project confidence when speaking to a stranger (the respondent). These are just general guidelines, as there is a tremendous range of variation in the voices of successful interviewers.

However, there are certain circumstances where interviewer characteristics can bias election poll data. Extensive research has shown that although the demographics of skilled interviewers are generally unrelated to the data they elicit from respondents, the exception is with surveys that ask substantive questions about topics such as gender issues, race relations, and the like. In these cases, the demographics of the interviewer—including what can be visibly observed about an in-person interviewer, what can be observed about an interviewer who conducts video-assisted internet interviewing, and what can be deduced from the voice of a telephone interviewer—and the respondent may interact in ways that can unintentionally bias the data. In some polls that measure the so-called *Gender Gap*, for example, male interviewers may elicit consistently different answers from male respondents than female interviewers do and vice versa. This can complicate the measurement of candidate preference when a woman is running against a man. For example, in 2016, in the race between Hillary Clinton and Donald Trump, pollsters that used interviewers to gather election polling data needed to pay close attention to how the voting preference data varied by interviewer gender and respondent gender.

HOW ARE INTERVIEWERS TRAINED AND MONITORED?

Polls that have interviewers recruit respondents and gather data are highly dependent on the quality of their interviewers. In terms of the success of an interviewer during the recruitment of respondents in order to gain their cooperation, interviewers are trained how to be persuasive with reluctant respondents by trying to (1) initially engage the respondent in a conversation that allows the interviewer to diagnose the basis of any reluctance a respondent may express and (2) tailor the information that is provided to the respondent so that it addresses the reasons why that particular respondent may or may not want to cooperate with the poll. Doing this well requires a natural ability for conversation, a solid understanding of the subject matter of the poll and the methods used to design the poll, a good deal of intelligence, and a lot of practice.

Skilled interviewers also must be trained to read the poll's questions exactly as they are worded. They also must learn to use *nondirective probing* to follow up responses to open-ended questions and ambiguous responses to closed-ended questions. Nondirective probing takes place when an interviewer encourages a respondent to answer a question more fully, but does so in a manner that is neutral and does not bias the response that is elicited from the respondent. Polling organizations concerned about the quality of their interviewers' work provide careful supervision of them. Prior to the COVID pandemic, telephone interviewers would generally work in a centralized facility and not at home, so supervisory personnel were able to closely monitor them and provide constant feedback and on-the-job training. But with the advent of the pandemic, telephone interviewing shifted to having the interviewers being apart from each other (normally at home). This put more burden on pollsters employing careful monitoring on the performance of their telephone interviewers. In many organizations, supervisors routinely monitor ongoing telephone interviews and live video interviewing in a manner that is unobtrusive to both the interviewer and respondent in order to gain a real-time assessment of interviewers' work. In other polling organizations, supervisors listen to recordings of a sample of calls that interviewers have with respondents. Despite what many think, this monitoring is not illegal. It is done for training purposes and to ensure quality control, not to learn anything about a particular respondent. Nevertheless, it is a courtesy (and in some states a legal requirement) to have interviewers inform respondents that monitoring or recording might/will occur while the interview is being conducted.

In the rare case that in-person interviewing is being used for data collection in an election poll, that same quality control rigor should be employed by the polling organization for hiring and monitoring. But the big difference is the inability to do real-time monitoring while an interview is being conducted. However, the computer-assisted personal interviewing (CAPI) and live interviewing software that interviewers use nowadays routinely has a feature that can record the entire verbal exchange between the interviewer and respondent. Supervisors then can monitor a sample of these recordings later.

HOW DOES CONTACT WITH A RESPONDENT TAKE PLACE?

Contacting a sampled respondent is the first step in gaining cooperation from her/him, and thereby having a chance of gathering their data. Simply put, if no contact is ever made, there will be no data gathered. Research shows that effective *advance contact* increases response rates. That is why the prudent pollster also uses multiple contact attempts when needed with harder-to-reach sampled respondents during the field period of the poll. Contact with respondents in a poll can be attempted via in-person, live video, the telephone, the mail, and/or by sending an e-mail or a text message. However, in the United States there are legal restrictions that prohibit unsolicited calls using computerized modems to cell phone numbers where the owner had not given prior permission to be called. Similarly, in the United States, text messages cannot legally be sent to smartphones without prior expressed permission from the owner. In many other countries throughout the world, these restrictions do not exist.

When interviewers are used for a poll, they are typically assigned at random to the respondents they try to interview. For example, most interviewers do not even know who resides at a telephone household before they dial the number, nor do they need to know. The initial contact with most respondents often occurs at their homes, although when calling cell phone numbers completed interviews are often done while the respondent is away from home. For the very rare election poll that uses in-person interviewing, contact is almost always made at the sampled respondent's home.

The interviewer begins the contact by using an *introductory spiel* that the pollster has crafted so the interviewer can briefly describe the poll and explain its purpose. This helps to gain the cooperation of the person within the household who is to be interviewed. The importance of this latter point—gaining cooperation of the so-called *designated respondent*—is often not understood or appreciated by people who are not researchers. If a survey does not use a systematic respondent selection technique to select one person from within each household to interview, then biases in the poll data are likely to result. This could take the form of interviewing too many women and older adults rather than a representative sample of the target population. Furthermore, if the wording of the introduction and the persuasive abilities of the interviewer do not induce respondent cooperation, then many will refuse; and experience shows that it is often certain types of respondents who are most likely to refuse when asked to participate in polls. An unrepresentative final sample of respondents can have disastrous consequences for a poll's accuracy.

The goal of most introductory sequences is to provide a minimum, yet adequate, amount of information about the study for the respondent to make a reasonably informed decision about whether or not to participate. It is at this time in a survey that researchers gain what is called *informed consent* from respondents; ethically, participation in a survey is voluntary. Ethical polling requires that respondents understand that their participation in the poll is voluntary, and their responses will be held in total confidence and reported only after being aggregated with the responses of the other respondents for statistical analysis. The purpose of this assurance is to make it clear that no harm will come to them, whether or not they choose to participate in the poll. The ethical guidelines that govern these procedures came into effect in the early 1950s, after WWII, because of the atrocities that the Nazis perpetrated in the name of "research."

However, an introductory statement should not provide too much information about the poll because it could bias subsequent responses to the questions. It has to provide enough information to inform the respondent about what he/she is being asked to do and to engage a respondent's interest in continuing. Polling organizations that strive for high-quality data collection will train their interviewers to use extensive persuasive material to help them explain more about the poll if a curious or reluctant respondent needs such information. For example, in random-digit dialing polls, some respondents ask, "How did you get my number?" or "How did you pick my address?" Interviewers must be able to provide a brief, informative, easily understood, and honest response to such a question, and they should be trained to do so with skill.

When contact attempts with a sampled respondent are made in polls without using a human interviewer, the same approaches apply, although the approaches are crafted to be communicated via mail, e-mail, or recorded IVR phone messages. Of course, under these modes of contact, there is no opportunity to answer any questions the respondent may have at the time. Because of that, prudent pollsters often provide a toll-free phone number or a webpage that a curious and/or concerned respondent can use to learn more about the poll before deciding whether to participate.

HOW LONG DO ELECTION POLL QUESTIONNAIRES TAKE TO COMPLETE?

The length of time a respondent can expect to be interviewed by an interviewer in the typical election poll conducted on the telephone will generally range between ten and twenty minutes, although there will be a good deal of variation among respondents in the same poll. An interview of this length will generally consist of somewhere between fifty and one hundred closed-ended questions. The purpose of the poll and the amount of funding it has available will determine how lengthy a questionnaire can and will be used. Telephone polls administered by interviewers that are shorter than five minutes are uncommon because a significant portion of polling costs involves the effort made to contact respondents and gain their cooperation. Once contact is made, there is little cost-savings incentive to avoid asking upward of fifty questions or so because each additional question can be asked for a relatively small marginal cost when interviewers are involved. Including the many demographic and political background questions that will be asked in most polls, it is surprising how quickly a questionnaire will fill up with items that need to be asked for the poll's main purpose. Of note, for the purposes of many of the election polls, the sponsors (in particular the news media and candidates) often want the data collected and analyzed very quickly (within a week, or even faster). And, because of that, it often makes little sense to gather a great deal of data, as it is unlikely that there will be time to properly analyze it.

Using a telephone questionnaire that takes longer than thirty minutes also is uncommon because for many respondents this is just too long to engage in an interview, and they tire and break off the interview. It is also true that the quality of answers often suffers in the last parts of a long interview. The initial contact an interviewer makes to explain the survey and elicit the cooperation of the designated respondent often takes less than one minute. After the interview begins, the time it takes to administer the questionnaire will vary across respondents by a factor of about two; that is, the fastest interviewers and respondents, working together, will take about half as much time to go through an interview as the slowest pairs.

Another factor that affects the time it takes for an individual respondent to be interviewed will be the number of *contingency-question* sequences the questionnaire contains—that is, linked questions that are not asked of everyone because they do not apply to everyone—and how many of these sequences an individual respondent's answers will invoke. For a contingency question, a particular response to one question results in a follow-up question being asked. A different response to the initial question will just move the respondent on to the next section of the questionnaire. In the case of a questionnaire that has several contingency sequences, respondents whose pattern of answers causes them to be "skipped out" of each linked sequence will complete the questionnaire much sooner than those whose answers invoke all the linked sequences.

When election poll data are gathered by in-person interviewers, it is not unusual for the questionnaire to take thirty minutes or occasionally even an hour or more to complete. Decades of in-person interviewing has shown that respondents do not seem to mind when they are asked to complete such long questionnaires that are administered to them face-to-face. This may be related to the social context of in-person interviewing, whereby the interviewer is allowed into the respondent's home at a time that is convenient for the respondent.

Telephone data collection that is conducted via IVR technology normally involves very few questions. Thus, the amount of time for such polls is almost always less than five minutes and often may be only a minute or two.

For mail questionnaires that can be completed at the respondent's leisure, the time required can be broken up over more than one sitting or session. This allows longer questionnaires—those exceeding twenty minutes in length—to be viable for mail election surveys.

Internet (computer-assisted web interviewing, or CAWI) questionnaires can be completed over more than one sitting by the respondent, and yet the "ethos" of the internet often creates expectations among its users that things are going to happen very quickly. This is especially the case when a respondent is completing CAWI election poll questionnaires on her/his smartphone. So, most CAWI election polls keep the questionnaire to less than ten minutes, and many try to make the task of completing the questionnaire take no more than five minutes.

In light of these parameters, the reader may find it interesting to learn that follow-up research with recent poll participants shows that most of them significantly underestimate the time it took for them to complete the interview or questionnaire. It is probably an overstatement to invoke the saying that "time flies when you are having fun" to explain this phenomenon, but many election poll respondents do enjoy having their opinions taken when done by a competent polling organization.

It also may surprise the reader to learn that experience in the past four decades with computer-assisted interviewing using interviewers to gather the data has shown that it takes approximately 20 percent longer to ask a series of questions in this mode than to ask the same questions as a *paper-and-pencil interview (PAPI)*. This appears to be related to the fact that an interviewer has more direct control of the pace of questioning when using paper and pencil than when using a computer. On the computer, a subsequent question comes onto the screen only after the previous response has been recorded. With paper and pencil, the interviewer often starts reading the next question on the page while recording the answer to the previous question. Of course, this leads to some coding errors with paper-and-pencil interviewing that no longer occur with computer-assisted interviewing.

CAN INTERVIEWERS AFFECT THE KINDS OF ANSWERS RESPONDENTS GIVE?

Yes, they definitely can. Quality pollsters strive to employ interviewers who have the skills and the willingness to engage in *standardized survey interviewing*. Simply put, standardized survey interviewing refers to interviewers who ideally read questions exactly as written—thus exposing all respondents to the same stimulus (the same question wording). These procedures also include following up incomplete or ambiguous responses with nondirective probes—follow-ups that merely encourage a fuller response instead of conveying to respondents that they are giving a "right" or "wrong" answer.

Without disciplined interviewers who standardize their administration of the poll questionnaire, data in polls may have errors caused by the interviewers in the form of bias and/or variance. In this context, biased data means that the interviewer has done something to "push" answers from respondents in one direction or the other compared to what the respondents would have reported had the interviewer not affected them. Even something as simple as an interviewer saying "That's good" to a respondent as a simple expression of thanking the respondent for answering the question may convey to the respondent that s/he just gave an answer of which the interviewer approved. If this were the case, the respondent may be influenced, even unconsciously, to continue to try to give "pleasing" answers to the interviewer that differ from the respondent's own true opinions. Interviewers also can add error (variation) in the data they gather by being inconsistent or otherwise careless across respondents in how they administered the same question to different respondents. Good pollsters consciously try to avoid their interviewers adding bias and variance to the data they gather.

The best pollsters also strive to create a work environment that will promote standardized interviewing in their data collection staff. Interviewers are human, however, and even the best will unintentionally, yet nonetheless occasionally, contribute error to the data they gather. Given that many polls are conducted by interviewing staffs that are neither well trained nor well supervised, it is probably the case that a good deal of error in polls is caused by interviewer-related behavior. Some additional examples further illustrate how this happens. First, interviewers might unconsciously and unintentionally reinforce certain types of answers that a respondent gives later in a questionnaire by making negative comments ("Oh, that sounds bad") after some answers. Second, interviewers may let their own politics or morals bias the way they read a question, conveying with their voice that they expect a certain "correct" answer to an *opinion question*. However, even in cases where an interviewer hears a respondent give what the interviewer considers to be an abhorrent racist or sexist response in answer to a question, for example, the standardized interviewer must remain professional and neutral, and not convey anything to the respondent that suggests the interviewer agrees or disagrees with the response.

Accurate measurement of public opinion using polls depends on respondents sincerely believing that there are no right or wrong opinions, at least not as far as the pollster and the interviewers are concerned. Anyone who participates in an election poll and encounters an interviewer who appears to be poorly trained or biased should ask to speak to the interviewer's supervisor or consider contacting the polling organization. The supervisor and pollster should thank any respondent who brings these kinds of problems to their attention because correcting them will improve the quality of the data.

WHAT HAPPENS IF INITIAL CONTACT WITH A RESPONDENT IS UNSUCCESSFUL?

As discussed in chapter 5, survey nonresponse occurs whenever a completed questionnaire or interview is not obtained from a sampled household or designated respondent. The two primary causes of nonresponse are (1) never contacting people who have been sampled at a time when they are willing and available to complete the questionnaire or (2) having the sampled person refuse to participate. In order to lessen the chance that nonresponse will contribute to the inaccuracy of the poll—which can happen whenever nonrespondents as a group hold significantly different opinions and intentions than the respondents—a good polling organization will work hard to reduce nonresponse in their surveys.

The simplest way to reduce the potential problem of noncontacts is to have interviewers try and try again, at different times of the day and on different days of the week, to reach the respondent at a convenient time. Or when contact with a sampled person or household is done via the mail or e-mail, the survey organization will resend the invitation to participate at least once and possibly more times, depending on how long the field period for the poll lasts. It is not unusual for academic surveys to try to reach a person who has been sampled via the telephone ten or more times before giving up. And in the case of a survey conducted via mail or e-mail contact, to re-mail the materials three or more times to those who have not already responded. On the other hand, most media polls must be completed within a field period of two or three days, making it very difficult to reach many of the sampled people because only one or two recontact attempts are practical in a telephone or internet poll; and in mail surveys with such a short field period no recontact attempts are feasible. Experience shows that males and younger adults are the hardest respondents to reach in polls, especially those with brief field periods.

To reduce the potential problem of refusals in polls that use interviewers, the best pollsters train their interviewers to try to avert refusals by diagnosing why someone is reluctant to participate and to use persuasion that is targeted to the specific person to whom they are speaking. The better pollsters sometimes also have a group of especially talented interviewers who try to "convert" sampled respondents who told a previous interviewer that they would not participate in the survey. Sometimes the original refusal occurred because the interviewer called at an inconvenient time, when a person was working around the house or engaged in an activity he or she did not want to interrupt (e.g., driving their car). These people were indisposed to be interviewed when first called, but they may have the time when called a second or third time. Once again, this process may be impractical for most media polls, where the field period extends only over a few days. In surveys with longer field periods, *refusal conversions* can yield somewhere between a 20 to 30 percent success rate; that is, one-fifth or more of initial refusals eventually can be converted to completed interviews. Experience shows that initial refusals are more likely to come from women and older adults, but these are also the two demographic subgroups that subsequently are most likely to agree to an interview when skilled refusal-conversion interviewers recontact them. For polls that contact their respondents via the mail, regardless of how the poll tries to gather its data, pollsters are very hard-pressed to know whether contact was ever made versus whether it was made and the recipient of the mailing just threw it away unopened or read it and decided not to respond. If a field period is long enough (e.g., greater than two weeks), the pollsters can consider doing a second (or more) mailing with a small cash incentive to try to "convert" initial refusals. But this practice is very rarely used when conducting election polls.

One method that scientific surveys do not use to compensate for cases of noncontact or refusals is to replace (i.e., substitute) another household or person for the one sampled originally. Sampling with replacement can create serious problems of bias in the poll results if people who refuse to participate or cannot be located are systematically different from those who do respond, and they are replaced by more "willing" respondents. Poorer quality polling organizations may employ this substitution approach, but only with serious risk to the accuracy of their polls.

HOW DOES INFORMATION FROM A RESPONDENT GET RECORDED INTO A COMPUTER?

The process of gathering data in a poll is motivated by an interest in quickly having data to analyze in order to answer a research question. Poll data are analyzed with computers using statistical software. In order to analyze the data, the answers that respondents provide are almost always represented as numbers on the questionnaire and in a data file. These numerical data files are what pollsters analyze to determine the poll's results.

The traditional way that respondents' answers were entered into a computer-friendly form was to have them transferred from a printed questionnaire to a computer file by data entry workers. Prior to the 1980s and the microcomputer revolution, this was mostly done by key punching the numbers onto computer cards, which in turn were read into a mainframe computer by various means. Nowadays, when a poll is taken via a paper-and-pencil questionnaire, which still sometimes happens, the data are transferred directly into a computer file, using a scanner and then a program such as Excel or SPSS. For most telephone (CATI) polling, data entry occurs simultaneously with the data-gathering process. For internet (CAWI) data collection the data always are captured immediately as the respondent is providing answers to the poll's questions. However, with a survey that gathers data via the mail mode, with completed questionnaires being mailed back to the polling organization, there will need to be a data entry stage before the analysis stage can begin whereby the answers on the questionnaires are transferred into a digitized format.

The changes in computer technology in the past four decades have radically improved the speed at which polls can be analyzed, as well as the accuracy of the data, because there is less likelihood of human error in the data entry process. In addition to recording and analyzing the responses given to closed-ended questions (which typically are pre-coded with numeric values such as Yes = 1, No = 2, and Uncertain = 9), many polls gather responses to open-ended items in which the respondent's own words are the answers. While these verbatim responses used to be coded and transcribed into meaningful and reliably quantified categories by humans before they could be analyzed, there is now a variety of Natural Language Processing software available to complete this task. These procedures may result in an increase in the use of open-ended questions in future polls. However, if the pollster's client simply wants to use the respondents' verbatim responses as interesting quotes, then none of these coding procedures is necessary.

DO RESPONDENTS HAVE TO GIVE THEIR NAMES WHEN THEY ARE INTERVIEWED?

The short answer to this question is "No," but there are some legitimate instances in which respondents might want to agree to giving their names and other contact information to the researchers. If a pollster knows someone's name or any other identifying information, it means the poll is not anonymous. But the polling organization should nonetheless guarantee confidentiality by pledging that the data a respondent provides will not be released to anyone except in aggregated form where all answers are pooled together and summarized in statistical tables or figures. In this way, no one's identity can be linked to her/his responses.

There are several reasons why a polling organization might want to be able to recontact a respondent. Pollsters may want someone's name if the client would like to re-interview the respondent at some later time. In most media polls, contact information is requested so that a reporter may call back to talk to a respondent at greater length about his or her views. This respondent could even end up being quoted by name (and with a photograph or video interview) in a subsequent news story, pending the respondent giving permission for this usage. When interviewers are used to gather poll data, they usually will have given each respondent a pledge of confidentiality at the beginning of the interview, so respondents will need to be asked to waive this guarantee before providing their names and contact information. Similarly, when data are gathered via mail or the internet, a written disclosure and confidentiality waiver statement should be provided to the respondent explaining the terms of what is being requested of the respondent by seeking her/his name and contact information.

Respondents should also understand that the polling organization often knows something about their household before the interview begins. A sample for a mail survey often is based on a list of names and addresses. In *face-to-face interviewing* at a person's home, the interviewer will always know the address of the home, but not necessarily the household's or respondent's name, unless it is asked and given. In telephone polls that use random-digit dialing, the name of the household is not usually known unless it is asked and given, or unless the telephone number has been matched against one or more of the many commercial databases with such information. Polls that sample individuals from voter registration lists, whether conducted by mail, internet, in person, or via telephone, will know the sampled respondent's name and past voting history in advance (i.e., whether the person voted, but not for whom s/he voted), and the questionnaire will either be sent to that person, or the interviewer will ask to speak with that person (and no one else).

Furthermore, there are times when poll respondents should be concerned about whether a private poll is really a fund-raising gimmick or a way to construct a mailing list for a subsequent sales pitch. And they do not have to supply any personal information that might be used for such purposes. So, if you are contacted and asked to participate in an election poll, it is only prudent to think at least briefly about whether the pollster is likely to know your name and, if so, whether you should have any reasonable concern about that.

We can neither automatically encourage everyone to release their names to pollsters nor discourage everyone from doing so. We do encourage readers to use common sense in deciding whether or not they should give out their names if they are asked in an election poll. Here, a good rule of thumb is: If you are uncertain, ask the interviewer to clarify why your name is being requested. If you are mailed a questionnaire or an invitation to participate in an internet poll, and are asked for such identifying information, you may want to first contact the polling organization to inquire about this. But if you do give your name, make certain you understand whether or not you also are waiving your right to have your responses kept confidential.

NOTES

1. Fivethirtyeight.com is one source of pollster ratings, based upon their historical record of accuracy. See https://projects.fivethirtyeight.com/pollster-ratings/ for the latest set of evaluations.

2. See https://www.linkedin.com/pulse/does-searching-political-yard-signs-predict-how-state-hoplamazian?articleId=6722881235133243393 and https://www.nyu.edu/about/news-publications/news/2020/november/biden-leads-trump-in-online-searches-for-yard-signs.html.

Chapter 8

How Do Media Organizations Analyze Polls?

Poll data support a different kind of news story than do traditional forms of reporting. Most election news stories are based on interviews with a few key individuals, usually political elites. They often provide an organizational perspective on a story that is based on strategic interests. When a reporter interviews the Democratic or Republican Party chairperson, the interviewee provides spin on a story to support his or her party's interest. In contrast, when stories are based on poll results, they are meant to give a voice to the feelings, attitudes, or intended behavior of the public.

This can be more informative for readers and voters, if the poll is appropriately analyzed. Media organizations have to analyze and present the results of polls in a way that is understandable and intelligible for readers and viewers with limited methodological research and statistical training. Usually, this means that poll data are presented one question at a time. Sometimes there is limited analysis of the data by the demographic characteristics of the respondents, such as age, party identification, race, or gender. Often, however, there is no analysis by relevant subgroups. Then the reader or listener is left with a statement of gross percentages or rates that are technically accurate but do not provide much politically useful or relevant basis for interpretation. A general problem with many media polls is that a good deal of time and money is invested in collecting the data, but neither enough effort nor time is allowed for analysis.

This situation tends to be worse for data presented on television than for data in a print or web format. Television stories are shorter and require that some of the content be devoted to graphics. In some cases, for poll findings that are reported via the internet, for example on a newspaper's website, a great deal of thought and work goes into a very sophisticated analyses and presentation of a poll's findings. But these reports often come out a week or more after the poll has been conducted. In other cases, with internet reporting of a poll result, a very superficial presentation is given in a rush to get out the findings to the broadest audience possible. Some critics of the analysis of media polls describe them as "data rich but analysis poor," reflecting the fact that more informative and newsworthy stories could often be told with the data available if more skillful analyses were conducted and presented.

WHAT IS A VARIABLE?

A *variable* is a measure that contains the range of responses to a poll question. By definition, a variable consists of different values associated with different response categories, as opposed to a constant, in which all of the values are the same. In a simple case, information may be recorded about respondent characteristics, such as gender or age. Traditionally, every respondent to a survey has been treated as either male or female, so gender has traditionally been treated as a variable with two categories. But some polls nowadays are providing more "gender" choices for transgendered individuals and others. Although this is being done, even polls with a thousand people providing information, for example, have far too few respondents who report being neither female nor male to provide reliable findings broken out by these other gender categories.

A respondent's age can be recorded in several ways. One would be to record actual years of age. In a survey of teenagers, where the age range is highly constrained, this might be useful for analysis. But in a general population survey of adults, this coding will produce far too many categories and complicates analysis because of the sheer number of values. In these instances it is common to bracket or collapse ages into groupings such as 18 to 29 years of age, 30 to 49 years of age, 50 to 64 years of age, and 65 years of age or older. In these examples of demographic variables (gender and age), the categories for each variable are inclusive (and thus exhaustive) of all the possible responses, and each category is mutually exclusive of the others. That is, each response can fall into one and only one category.

HOW IS A POLL ANALYZED?

Each question in a poll is converted to one or more variables that can be analyzed by statistical software. In modern polling, where most of the data are collected through telephone interviews or via the internet, the questionnaires themselves are computerized. As the interviewer or respondent records the answers, they go directly into the computer. This means that in these computer-assisted telephone interviewing (CATI) and computer-assisted web interviewing (CAWI) applications, the data are available for analysis almost as soon as the last interview is completed.

The use of CATI and CAWI applications also means that the results can be analyzed and reviewed at various stages during the data collection period, such as at the end of each day. This is especially important to news organizations because these interim analyses help reporters to think about, anticipate, and structure their stories in advance and to discuss this coverage with their editors or producers. Of course, the preparation of the final story must wait until all the data are in; but interim analyses are an important part of the news-making process. However, a final dataset is usually weighted before analysis begins.

WHAT ARE THE FREQUENCIES?

Frequencies consist of the raw numbers of cases (counts of interviews or respondents) coded with each value of a variable. The raw numbers are not usually as important analytically as are their relative occurrence, which is most easily presented and interpreted as percentages or proportions. For example, it is not important to know that 356 respondents approve of the way President Joe Biden is handling his job because the significance of that number depends entirely on how many people were interviewed. Instead, it is more useful to know that 31 percent of the respondents approve of Biden's handling of his job as president, 48 percent disapprove, and the remaining 21 percent are undecided or don't know how they feel about him. Therefore, most news articles report poll data as percentages. Good reporting will provide the percentages for each value or category of the variable, except when there are only two categories (such as in a "Yes/No" question) and the assumption can be made that the second percentage is 100 percent minus the first (e.g., Percent No = 100 - Percent Yes) unless there are also Undecided responses.

WHAT IS AN ESTIMATE?

An estimate is a number calculated from a sample interviewed in the conduct of a poll, and it represents a statistical statement of what the "true value" is likely to be in the poll's target population, if everyone were to be interviewed. A pre-election poll can be used to estimate the turnout in next week's election, for example. Or an economic labor force survey might estimate the unemployment rate in the population during the past month.

Assuming a probability method of sampling was used, the precision of these estimates is based largely on the size of the sample from which the data were collected, as described in chapter 5. A sample estimate has some imprecision associated with it (i.e., the *margin of sampling error*, or MOSE) due to chance alone. This translates into a level of confidence that the estimate accurately reflects the true population value of the statistic. For example, a poll might produce an estimate of turnout in the election that is stated as 52 percent, with a MOSE of ± 3 percentage points (plus or minus 3 percentage points) and a 95 percent confidence level. The translation of this is that 52 percent of the survey respondents indicated that they are likely to vote. Probability theory suggests that 95 out of 100 samples of the same size would produce an estimate of turnout between 49 and 55 percent (52 ± 3) and that the true value in the population is highly likely to lie within this *confidence interval*.

WHAT IS A RELATIONSHIP BETWEEN TWO OR MORE VARIABLES?

The essence of analysis is comparison; one variable, sometimes called an *independent variable*, can be used to predict or explain why some subgroups in the sample are different from each other on a second variable, called a *dependent variable*. Using appropriate explanatory (independent) variables makes analysis of poll data politically relevant and interesting. For example, the Gender Gap is a concept that suggests that men and women evaluate candidates differently and frequently support them to different degrees. In order to analyze the Gender Gap, pollsters look at a candidate preference question by gender to see whether or not the proportion of women who prefer Candidate A is greater or less than the proportion of men who prefer Candidate A. If there is a meaningful difference, then the Gender Gap is present; if there is no such difference, then the Gender Gap is absent. This principle of analysis is illustrated in tables 8.1 and 8.2 in a comparison between hypothetical pre-election poll and data from the final NEP exit poll in the 2020 presidential contest between Joe Biden and Donald Trump.

In the hypothetical pre-election poll shown in table 8.1, Joe Biden is preferred over Donald Trump by a 51 to 39 percent margin with 10 percent yet undecided. In the table, there is no real difference (at least none that is statistically reliable) in the proportion of men and women who prefer Biden; since men and women are about equally represented in the electorate, there is no difference in the support for Biden that appears in the population as a whole, and there is no meaningful gender gap.

Table 8.1 2020 Presidential Candidate Preference by Gender in a Hypothetical Pre-election Poll

	Prefer Biden	Prefer Trump	Undecided	Total
Men	50%	41%	9%	100%
Women	53%	37%	10%	100%
Total	51%	39%	10%	100%

Table 8.2 Candidate Preference by Gender in a Hypothetical 2020 Presidential Exit Poll

	Prefer Biden	Prefer Trump	Other	Total
Men	45%	53%	2%	100%
Women	57%	42%	1%	100%
Actual Result	51%	48%	1%	100%

In table 8.2, however, the final vote totals estimated by the NEP exit poll showed that Biden was the clear choice of women by 15 percentage points, while Trump was the clear choice of men by 8 percentage points. The net Gender Gap in preference for Biden was a whopping 23 percentage points, important because more women voted in the 2020 election than men.

Significant differences in political attitudes and preferences sometimes exist beyond what is shown by two-way comparisons, such as those above. Analyses of 15,590 exit poll respondents in the 2020 election showed that both candidate preference and the Gender Gap are highly related to educational attainment.[1] Among White respondents without a college degree, 54 percent of women preferred Joe Biden, whereas 28 percent of men did, a Gender Gap of 26 percentage points for this educational cohort. For those who graduated from college, this Gender Gap grew to 29 percentage points favoring Joe Biden among women and was just 3 percentage points in favor of Donald Trump among men.

HOW DO THE MEDIA TYPICALLY PRESENT POLL RESULTS?

A typical poll story in the news media is organized around the main finding from the survey and sometimes is embellished with information from standard reportorial techniques such as in-depth interviews with candidates or their campaign managers. If there is time or space available, additional data may be presented from other questions that were part of the poll. The most common form of data presentation includes the marginal frequencies for the main horse race question and perhaps some breakdown of those data by demographic groups, including party identification and sex.

One problem with emphasizing a particular percentage or statistic from a story is that most readers or viewers do not have any frame of reference to use to interpret that result. It would be more useful to poll consumers if such news stories contained at least one reference to another measurement of the same variable or statistic. This would eliminate a lot of the "gee whiz" flavor of poll-based reporting by providing context for how to interpret the current data.

Often a news organization is interested in adding a human dimension to the rather sterile presentation of statistical data. As a result, reporters may interview people and add photographs or video to the story. In many cases, they interview people who were part of the poll's sample after these respondents waive their right to confidentiality. In other instances, reporters just go out to get useful quotes by interviewing as many people as are necessary. The representative attitudes are obtained from the poll by employing scientific sampling techniques. Knowing what the poll results are, a reporter can reach out to interesting and appropriate prototypes of the respondents who can provide good quotations or sound bites. Most people interviewed in media polls agree to give their names and other contact information so a reporter may call or e-mail/text them back.

Furthermore, there are some differences in the way results from the same poll will be presented on television, in a newspaper or magazine, or on the internet. Most televised presentations of poll data involve only a single story because space is much scarcer in the news hole of a twenty-two-minute evening news broadcast (a half hour minus the commercials) than it is in a newspaper. The televised version of the story usually will include tabular presentation of data, but print stories often do not contain data tables. Newspapers often will print a *methods box* containing some of the details of how the poll was conducted. Television stories usually provide only the sample size and an indication of the size of sampling error. On the internet, a news organization can provide more extensive analysis and more detailed methodological information since space is essentially unlimited there. An interesting natural experiment occurs whenever media polling partners, such as the *New York Times* and CBS News or the *Wall Street Journal* and NBC News, collaborate to conduct a poll. Although the partners plan the poll's sampling design and questionnaire together, and then have access to all the same data, each respective news department does its own analyses and write-up of the findings and determines the presentation for each output format. In this way, each organization serves as an independent check on the other in terms of the interpretation and news emphasis that is taken in reporting the poll.

WHAT ARE MARGINALS AND CAN THEIR PRESENTATION BE MISLEADING?

Marginals are percentages that appear "on the margins" of frequencies or cross-tabulation tables such as in tables 8.1 and 8.2. They provide the total percentages for the rows and columns of the table. For example, in table 8.1 the values along the bottom row of the table, 51 percent and 39 percent, are the column marginals for this table and show the portion of the entire sample that was used for this table that prefer each of the two candidates (i.e., 51 percent for Biden and 39 percent for Trump).

The presentation of marginal frequencies (aka percentages) for how many people in the sample overall answered a question in a particular way can be misleading if it gives the impression, often false, that public opinion is solidified or that views are strongly held. Providing marginals without any breakdown by relevant subgroups may also produce a less informative and interesting news story than one that has the nuance of appropriate analysis.

As an example, a recent Gallup Poll showed that President Biden's approval rating was at 37 percent approve and 59 percent disapprove, with 4 percent providing other responses.[2] We are currently in a period of extensive political polarization, where Democrats and Republicans often have sharply divergent views on many issues. In the case of presidential approval, this poll showed that 4 percent of Republicans approved of President Biden's handling of his job while 83 percent of Democrats did. For Independents, his approval rating was at 31 percent. The inclusion of the approval ratings by party identification provides additional meaning about where support for President Biden's job performance stands in the American public.

WHAT IS A TREND?

A trend reflects the analysis of the responses to a single question administered repeatedly over different surveys. That is, if a series of polls contains questions on presidential approval, the trend in the data can be analyzed to see whether over time the approval is increasing, decreasing, or staying about the same.

Trend analysis is a simple and important way to provide a context for interpreting a current poll result. A very common form of trend analysis in election polls involves looking for changes in the trial-heat question, the question that measures the relative standing of the candidates. Figure 8.1 shows the trend in aggregated pre-election polls for presidential preferences in the 2020 campaign between September 3 and Election Day for Joe Biden

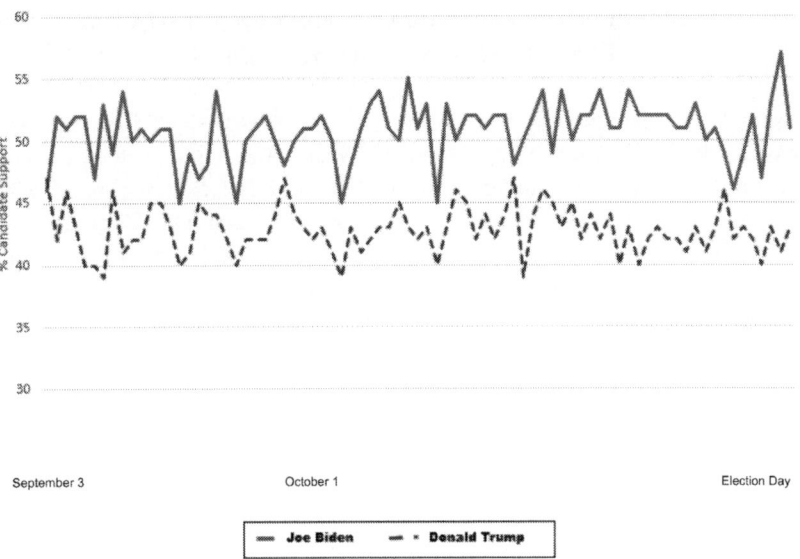

Figure 8.1 Support for Joe Biden and Donald Trump from Labor Day to Election Day, 2020.

Source: This chart was developed from the time series of aggregated poll results available from RealClearPolitics at https://www.realclearpolitics.com/epolls/2020/president/us/general_election_trump _vs_biden-6247.html.

and Donald Trump. A political campaign is all about swaying public opinion to put together a winning coalition on Election Day. Furthermore, this form of analysis is consistent with the media's preoccupation with horse race journalism (who is ahead and who is behind) and the use of sporting metaphors to characterize the strategy and performance of the competitors.

HOW ARE TRENDS ANALYZED?

There actually are two ways that polls are used to identify trends. One is through the administration of the same question to different samples at different points in time, and the other is through the administration of the same question to the same sample of respondents interviewed at more than one point in time.

The first method employs an analytic design involving what is known as "repeated cross sections," whereby the same question is asked in successive polls, each involving its own independent sample (i.e., the same people are not interviewed each time data are gathered). One can have the greatest confidence in trend analysis when the amount of change is relatively large (greater than the margin of sampling error) and when the time series of polls involves more than two measurements. Looking at trends over time is complicated with only two data points because they always result in a straight-line projection that must suggest movement upward, downward, or at a constant (unchanged) level. If the longer-term movement is much more complicated than that, measurements from only two polls will not adequately reflect that complexity. In 2020, there were literally hundreds of polls that measured President Biden's approval ratings. Websites like RealClearPolitics.com or fivethirtyeight.com compute daily averages of these polls and graph them continuously.

In order to estimate the full amount of change, pollsters must employ a panel design in at least two studies. In a panel, the same people are interviewed at more than one point in time and are asked the same question. The full extent of change at the individual level can be measured in this fashion. This is the second, and more informative and more powerful, method that is used to analyze trends, since in this method change is measured within the same individuals. For example, in the first (cross-sectional) method knowing that support for the president changed from 31 to 35 percent during a two-week period only indicates that a 4 percentage point net change overall occurred. In the second (panel) method, that 4 percentage point change can be much better understood as being made up of a combination of shifted opinions, such as learning that approximately 20 percent of the people who previously disapproved of the president now approve whereas approximately 3 percent of the people who previously approved now disapprove, adding up to the overall 4 percentage point shift towards approval.

HOW CAN SURVEYS MEASURE CHANGE?

Understanding the different ways that repeated cross sections and panel designs measure change is an important tool in interpreting poll results, especially as they apply to politics. For example, the president's approval rating may be 28 percent one month and 35 percent the next. If the two independent polls have sufficiently large sample sizes so that the margin of sampling error is, say, plus or minus 3 percentage points, then we are reasonably confident in concluding that the president's approval rating has risen because the range from 25 to 31 percent does not overlap with the range from 32 to 38 percent. But this initial change of 7 percentage points is an aggregate measure, reflecting the net difference between people who felt more positive about the president across thirty days and those who felt less positive about him. By interviewing the same people in both months and comparing their answers from each survey, pollsters can identify four groups of respondents: (1) those who approved of the president in both months, (2) those who disapproved of the president in both months, (3) those who approved at first and then disapproved, and (4) those who disapproved at first and then approved. The size of the latter two groups in this example is greater than the 7 percentage point difference, although their combination is where the difference came from. These groups can be analyzed thoroughly only when the same people are interviewed in a panel survey at more than one point in time.

WHAT DOES IT MEAN THAT PUBLIC OPINION HAS CHANGED?

This is a more complicated issue to deal with because one form of change refers to different proportions of the public holding attitudes on an issue. That is essentially what is involved in the trend analysis discussed above.

Another form of change refers to the public holding different attitudes. And the notion of holding different attitudes can be a direct result of the use of different questions in different surveys. This is one of the most difficult matters of interpretation of multiple polls on the same issue. To make direct and accurate comparisons of change, the exact same questions must be asked of similar individuals with the results coded in the same fashion. Recently, many polls are reporting more negative attitudes toward China, but the size of the decline varies by polling firm and the question asked. Since 2020, Pew has reported a 3 percentage point increase in those saying they have an "unfavorable" view of China, from 79 to 82 percent. In this same period, Gallup reports that there was an 18 percentage point decline in those who have a "favorable" view of China, now standing at 15 percent. Each firm asks a similar question but emphasizes a different response category trend in their reporting.

IS IT POSSIBLE TO COMPARE DATA COLLECTED IN DIFFERENT POLLS?

The answer is, it depends. And the factors that make the answer conditional are (a) the question asked, (b) the sample of people who were asked the question, and (c) the significance of the time that elapsed between the surveys being compared.

One way to think about these issues is through the following example. You read a newspaper article that contains the statement that polls show that President Biden's popularity has declined in the last three months. This is a statement about change that appears to be based on polls. The central concept here is President Biden's popularity, which is typically measured in a single survey question. The minimum condition for comparing the president's popularity would be that the same question was asked in more than one survey, that is, that the question had the same wording and included the same response categories. If two different questions were asked, it is sometimes impossible to evaluate the meaning of the responses, even if the response patterns were apparently the same. Therefore, you would want to know the exact question wordings. The importance of this was discussed in greater detail in chapter 6.

An important issue is who was asked the question. If the responses in one survey were obtained from a representative sample of all Americans and those in another survey were obtained from a representative sample of Republicans, we would not be surprised to know that Republicans had less favorable views of President Biden than a sample that contained many Democrats and Independents. Finally, we would want to consider whether any significant events occurred in the period between the first and the second surveys. This might explain why attitudes toward President Biden had changed between the first and second surveys, suggesting that the change in fact was in an expected direction.

NOTES

1. See https://www.nytimes.com/interactive/2020/11/03/us/elections/exit-polls-president.html.

2. See https://news.gallup.com/poll/329384/presidential-approval-ratings-joe-biden.aspx.

Chapter 9

How Can I Evaluate Published Poll Results?

Many citizens are inherently skeptical about polls and poll results. As a poll consumer, you want to have confidence in the information you see, read, or hear.

There are only a few basic things you need to know in order to make an informed judgment about the quality of the data and the findings based on them. Some people are concerned about small sample sizes: How can I trust information obtained from so few people? Why should I believe poll results if no one I know has ever been interviewed? Some people are concerned about the presentation of biased data by individuals or groups who want to use polls to support views they already hold: How do I know they asked the right question? Which group of people responded to this poll? Still others are uncomfortable with statistical information because it is unintelligible to them: What do all these numbers mean? A few basic principles and rules will help any citizen to understand and evaluate poll results—if the report of the poll contains the appropriate information.

The preceding chapters introduced the essential elements of this information. Some readers may have skipped ahead to this chapter in order to find a short list of items they should consider in evaluating poll results. Here is a summary of information that will help readers perform a critical review of published poll results.

WHAT DO I NEED TO KNOW TO UNDERSTAND AND INTERPRET POLL RESULTS?

In order to interpret the published results of a poll, a reader or viewer should know who sponsored the poll, who conducted the poll, and a certain level of detail about how the poll was conducted. The latter information includes specific information about the questions asked, who the respondents were and how they were selected, and the dates when the poll was conducted. With this information in hand, poll consumers can better make up their own minds about what the data mean and how much faith they want to put in the results.

ARE THERE ANY STANDARDS FOR REPORTING POLL RESULTS?

Fortunately, the polling industry and those who work in it have been very concerned about standards for reporting survey results. The major national group of survey research professionals has developed such standards. Established in 1946, the American Association for Public Opinion Research (AAPOR) is an organization whose 2,500 members are individuals who produce and use survey data; they have both a Code of Professional Ethics and Practices as well as a compendium of Best Practices for Survey and Public Opinion Research, included in their Standards for Disclosing Information about the Methodology of Public Polls.[1] These are included in appendix A.

The AAPOR standards contain a long list of items that the organization believes should be disclosed in reports, press releases, or other public dissemination of poll results. They include the sponsorship of the survey and who conducted it; field dates for the data collection; the method (mode) of obtaining the data; the population sampled and how it was sampled, and the size of the sample and any relevant subsamples; the complete wording of questions asked; and the percentages on which the conclusions were based. The AAPOR standards further suggest including information about sampling error or precision and any information about weighting procedures. They also suggest including information about response rates, eligibility criteria, and *screening* procedures.

Starting in 2011, AAPOR began a Transparency Initiative to increase the availability of important information about how polls are conducted. The details are discussed in chapter 2, but the main goals of the initiative are to provide additional information about the methods of polls whose findings are publicly released, archive that information, and recognize polling firms that agree to provide it publicly. Currently there are more than one hundred organizations that have qualified and joined the AAPOR Transparency Initiative.

When the results from a poll are published in the newspaper, this type of information is sometimes placed in a methods box (or sidebar) found at or near the end of the article. When the results are used in a television broadcast, much less information of this kind is usually made available. Often, the viewer will only see the sample size and the margin of sampling error estimate. Nowadays, the greatest methodological detail is often provided when poll results are available on a website.

WHY SHOULD I WANT TO KNOW WHO SPONSORED THE POLL?

This information is a poll consumer's first, best guide to whether the results might be biased in some fashion. When candidates sponsor polls, for example, they might be used for strategic purposes in the campaign. For example, question wordings might be unusual in some way. Sometimes poll results are leaked to reporters on a confidential or exclusive basis that is clearly intended to get them published or broadcast. Under those circumstances, a reader should wonder whether only the most favorable results were released while others were withheld.

Sometimes a special-interest group interested in influencing proposed legislation will sponsor a poll. In 1999, a series of similar polls was sponsored by the Citizens Flag Alliance, a group that was supporting a constitutional amendment to prevent burning of the American flag. Separate surveys were conducted in ten states whose US senators had indicated they were undecided about this issue. These polls were conducted and released to the public to influence future votes in the Senate and citizens who might vote in the senators' reelection campaigns.

Another example of a sponsorship effect appears in current polling about gun control laws. Most current polls show support for strengthening gun control laws, including so-called "red flag laws," which create legal procedures that allow guns to be removed from certain individuals under some conditions. At the same time, polls conducted by the Crime Prevention Research Center, a conservative organization favoring gun ownership, reported public opposition to such laws.[2] Using something akin to a *push poll*, after asking whether respondents would support such a law (58 percent said they would), the follow- up question was "*Would you be more likely or less likely to support 'red flag laws' if you knew there are no hearings before an individual's guns are taken away and there are no mental health care experts involved in the process?*" Then support for such laws declined to 30 percent.

Recent research suggests that sponsorship is an important cue that poll consumers use in assessing a poll's accuracy. For those who have ready access to the internet, it is easy to check to see whether a group has sponsored previous surveys on the same subject and what the results were.

WHY SHOULD I WANT TO KNOW WHO CONDUCTED THE POLL?

Knowing who conducted the poll provides useful information about its likely quality. Polls are conducted by well-known national polling firms, as well as by other, far less skilled companies and individuals. The ease and low cost of collecting data through the internet by individuals with little or no formal training or experience in survey methods means that knowing the background and experience of individuals and firms in the polling business is more important than ever. It is polls conducted by inexperienced pollsters that once prompted Harrison Hickman, a prominent political campaign consultant, to observe that "any fool can become a pollster, and many have."

Most people cannot evaluate polling firms unless additional information is provided about their history or some of their recent clients. Nate Silver at fivethirtyeight.com provides ratings of firms based upon their recent record of accuracy in pre-election polls. Some firms produce results that tend to favor the Republican candidates over time while others produce results that tend to favor the Democratic candidates. These systematic differences between firms are known as *house effects*. Poll consumers who know the name and location or e-mail address of the firm can use this information to contact the company to request additional information about the poll or to do this kind of information search on the internet. If the poll results were released at a press conference, then the AAPOR Transparency standards suggest that the polling organization should answer poll consumers' questions about the methodology of the poll or the results.

WHY SHOULD I WANT TO KNOW WHAT MODE OF DATA COLLECTION WAS USED?

Information about what kinds of data collection were used can tell a poll consumer something about other important considerations, such as what frame was chosen to sample respondents and the likely response rate. Response rates to polls have declined across the last thirty years, and mixed data collection mode designs are increasingly used. Telephone polls usually will produce higher response rates than mail or internet polls, unless the mail polls use multiple mailings to or make multiple contacts with those who do not respond initially. But even telephone pre-election polls are usually conducted over a very short period, while mail polls take much longer, even when only one mailing occurs. Internet polls can have the shortest field periods. A relatively short data collection period is important for media polls because events may have taken place between the time the first and last interviews were obtained, influencing the interpretation of the results. However, the future viability of telephone polls for reaching a representative sample of US voters is uncertain given all of the new regulatory and telecommunications challenges that pollsters are now facing. Increasingly, it is important to know what proportion of the sample was contacted by landline or cell phones as Americans continue to switch more to personal devices.

Data that are gathered via interviewer-administered (in-person, live video, and telephone) modes typically have fewer answers that are missing, but other problems are more likely to exist, such as bias due to what is called social desirability, which is the reluctance of many respondents to give an answer to a live interviewer that would place the respondent in a bad light. In contrast, self-administered modes of data collection (internet, mail, and IVR) have relatively more answers to questions that are missing but are less likely to suffer from social desirability bias, since no live human is present to hear their answer. A poll consumer also should want to know whether information was obtained from people who volunteered their responses by calling an 800 or a 900 number to register their views, by clipping a questionnaire from a newspaper or a magazine, or by volunteering to respond to questions posted on a website. These *call-in*, *mail-in*, or *log-in polls* of self-selected respondents present substantial concerns of bias because they rarely represent any knowable target population. These issues are discussed more in chapters 7 and 10.

Currently, almost every American has access to the internet, whether through a broadband supplier or on their smartphone. All other things equal, this means that internet data collection can reasonably represent the American public, if high response rates are achieved and representative samples are drawn. But some internet polls may require extensive weighting algorithms to approximate the adult population of the United States, and even then the weighting may not improve the accuracy of the findings.

WHY SHOULD I WANT TO KNOW WHAT KIND OF SAMPLE WAS USED?

The two most important issues about a poll's sample are what sampling frame was used and whether a probability design was used to choose those people who were surveyed. If a probability sample was not drawn, then inferences from the sampled opinions to those of the *target population* cannot be made reliably. The laws of probability and inferential statistics can be used only when every member of the population (as reflected by the sampling frame) had a known, nonzero probability of selection. If that is not true, it is likely that biases were present in the sampling procedures.

Other information about the sampling frame is important too. Lists of US phone numbers are not good frames for telephone interviews, for example, because reliance on this source for numbers will exclude those millions who have unlisted numbers or cell phones or who have moved recently, which are people who happen to be more likely to vote for Democrats. By definition, *unlisted households* have to be sampled with special techniques. There is currently no sampling frame of e-mail addresses that exists that represents any target population of interest to those who want to conduct accurate election polls. Many news organizations, both television and newspapers, maintain websites that offer those visiting the site a chance to opt-in and respond to a "survey question of the day," which oftentimes is related to politics. None of these polls provide valid data about the attitudes and intentions of any knowable target population, and as such are of no value other than for the entertainment of those who respond to them. These issues are discussed more in chapter 5.

WHY SHOULD I WANT TO KNOW WHAT THE SAMPLE SIZE WAS?

Knowing the sample size for a probability sample will tell a poll consumer something about the margin of sampling error (MOSE) around estimates produced from the poll. The larger the sample, the smaller the sampling error is. A table of standard sampling errors for simple random probability samples is included in appendix B. But there are just a few numbers that a poll consumer might remember and use as a rule of thumb in evaluating poll data.

A useful guide is that the MOSE around an estimate for a sample of size 2,000 is ± 2 percentage points. For a sample of size 1,000, it is ± 3 percentage points; for a sample of size 500, it is about ± 4.5 percentage points; and for a sample of size 265, about ± 6 percentage points.

For nonprobability samples, calculating anything about sampling error is controversial and often unreliable. However, that does not stop many pollsters that use nonprobability samples from reporting a standard MOSE, even though their calculations are statistically meaningless. In writing this, we do not mean to suggest that nonprobability samples always yield incorrect findings, but rather that consumers need to be much more critical in their confidence in and other evaluations of polls using such sampling methods.

WHY SHOULD I WANT TO KNOW IF THE RESPONSES OF IMPORTANT SUBGROUPS WERE ANALYZED SEPARATELY?

The estimates of sampling error given above are based on analysis of all the data from the entire sample. The analysis of subgroups in the sample is the same thing as producing estimates from samples of that reduced size, so the sampling errors are larger.

In most surveys of the general population, for example, the sample will contain about as many men as women. An estimate of President Biden's approval rating in the full sample of size 1,000 will have an overall sampling error of ± 3 percentage points. For the subsamples of men or women, however, the margin of sampling error for an equivalent statistic will be ± 4.5 percentage points. Although each of the subsamples is half the size of the full sample, the margin of sampling error is only about 50 percent greater.

WHY SHOULD I WANT TO KNOW WHAT THE RESPONSE RATE WAS?

Traditionally, a survey's response rate has been used as one indicator of how well the survey design was carried out, including its recruitment and data collection. When the response rate is below 90 percent of the original sample—which is essentially always the case for election polls—there is a legitimate reason to wonder whether the final sample that provided data adequately represents the population from which it was drawn, even if a probability method was used. In current election polls using probability sampling that involve telephone interviews or internet data collection, response rates are now often in the single digits, meaning that more than 90 percent of those sampled to particulate did not provide any data. (And with nonprobability surveys, response rates are typically less than 1 percent.)

However, pollsters and other survey researchers have come to realize that the response rate in itself may signal nothing of value about the likely accuracy of the poll. In the past twenty years, more attention has been paid to the importance, or lack thereof, of the linkage between response rates and election poll accuracy. This research has shown that even with very low response rates, a poll that otherwise was well conducted can be very accurate in predicting an election outcome. This research also suggests that this happens because those people most likely to participate in the horse race–type polls also are the ones most likely to vote in the election.

Whenever you see that the data for a poll have been weighted to adjust for differences between the characteristics of the cooperating sample (such as for age, gender, race, and/or education) compared to the characteristics of the target population, this means that the researchers have tried to adjust the data to better reflect the target population because of a "low" response rate producing an unrepresentative sample. For example, almost all surveys and polls find it more difficult to gather data from sampled respondents who are younger, less educated, and/or racial or ethnic minorities (with the exception of Asians). If a sizable proportion of the voters in a given election will have any of these demographic characteristics, then a low response rate for a poll that is trying to predict the outcome of that election may signal that the findings may be inaccurate, even if the data are weighted.

In the 2012 election, turnout among African Americans exceeded turnout for Whites for the first time. Exit polls showed that 95 percent of Black voters supported Barack Obama. If the response rate for African Americans was lower than for White respondents, polls would have systematically underestimated support for Obama's reelection bid. Some analysts suggested that that actually happened in that election. With the increased predictive power of party identification and candidate vote choice, it is more important than ever that the internal balance of partisans in a sample is correct.

Currently there is an active discussion of these issues within the survey research community, and the coming years will likely produce a better understanding of these problems and what pollsters should do about them and how poll consumers should think about them.

WHY SHOULD I WANT TO KNOW WHEN THE DATA WERE GATHERED?

There are two issues here. Poll consumers should want to know whether the data being reported are current and whether any important intervening events occurred while the poll was being conducted or since the poll was conducted.

Poll consumers generally assume that data contained in a poll report are current, especially if the newspaper or television station sponsored the poll because of its assumed news value. One important criterion of newsworthiness is that the story relates to something that is of current interest or that happened recently.

On occasion, a poll story contains data collected some time ago, such as information from candidate polls conducted at the start of the campaign. Candidates may release such data because the poll was favorable to certain positions they hold or to them personally. But a lot may have happened in the campaign since the data were originally collected, making it reasonable to assume that the same question asked last week would have produced a different result.

It is also important to know when data were collected in order to assess whether any intervening events occurred that might have affected public opinion. If the president makes a major policy address to the American people, a news organization wants to assess public opinion after the speech. Or if a crisis occurs in foreign affairs, a news organization wants to know about public opinion following those events. Sometimes, journalists are interested in whether opinions have changed because of the speech or the crisis. Then they want to compare data that were collected before the event with new data collected after it.

WHY SHOULD I WANT TO KNOW THE EXACT QUESTION WORDINGS, INCLUDING THE RESPONSE CATEGORIES?

Knowing the exact question wording provides an indication of how well the question could be understood by the respondents, and it allows for an evaluation of potential bias in the question wording. If the question was closed-ended, the wording will show what response alternatives were offered. The full wording will also show whether an explicit "Don't know" category was included as an option. All of this information is useful for interpreting the meaning of the reported results for a question.

WHY SHOULD I WANT TO KNOW THE QUESTION ORDER?

Sometimes questions can be posed in a leading fashion, that is, in a sequence that is likely to produce a certain response to the last question in a series. Responses to a particular question should be evaluated, in part, by what questions came before it. And, it is often interesting to know what questions followed, to get an indication of whether the first set of responses might have affected some subsequent ones.

WHY SHOULD I WANT TO KNOW WHETHER THERE ARE REFERENCES TO OTHER POLLS ON THE SAME TOPIC?

If a published report of poll results contains a reference to other polls on the same subject, then it probably also contains statements about how opinions have changed over time. Provided with enough relevant information of the kind we have been discussing, a poll consumer can evaluate the previous results, especially if access to the internet is readily available. Most data are released as "new" findings, but they may reflect exactly the same results as many previous surveys on the same topic. Checking for previous results is the basis for assessing whether attitudes, opinions, or behaviors likely have really changed.

DOES THE ANALYSIS SUGGEST THAT CHANGES IN OPINION HAVE OCCURRED, AND ARE SUCH INTERPRETATIONS JUSTIFIED?

The meaning of change is a difference in "comparables," that is, comparing apples to apples and not to oranges. Sometimes, a discussion of change over time really reflects differences in measurement over time (completely different results) rather than change in the same measurement. To make direct and accurate assessments of change requires a comparison of the responses to the same question, asked of similar individuals, and with the results coded in the same fashion.

Poll consumers should look to see that the same question was asked of respondents in two similar samples, if not of the same respondents interviewed at more than one point in time. The same question wording means that the same concept, such as presidential approval, was measured, allowing those from whom the data were collected the same response options. If the same polling organization conducted both surveys, it is more likely that this is the case.

It is also important to note whether the same kinds of people were asked the question. Often the findings from two polls will be reported as presenting conflicting results. In the first poll, the question was asked of a representative sample of the entire population; but in the later one, it was asked only of partisans of one kind or another (Democrats or Republicans). Another common problem is that results from the trial-heat question appear to change because it was asked of a sample of adults or registered voters in an earlier poll, but it was asked only of likely voters as Election Day neared.

NOTES

1. Both authors of this volume are former AAPOR presidents, and each is the winner of AAPOR's Lifetime Achievement Award.

2. See https://www.nraila.org/articles/20221003/manipulated-public-opinion-polling-should-not-drive-public-policy-on-guns.

Chapter 10

What Are Some Common Problems and Complaints about Polls and the Media's Use of Them?

With all of the knowledge about polls and the polling process that you have gained by getting this far into the book, it is possible now to talk more about the promises and the pitfalls of polling.

On the positive side, the prospects for election polls contributing to a better-informed citizenry are virtually unlimited. In order for that potential to be realized, however, polls have to be conducted with care so that they produce reliable and valid data. They have to be analyzed carefully so that accurate and meaningful news stories are constructed from them. And these stories have to be produced and disseminated in ways that reasonably large numbers of sophisticated readers and viewers will be exposed to them. The main purpose of this book has been to provide readers with the background knowledge to become educated consumers of election polling information.

The pitfalls are numerous too. Many news organizations, especially individual television and radio stations and smaller newspapers, are enamored of polls as a news source. Editors and producers want to generate their own data at the lowest cost possible. In the polling business, just as in any other, you get what you pay for. One difference, however, is that you can disseminate an awful lot of bad data very quickly through the application of modern technology to the news business.

Many journalists attach a special importance to information obtained from press releases and press conferences that an individual or a special-interest group has called to discuss some new poll findings. When poll results are re-disseminated through news organizations in this manner, it is the responsibility of journalists to serve as the gatekeepers for data quality. Often, this will require additional training in basic polling methods and the elements of data analysis for most of them. And contrary to the standards for determining newsworthiness that place an emphasis on what has happened in the past twenty-four or forty-eight hours, journalists must learn that sometimes they will have to return to a poll-based story from some time ago to reexamine reports of public opinion at that time.

For example, at the end of 1995, a controversy arose over statements made in 1994 about public support for the Republicans' Contract with America. Information of some kind, perhaps from a combination of focus groups and a survey, was disseminated to suggest that at least six out of ten Americans supported every plank of the contract. Revisiting and reconstructing events at that time, Frank Greve, a reporter for Knight-Ridder, concluded that these statements, which formed the basis for stories on the Associated Press wire and in the *Wall Street Journal* that subsequently appeared in innumerable other news stories and the *Congressional Record*, were misleading at best and possibly false. There was no representative sampling of adult Americans who were asked balanced and unbiased questions about the policy preferences on these matters. This lack of true public support is one factor among many that appear to explain why the Republicans in Congress had such difficulty in converting the contract into legislation, and the party in general and some of its former leaders in particular, especially Newt Gingrich, suffered in subsequent measures of public opinion as a result. Of note, after their narrow victory securing control of the House in 2022, the Republicans rolled out their new "Commitment to America"; but there were no claims of poll-based public support this time.

These kinds of issues, and many others like them, are dealt with in the answers to the following questions.

DO POLLS MEASURE "REAL" ATTITUDES?

A main purpose for election polls is to measure the electorate's thoughts and feelings on a wide variety of social policy issues, such as balancing the federal budget, health care costs and insurance, abortion, capital punishment, gun ownership rights, and Social Security reform. Pollsters often refer to the ideas that the public holds about these policy issues—an aggregated kind of public opinion—as the public's attitudes.

A common concern that poll critics (and many pollsters themselves) have about measures of attitudes taken in polls is whether or not they represent anything real beyond the context of the poll itself. There is wide variation in any population in terms of how interested people are in public policy issues and how much thought they have given to specific policy proposals. Experience with polls has demonstrated convincingly that many adults answer an opinion question in a poll, such as *"Do you agree or disagree that the United States should send additional weapons to Ukraine?,"* without having given much thought to the specific issue prior to being asked the question. Under these circumstances, some critics argue that the attitudes measured in the answers to the question do not reflect real public opinion but so-called "measured opinion"—specific responses offered to a particular question that are associated with the set of response options offered. The responses do not reflect any kind of considered opinions on the issue because most respondents had hardly thought about it before they were asked the question in a poll.

Respondents who answer a question inaccurately produce one form of *measurement error*. There are many reasons why this might happen, including not wanting to appear uninformed or ignorant. Therefore, some respondents choose one of the answers (such as "strongly disagree") offered in the poll question rather than admit they are uninformed about an issue by saying "I don't know."

An interesting case of mistaken public beliefs occurred after the US invasion of Iraq in 2003. Although then president Bush had indicated that Saddam Hussein's possession of weapons of mass destruction and links to al Qaeda were two of the justifications for the invasion, an extensive search had not turned up any indication of such weapons. And the terrorist links were based upon disputed intelligence that later was found to be unreliable. Nevertheless, polls showed that substantial minorities of the US population believed that weapons had been found and the links to terrorism had been established. During the summer of 2003, a poll showed that 34 percent of Americans believed that weapons of mass destruction had been found in Iraq after the war ended. And that fall, 43 percent of Americans had the impression that the United States had found clear evidence of links between Saddam Hussein and al Qaeda. These poll findings first prompted a statement from Secretary of State Colin Powell that no weapons had been found and eventually a statement that they were unlikely to be found and there was no clear link between Saddam Hussein and al Qaeda. And even four years later in the summer of 2007, a *Newsweek* poll showed that 41 percent of Americans still believed that Saddam Hussein's regime in Iraq was directly involved in planning, financing, and carrying out the terrorist attacks on September 11, 2001.

The issue of whether the attitudes that pollsters measure are real has been the subject of much research and debate—too much to review here. Nevertheless, pollsters have one fairly easy-to-implement solution to help cope with the problem of respondents expressing attitudes on issues they know little or nothing about. They can add questions to polls to test the accuracy of respondents' knowledge about an issue and then they can conduct subsequent analysis by dividing respondents who are relatively informed or uninformed into subgroups. The purpose of this is to investigate differences in the opinions and policy preferences they hold. Such a comparison does not directly answer the question of whether the attitudes are real, but it does go a long way in providing a broader understanding of attitudes that are expressed. Unfortunately, this straightforward approach is often judged impractical by pollsters (and their sponsors or clients) because it lengthens interviews, thereby adding to costs.

There are also many times when knowledge is irrelevant to the poll's purpose. Candidates often sponsor private polls to learn what the public thinks about an issue, not necessarily whether citizens know much about it or not. The reason these private polls treat these attitudes as real is that they can affect the way that citizens will vote, regardless of whether or not they are well informed on an issue. Even uninformed attitudes can have very real consequences for candidates!

CAN POLLS BE DESIGNED TO FIND WHATEVER THE SPONSOR WANTS?

As explained in chapter 6, there are many ways that a questionnaire can be formulated that can lead to biased findings, including some findings that are "preferred" by the poll sponsor. Thus, the flaws are sometimes intentional because they are explicitly planned by the pollster (and possibly the sponsor) to lead to a knowingly biased but nonetheless desired result. This practice is abhorrent to any ethical pollster, but that does not mean that the practice does not take place. In fact, professional organizations like the American Association for Public Opinion Research work to root out such practices and censure those who engage in these unethical practices. Their enforcement procedures are limited, but their efforts at exposing such practices are important for maintaining public confidence in the polling business.

An example will help illustrate how poll questions can purposely be written to lead to desired findings. Imagine an unscrupulous pollster who wanted to publicize poll results unfavorable to an opposing political candidate. The pollster would merely need to word certain attitude questions in such a way that Candidate X's policy positions appeared to be at odds with some revered figure in American politics, even if that person never really held such a position. By explicitly linking a policy position with a respected public figure, the pollster would lead many respondents to be more likely to side with that position and against Candidate X's position, even if they were generally supportive of the same side of the issue as Candidate X. The unscrupulous pollster might then hold a press conference or issue a press release to report the opposition to Candidate X's position, without an explicit reference to the leading and unbalanced question that was asked. In this way, the pollster would have manipulated and biased the measures in order to create a certain result, and the misleading result would be entered into the news stream by further deceit and ignorance.

WHEN IS A SURVEY NOT A SURVEY?

Another unscrupulous practice in which some "pollsters," political campaigns, and telemarketers engage is to pretend that a legitimate survey is being conducted when in fact it is not a survey at all! This flagrant violation of business ethics is different from the problem of purposely biasing the wording of poll questions in order to shape the answers that are likely to be given. In these instances, we are talking about someone pretending to conduct a survey when something else entirely is really occurring.

One such unethical practice is a form of the infamous push polls. This type of poll mimics a legitimate survey, but its real purpose is to manipulate the opinions of individual voters for strategic purposes. Pretending that the respondent has been contacted for a legitimate poll and then using purposely biased questions that are laden with propaganda supportive of the candidate accomplish this, as do questions worded to favor the issue position the poll sponsor is trying to push voter sentiment toward. Unsophisticated respondents in a push poll may never realize that they were not interviewed for a poll in which there was sincere interest in their opinions; instead, they were interviewed because the sponsor wanted to expose the respondents to propaganda masquerading as survey questions.

This also happens with some issue polls. There is a recent example of sponsorship effects that appeared in recent polling about gun control laws, as described in detail in chapter 9. An organization opposed to strengthening gun control laws tried to move poll respondents in that direction by raising a hypothetical condition in a follow-up question that made it seem that the proposals would be unfair to gun owners. It produced a decline in support for such laws of about 28 percentage points, from a majority to minority support.

When telemarketers and political campaigns engage in a similar practice, it often is referred to as SUGing, or "soliciting under the guise" of polling. In these cases, telemarketing sales personnel pretend to be legitimate telephone interviewers calling to conduct a survey. But they are really using the simulated survey to establish enough interviewer-respondent rapport to give the respondent a sales pitch. Telemarketers who engage in this unscrupulous practice have found that many more people will stay on a telephone line long enough to hear the sales pitch if they start out thinking they have been called for a survey than if the sales pitch is made explicit right from the start of the conversation. Deceptive telemarketing practices such as these contributed to the groundswell of support for the establishment of a federal Do Not Call List in 2004, on which more than three-quarters of US residential telephone numbers are currently enrolled.

The same principle applies when a pseudo poll is used to raise money for a special-interest group. A series of unbalanced questions is asked that leads many of the respondents to conclude that the special-interest group needs financial assistance. This practice is known as FRUGing, or "fund-raising under the guise" of survey research.

WHAT IS AN AUDIENCE CALL-IN POLL?

During the past four decades, more and more radio and television stations have started to conduct call-in polls of their listeners and viewers; candidates began to use this technique as well. The basic approach is to pose a single question designed to elicit opinions from the audience and to provide telephone numbers for the audience to call. Usually two numbers are offered, each associated with a different answer to the poll question, such as "agree" and "disagree." Daily newspapers also occasionally use this method; in these cases, the newspaper typically prints two telephone numbers associated with an equivalent two-choice decision, such as agreement or disagreement with an issue.

Typically, these numbers are provided so that callers can register support either for or against an issue, but the method also can be used to register preferences for different candidates contesting an election. Sometimes the telephone numbers are ones for which the caller does not pay anything. But still other call-in polls, some of which border on questionable ethics, use 900 numbers, which cost the caller a fee, often less than one dollar but sometimes a lot more. These polls are used for fund-raising purposes by whoever is conducting the poll. Billionaire Ross Perot used such a technique in his 1992 presidential campaign.

Audience call-in polls suffer terribly from major sources of survey error. In particular, there is absolutely no control over who is "sampled," since callers are self-selected and may call in as many times as they choose without the pollster knowing this has happened. Furthermore, the questions posed usually offer response alternatives that are too restrictive, typically only two options from which to choose.

Although a count might be taken of the number of agree or disagree calls, these polls typically ignore any measurement of the undecided sentiment, which can sometimes be of considerable size. As a result, the responses are typically biased by calls from people who have strongly held views on the issue.

One interesting application of the call-in poll in 1992 illustrates the problems the practice presents. After President Bush's State of the Union address on January 28, CBS News sponsored a call-in poll to get viewer reactions. For some measures, they had results from a scientifically conducted poll from just a few days earlier. All told, they tallied about 315,000 responses out of 24.5 million calls attempted. Among the call-in poll respondents, 29 percent said they were better off than they had been four years ago, 53 percent said they were worse off, and 18 percent said they were the same. From the regular CBS poll conducted from January 14 to 19, 1992, that used a probability sample, the responses were 24 percent who said they were better off, 32 percent who said worse off, and 44 percent who said the same. Not surprisingly, the people who dialed and made it through to have their opinions registered were much more concerned about their personal financial circumstances than was the public as a whole.

Newer versions of this now take place over social media. In 2017, Donald Trump retweeted a poll conducted on X, formerly known as Twitter, from @ProgressPolls consisting of a single question: *Who is the better president of the United States?* It may not be surprising that the results, based upon 125,000 followers of the account, favored Donald Trump (61 percent) over Barack Obama (31 percent).

Call-in polls might be considered legitimate vehicles for building audience interest in a radio or television program or among a newspaper's or website's readership, but they have no scientific value whatsoever for anyone who wants to sample voters' opinions or preferences with any accuracy. This is not to say that the results of call-in polls are always wrong; however, the people who conduct these polls and those who see the results have no way of knowing whether they are right or wrong.

WHAT IS AN INTERNET LOG-IN POLL?

Some websites for news organizations use a similar approach by posting a simple question that allows website visitors to express their opinion of the issue. These web-based "polls" suffer from the same problems inherent in call-in polling.

An internet log-in poll is the same thing as an audience call-in poll but employs the technology of a website to gather data. Sometimes called "instant polls," they allow self-selected citizens with an interest in an event or a candidate to contact the website, usually as many times as they want, in order to express their views. Just as with call-in polls, sampling errors cannot be measured.

One good example of the problems of internet log-in polls occurred after the first presidential debate in the 2000 Bush-Gore election campaign. A number of organizations sponsored post-debate assessments of who won that debate. A comparison of seven post-debate polls showed that four network polls—ones that employed RDD telephone samples—suggested that Al Gore was the winner, by margins that ranged from 3 to 14 percentage points. But three other log-in polls produced results that indicated George W. Bush was the winner, by margins that ranged from 8 to 76 percentage points. This difference could be attributed to the fact that the chairman of the Republican National Committee contacted party members before the debate, gave them some web addresses of post-debate assessment sites, and encouraged them to support George W. Bush.

HOW SHOULD I TREAT POLLS THAT ARE MAILED TO MY HOME OR POLL INVITATIONS I RECEIVE VIA E-MAIL?

Receiving a questionnaire in the mail or getting an e-mail invitation to go to a website to participate in a poll provides the recipients with the opportunity to exercise the option of whether or not to respond without the pressure they might feel if the contact were made by an interviewer via telephone or by someone knocking on their front door. The decision to participate in a poll should always be viewed (and presented) as a voluntary act—one that will bring no harm to potential respondents, regardless of whether they agree to participate or not.

In deciding whether to take the time to respond to a mail or internet survey, you should consider the same basic factors that would affect your decision to participate in any survey. The most important of these are as follows:

- Is there an explanation of who is conducting and sponsoring the study?
- Is there an explanation of the purpose of the study?
- Is there an assurance that your answers will be kept confidential?
- Is there an explanation of who is being sampled and how the sample was chosen?
- Is there a telephone number that you can call or an internet site to check if you have any questions or want to check on the legitimacy of the study?
- Does the questionnaire appear to have been crafted in an unbiased fashion, with questions that are easy to understand and response choices that logically fit the questions being asked?

For any of the above questions, a "No" answer is a strike against the pollster and/or sponsor. When reviewing this list in the context of a particular request to be interviewed, citizens will ultimately need to make their own decisions depending on how the poll scores on this list. We suggest that if even a few of these questions are not addressed in the *cover letter* or instructions you receive with the mail poll, e-mail invitation, or on the website, you should err on the cautious side and not cooperate. We say this with confidence because almost all well-conceptualized and legitimate polls will more than adequately meet these standards.

Some additional considerations you can use to make a final decision about whether or not to respond to a mail poll include whether or not a stamped self-return envelope was provided. A "No" is a strike against the pollster. Was a company letterhead used on the correspondence? Again, a "No" should make you wonder about the professionalism and legitimacy of the pollster. Finally, if you do not respond initially, does the poll follow up with a postcard or some other second (or third) mailing to encourage you to respond as soon as possible? Once again, a "No" suggests a poll that is not striving for accuracy. Any poll that does only one mailing, without follow-up contacts, is likely to have a dismally low response rate and is unlikely to produce valid and reliable data. Why would you want to participate in a poll that is not likely to be accurate?

When deciding whether or not to cooperate with an e-mail request to go to a website to participate in a poll (a technique that is called "*push to web*"), another factor to consider is whether you are given a password to log on once you get to the website. If not, then anyone who stumbled onto the website could participate. This would suggest the pollsters do not really care about who is generating their data. In addition, once you get to the website, is there any indication that once you complete the questionnaire you won't be able to participate a second, third, or more times? If not, then this is another indication that the pollsters do not really care about the quality of their sample data. Here again you should ask the question, "Why would I want to participate in a poll that is not likely to be gathering representative data?"

HOW ACCURATE ARE INSERT POLLS IN MAGAZINES OR NEWSPAPERS?

Newspapers and magazines are constantly striving to build reader loyalty, and one way they have found to do this is to provide readers with opportunities to participate in the news process. Encouraging readers to write letters to the editor has been the traditional mode for this. With the explosion of access to the internet, readers nowadays are often given the e-mail addresses of editors so they can more quickly and easily express their opinions.

Yet another technique to create audience involvement is to let readers fill out a survey questionnaire that is printed in the newspaper or magazine or available on a website. Low response rates that result in unrepresentative samples undermine the accuracy of many mail polls, especially those inserted into newspapers, magazines, or websites. Even when many of these *insert polls* now provide readers with the opportunity to e-mail in the questionnaire (which is almost always a single page in length), this does not appreciably increase the proportion of readers who respond or their representativeness. Thus, the people conducting insert polls have no way of knowing whether or not the responses they receive are even representative of their readership, let alone the public as a whole.

As with call-in polls, those conducting an insert poll will neither have a good idea of which readers have selected themselves into the sample nor how many times any one person has done so. Sometimes basic demographic questions are printed on insert polls, but these demographics cannot be used with any confidence to determine whether or not the sample accurately reflects the opinions and preferences of the target population (whatever that is). This information can be used only to show whether the demographics of the sample match the larger readership, if it is the newspaper or magazine's readership that is defined as the target population. There is no way to calculate the margin of sampling error for such nonprobability samples, further eliminating any clue as to the likely accuracy of the results.

Polls inserted into newspapers and magazines are vehicles for engaging readers and building reader interest in, and loyalty to, the publication. They are not a method that can be used to measure people's opinions and preferences in any reliable fashion.

HOW ACCURATE ARE INTERNET POP-UP POLLS?

Similar to audience call-in polls and insert polls, *internet pop-up polls* are unreliable. These polls appear on some news websites while visitors are using the site for other purposes. There is no way to know anything about the representativeness of the sample of respondents who answer the set of questions, and thus their value as a source of reliable information about election preferences or other public opinion is essentially zero.

IF I RECEIVE A TELEPHONE CALL TO BE INTERVIEWED, SHOULD I PARTICIPATE?

Some readers might be surprised to learn that many people who are interviewed for well-conceived and well-executed polls enjoy the experience. The reason for this is that professional interviewers who work for a high-quality polling organization tend to enjoy their work, and this is reflected in the manner in which they interact with respondents. They respect and value respondents' rights to express their opinions honestly, and they sincerely convey their appreciation when a respondent participates.

There is a variety of legitimizing information that a high-quality telephone poll should readily provide to a potential respondent when the respondent asks a question. Even if the interviewer's introductory statement does not explicitly contain the types of information enumerated in the discussion of that question, the interviewer should be trained (and authorized and instructed) to provide such information to every respondent who requests it. Any time an interviewer cannot or will not provide reasonable answers to reasonable queries posed by a respondent, respondents have good cause to wonder whether or not their time should be spent responding to the poll.

High-quality telephone polls will be conducted in a way that there is a supervisor on duty to oversee the work of interviewers. A curious respondent should always be able to speak to the supervisor if desired. Interviewers who state that they do not have a supervisor should be considered suspect, either because they may not work for a high-quality polling organization or because the caller may not really be an interviewer.

Many potential respondents to telephone polls are concerned about how their telephone number was chosen, especially if they have an unlisted or unpublished telephone number. The interviewer should be able to explain the process of random-digit dialing—as discussed in chapter 5—to the potential respondent's satisfaction. Otherwise, the respondent has good cause to choose not to participate.

Ultimately, respondents should be certain that their answers to survey questions will be kept confidential and that no harm will come to them from participating in a poll. If respondents do not have this level of confidence, then they should not answer questions posed by the interviewer-stranger.

SUPPOSE I AM CALLED AT A BAD TIME, LIKE WHEN I AM SITTING DOWN TO DINNER OR ON MY CELL PHONE WHILE DRIVING?

Pollsters conducting high-quality telephone polls will try hard to complete interviews with everyone in the sample. They are interested in achieving a high response rate that results in a representative sample, thereby lessening the chance for nonresponse error. One way this is done is by making *callbacks* to reach people when they are available and at a time that is convenient for them. So, if you are eating dinner or otherwise engaged, and it is not convenient for you to be interviewed at that time, feel free to explain the poor timing of the call. An interviewer should simply respond by apologizing for the inconvenience and asking when a good time would be to call back. Any other response is simply not good interviewing practice, and you should be suspicious.

In 2024, many election pollsters will be conducting surveys with people reached on their cell phones. If you are contacted on your cell phone to participate in a poll, one of the first things the interviewer should ask you is whether you are in a safe location to be interviewed. If you are not, and even if the interviewer fails to ask you about this, then you should immediately inform the interviewer and ask them to call you back at another time, assuming you want to participate in the poll. If you are not asked about your safety, the quality and legitimacy of the poll should be suspect.

HOW DO I KNOW IF A POLL IS BEING CONDUCTED BY A REPUTABLE SURVEY ORGANIZATION?

If you have never heard of the survey organization that is conducting the poll, then you may feel the need to confirm that the group is legitimate. A simple way to do this is to ask the interviewer for additional information about the organization, such as where they are located, and for a telephone number that you can call or an internet site you can check to verify that information. Many polling organizations now maintain 800 numbers that are toll-free and/or internet sites, just for this purpose. Even if you think you know or recognize the group doing the poll, you may still want to verify its legitimacy (and existence) before proceeding with the interview.

Ultimately, you will have to rely on your common sense to decide whether or not the group is legitimate and whether you should participate in the survey.

WHAT CAN I DO IF I AM CONTACTED BY A PSEUDO POLL?

There are several professional associations of market research and polling organizations that try to root out poor-quality and unethical polling practices. The most prominent of these groups is the American Association for Public Opinion Research (AAPOR). It welcomes questions from the public about survey practices and comments on questionable polling practices, such as pseudo polls. You can contact AAPOR about a potential code violation at https://www.cognitoforms.com/AmericanAssociationForPublicOpinionResearch/reportanaaporcodeviolation.

WHAT ASSURANCES SHOULD AN INTERVIEWER GIVE THAT NOTHING BAD WILL HAPPEN TO ME IF I PARTICIPATE IN A POLL?

Interviewers who work for high-quality polling organizations should be thoroughly trained to explain to respondents that their cooperation is entirely voluntary. They should also explain that their responses will remain totally confidential and that the poll data will be reported only in aggregated statistical form. These pledges mean that your answers will not be seen by anyone other than the interviewer and the people at the polling organization who process the data for computer analysis. Furthermore, employees of the polling organization should have signed their employer's confidentiality statement, in which they pledge never to violate the confidentiality of the information that respondents provide.

On occasion, a polling organization may want to deviate from these common ethical practices, but the legitimate poll will always seek and receive the explicit approval of the respondent beforehand. One example is a media-sponsored poll in which the news organization often will be interested in having a reporter call back some respondents for in-depth interviews to gather quotes to use along with some of the respondents' answers to the poll questions as reported in a news story. The interviewer should ask whether or not you would be willing to speak to a reporter, and the reporter should always get your explicit permission to interview you and your agreement that the conversation will be on the record.

Epilogue

As we noted at the beginning of this book, election polls play a powerful role in contemporary American democracy. They can and do affect the candidates and their campaigns; reporters, editors, and the campaign coverage that their news organizations provide; and the attitudes, candidate preferences, and voting behavior of the public.

We believe that election polls used to their best and fullest potential could have a significant positive impact on the American electorate, in part because of their singular ability to provide an accurate reflection of the attitudes and preferences of the people on a timely basis. Too often, though, their potential for good is not realized, whereas their potential for harming democracy seems to manifest itself routinely.

Candidates and campaign strategists appear to use polling more often to determine merely how to beat an opponent rather than how best to serve the public. Journalists and their news organizations appear to use polling more often than not to help identify likely winners, whom they then decide will merit news coverage, rather than to identify, investigate, and portray the appropriate complexities of issues that can and should affect public policy formulation. Given the typical content and format of reporting based on media polls, the electorate appears to use polling results too often to decide whether or not to vote rather than to further educate themselves about their own domestic and foreign policy opinions and inform themselves before making their final candidate choices.

The rapid pace of technological change, budgetary constraints in the news business, and the proliferation of polls in a period of declining response rates have created tremendous challenges for pollsters. While overall the accuracy of final pre-election estimates has improved over time, there have been some recent notable misses, as in the Michigan primary in 2016, the British election in 2015, the 2016 Brexit vote in the United Kingdom, and the 2019 federal election in Australia.[1] It is important to remember that survey research is a scientific enterprise, and there is continuous research on refinements in sampling, recruiting respondents, questionnaire design, data collection procedures, and data processing, including weighting, to keep up with new developments in technology and social and cultural patterns of daily living.

We believe that an educated public must demand better from political activists, news organizations, and itself. One of the ways this can happen is for more citizens to develop a better understanding of the strengths and weaknesses of election polls, in part so they can make better use of this information in forming their own political judgments.

Journalists are an important part of the process because they are the main conduit of polling information to the public. But they too need to become better informed about polling methodology and how to report poll results so they can help the public form more reasoned judgments that will enable them to exercise their democratic rights and responsibilities better.

1. https://dataandinsights.com.au/amsro-polling-inquiry-final-report/. The second author of this book was a co-author of the 2019 Australian post-election report.

Appendix A

Standards for Disclosing Information about the Methodology of Public Polls

AAPOR BEST PRACTICES FOR SURVEY AND PUBLIC OPINION RESEARCH[1]

Section III of the AAPOR Code of Professional Ethics & Practice (April 2021) specifies:

III. Standards for Disclosure

Broadly defined, research on public opinion can be conducted using a variety of quantitative and qualitative methodologies, depending on the research questions to be addressed and available resources. Accordingly good professional practice imposes the obligation upon all public opinion and survey researchers to disclose sufficient information about how the research was conducted to allow for independent review and verification of research claims, regardless of the methodology used in the research. Full and complete disclosure for items listed in Section A will be made at the time results are released, either publicly or to a research client, as the case may be. As detailed below, the items listed in Section B, if not immediately available, will be released within thirty days of any request for such materials. If the results reported are based on multiple samples or multiple modes, the preceding items (as applicable) will be disclosed for each.

A. Items for Immediate Disclosure

Data Collection Strategy. Describe the data collection strategies employed (e.g., surveys, focus groups, content analyses).

Who Sponsored the Research and Who Conducted It. Name the sponsor of the research and the party(ies) who conducted it. If the original source of funding is different than the sponsor, this source will also be disclosed.

Measurement Tools/Instruments. Measurement tools include questionnaires with survey questions and response options, show cards, vignettes, or scripts used to guide discussions or interviews. The exact wording and presentation of any measurement tool from which results are reported as well as any preceding contextual information that might reasonably be expected to influence responses to the reported results and instructions to respondents or interviewers should be included. Also included are scripts used to guide discussions and semi-structured interviews and any instructions to researchers, interviewers, moderators, and participants in the research. Content analyses and ethnographic research will provide the scheme or guide used to categorize the data; researchers will also disclose if no formal scheme was used.

Population under Study. Survey and public opinion research can be conducted with many different populations including, but not limited to, the general public, voters, people working in particular sectors, blog postings, news broadcasts, an elected official's social media feed. Researchers will be specific about the decision rules used to define the population when describing the study population, including location, age, other social or demographic characteristics (e.g., persons who access the internet), or time (e.g., immigrants entering the United States between 2015 and 2019). Content analyses will also include the unit of analysis (e.g., news article, social media post) and the source of the data (e.g., X, formerly known as Twitter, Lexis-Nexis).

Method Used to Generate and Recruit the Sample. The description of the methods of sampling includes the sample design and methods used to contact or recruit research participants or collect units of analysis (content analysis).

Explicitly state whether the sample comes from a frame selected using a probability-based methodology (meaning selecting potential participants with a known nonzero probability from a known frame) or if the sample was selected using nonprobability methods (potential participants from opt-in, volunteer, or other sources).

Probability-based sample specification should include a description of the sampling frame(s), list(s), or method(s).

If a frame, list, or panel is used, the description should include the name of the supplier of the sample or list and nature of the list (e.g., registered voters in the state of Texas in 2018, pre-recruited panel or pool).

If a frame, list, or panel is used, the description should include the coverage of the population, including describing any segment of the target population that is not covered by the design.

For surveys, focus groups, or other forms of interviews, provide a clear indication of the method(s) by which participants were contacted, selected, recruited, intercepted, or otherwise contacted or encountered, along with any eligibility requirements and/or oversampling.

Describe any use of quotas.

Include the geographic location of data collection activities for any in-person research.

For content analysis, detail the criteria or decision rules used to include or exclude elements of content and any approaches used to sample content. If a census of the target population of content was used, that will be explicitly stated.

Provide details of any strategies used to help gain cooperation (e.g., advance contact, letters and scripts, compensation or incentives, refusal conversion contacts) whether for participation in a survey, group, panel, or for participation in a particular research project. Describe any compensation/incentives provided to research subjects and the method of delivery (debit card, gift card, cash).

Method(s) and Mode(s) of Data Collection. Include a description of all mode(s) used to contact participants or collect data or information (e.g., CATI, CAPI, ACASI, IVR, mail, web for survey; paper and pencil, audio or video recording for qualitative research, etc.) and the language(s) offered or included. For qualitative research such as in-depth interviews and focus groups, also include length of interviews or the focus group session.

Dates of Data Collection. Disclose the dates of data collection (e.g., data collection from January 15 through March 10 of 2019). If this is a content analysis, include the dates of the content analyzed (e.g., social media posts between January 1 and 10, 2019).

Sample Sizes (by sampling frame if more than one frame was used) and (if applicable) Discussion of the Precision of the Results.

Provide sample sizes for each mode of data collection (for surveys include sample sizes for each frame, list, or panel used).

For probability sample surveys, report estimates of sampling error (often described as "the margin of error") and discuss whether or not the reported sampling error or statistical analyses have been adjusted for the design effect due to weighting, clustering, or other factors.

Reports of nonprobability sample surveys will only provide measures of precision if they are defined and accompanied by a detailed description of how the underlying model was specified, its assumptions validated, and the measure(s) calculated.

If content was analyzed using human coders, report the number of coders, whether inter-coder reliability estimates were calculated for any variables, and the resulting estimates.

How the Data Were Weighted. Describe how the weights were calculated, including the variables used and the sources of the weighting parameters.

How the Data Were Processed and Procedures to Ensure Data Quality. Describe validity checks, where applicable, including but not limited to whether the researcher added attention checks, logic checks, or excluded respondents who straight-lined or completed the survey under a certain time constraint, any screening of content for evidence that it originated from bots or fabricated profiles, recontacts to confirm that the interview occurred or to verify respondent's identity or both, and measures to prevent respondents from completing the survey more than once. Any data imputation or other data exclusions or replacement will also be discussed. Researchers will provide information about whether any coding was done by software or human coders (or both); if automated coding was done, name the software and specify the parameters or decision rules that were used.

A General Statement Acknowledging Limitations of the Design and Data Collection. All research has limitations and researchers will include a general statement acknowledging the unmeasured error associated with all forms of public opinion research.

NOTE

1. Additional elements of disclosure are indicated within thirty days of the release of study results; see https://aapor.org/standards-and-ethics/disclosure-standards/#1667933142558-b5099a52-a1eb.

Appendix B

Sample Tolerances (Sampling Errors) for Samples of Different Sizes

The data in the following table can be used, under an assumption of simple random sampling, to calculate the confidence interval around estimates based on samples of different sizes. It is based on a sample that is evenly divided in two halves on a measure, that is, 50 percent each. This produces the maximum confidence interval. The confidence interval would be smaller for proportions that are more extreme or divided, say 80 percent to 20 percent, in an equivalent sample of the same size. These calculations also assume that the samples are drawn from a population of at least 10,000.

Suppose a 2020 pre-election survey based on a simple random sample of 1,500 respondents reported that 52 percent support Joe Biden and 48 percent support Donald Trump. Using this table, you could conclude that for 95 percent of such surveys, the proportion of people in the population who support Biden lies between 49.5 percent and 54.5 percent (52 percent ± 2.5 percent).

It is important to remember that analysis of subsamples implies that a different row of the table must be referenced for the appropriate confidence interval. For example, the typical sample of adults in the United States would include approximately half male and half female respondents. So a sample of 1,500 respondents would consist of approximately 750 males and 750 females. While the confidence interval around an estimate of Biden support in the entire sample should be ±2.5 percentage points, for the subsample of either men or women, it would be ±3.6 percentage points.

On some occasions, published polls report differences in the proportion of the sample that supports each candidate. In this case, the sampling error for this difference in proportions is about twice the sampling error for the estimate of each individual candidate's support.

Table Appendix B1. Confidence Intervals for Simple Random Samples

Sample Size	Confidence interval at the 95 percent level (± in percentage points)	Confidence interval at the 99 percent level (± in percentage points)
50	13.9	18.8
100	9.8	12.9
250	6.2	8.2
500	4.4	5.8
750	3.6	4.7
1,000	3.1	4.1
1,250	2.8	3.7
1,500	2.5	3.3
2,000	2.2	2.9
2,500	2.0	2.6
5,000	1.4	1.8

Glossary

800 poll An audience or reader call-in poll to a 1–800 telephone number that involves no cost to the caller. These are most often sponsored by a media organization that produces news, and they typically ask opinions about a single topic or question. Callers who agree and those who disagree with whatever issue position is being surveyed use separate 800 numbers. Such polls are totally unscientific because there is no way to know what target population is represented by those who choose to dial in. (See also *900 poll*)

900 poll An audience or reader call-in poll to a 1–900 telephone number for which the caller must pay a charge, sometimes a very expensive one. These are most often sponsored by a media organization that produces entertainment programming, and they typically ask opinions about a single topic or question. Otherwise, they are similar in method to 800 polls and are just as limited in terms of unknown accuracy. (See also *800 poll*)

AAPOR The American Association for Public Opinion Research. A professional organization whose members are engaged in the study of public opinion and improving public opinion research methods. This includes individual private sector, academic, and government survey researchers. AAPOR was founded in 1946 to promote high-quality public opinion research and to encourage public disclosure of the methods and purposes of polls and surveys.

Advance contact An attempt to alert or warm up sampled respondents to the fact that they have been chosen to participate in a poll. This is typically done when sample addresses are used by sending a postcard or letter notifying them that an interviewer will soon contact them. Advanced contact usually explains the nature and purpose of the study, who is sponsoring it, who is conducting it, and what assurances of confidentiality the respondents can expect. (See also *Cover letter*)

Anonymity In terms of polls and surveys, this is a condition in which the pollster has no information whatsoever about the respondent's identity, including her/his telephone number or internet address. Pollsters pledge anonymity to respondents when privacy issues are thought to affect their decision to participate in the poll. It is most easily built into mail surveys, which provide respondents with a means of sending back their completed questions without providing their name or address, thus leaving the pollster no means of knowing which sampled person actually responded. Assuring anonymity in polls has serious trade-offs for the pollster, as one cannot do follow-up mailings, for example, to only those who are late in responding. Anonymity is often confused with confidentiality. (See also ***Confidentiality***)

Approval ratings Closed-ended poll questions used to measure the extent to which the public approves of the way the president (or some other elected official) is handling current domestic and foreign policy issues facing the nation. The questions employ responses that often range from strongly approve to strongly disapprove. These measures have been taken several times each year for longer than half a century and often are used to contrast approval levels of a current elected official with previous holders of the same office. (See also ***Favorability ratings***)

AP VoteCast The name of a data collection and statistical model for estimating election outcomes and explaining voting behavior on election night. It was developed in 2020 by statisticians and analysts at the National Opinion Research Center at the University of Chicago for the Associated Press, and it is used recently by Fox News, the *New York Times*, National Public Radio, PBS NewsHour, Univision News, *USA Today* Network, and the *Wall Street Journal*.

Attitudinal questions Closed-ended poll questions used to measure enduring or general beliefs about various political issues. Often posed as statements to which a respondent is asked to agree or disagree. For example, *"A woman should be able to get a legal abortion for any reason of her choice. Do you strongly agree, agree, disagree, or strongly disagree?"*

Balanced question A closed-ended poll question with a question stem that poses both sides of an issue (e.g., *"Some people favor an amendment that would require the federal government to have a balanced budget, whereas other people oppose such an amendment . . . "*) and/or one that uses a range of responses that has a true midpoint (e.g., very good, good, fair, poor, or very poor).

Bandwagon effect A going-with-the-winner effect that causes some voters who otherwise would be expected to vote for another candidate to support another candidate whom the pre-election polls predict will win the election. Definitive research on this effect is very difficult to conduct and therefore not much is known with certainty about the effect. (See also ***Underdog effect***)

Bias Systematic error in poll data that consistently produces findings that differ from the true results or the value that exists in the entire target population. This can be caused by any of several factors, such as poor question wording, poor interviewing, low response rates resulting in unrepresentative samples, or poor sampling designs. Poll bias is like a bathroom scale that consistently overweighs everyone who steps on it by ten pounds. In some cases, unscrupulous pollsters can devise methods that purposely bias findings in desired directions.

Biased question A poll question with wording that consistently causes respondents to answer in a way that distorts their true opinions or preferences, thus leading to inaccurate measurements of the topic of interest. For example, the question wording "*Do you favor or oppose a woman's right legally to kill her fetus by having an abortion?*" would cause fewer people to say favor than would be the case with less extreme (biased) wording.

Bivariate frequencies A statistical presentation of data that compares answers to two questions simultaneously. In election polls this is typically done by comparing responses to an opinion or preference question (the dependent variable) by the responses to a demographic question (the independent variable). For example, a report of poll results might contain a comparison of the proportion who say they approve or disapprove of the president's policies by the age of the respondents (those who are 18 to 29 years old, 30 to 44 years old, 45 to 59 years old, and 60 years or older).

Callbacks In face-to-face household polls and in telephone polls, the attempts made by interviewers to reach respondents who were not contacted in previous stops at the household or in previous dialings. Callbacks lessen survey nonresponse and may therefore lower nonresponse error. Media polls typically can manage few callbacks because news deadlines force the polls to be conducted over just a few days' time, sometimes even less.

Call-in polls Unscientific polls, most often sponsored by the news or entertainment media, that publicize telephone numbers that a self-selected respondent can call to register an opinion on a specified topic. Some use 800 or 900 numbers, while others simply use local phone numbers. Their value as accurate measures of public opinion is nil, but they do serve an audience engagement purpose. (See also *800 poll*; *900 poll*)

Candidate preference An expression of a respondent's (likely) vote choice, at least as of the time the poll is conducted. Some undecided respondents are asked follow-up questions to determine toward which candidate they are leaning. (See also ***Trial-heat question***)

Candidate recall The ability of respondents to remember the name of a political candidate on their own, in response to the question *"Can you tell me the names of the candidates who are running for (an office)?"* (See also ***Candidate recognition***)

Candidate recognition The ability of a respondent to recognize a candidate's name when it is presented. This is the lowest level of a respondent's knowledge about a candidate. Recognition of the candidate's name is a necessary condition for having opinions about the candidate. Respondents are more likely to have difficulty in recognizing candidate names early in the campaign or at the time of primaries, as well as those of candidates running for down-ballot offices compared to such offices as president, governor, or US senator. (See also ***Candidate recall***)

Candidate viability This is a concept often discussed in the news during the primary and caucus phase of the campaign. It refers to the chances or prospects that a candidate has of gaining the nomination of their party or winning the general election. Viability is a composite of a number of factors, including how much money a candidate has, how well organized their campaign is, and the quality of their staff. But it also includes how well they are doing in the polls, in terms of their standing in relation to their opponents.

Cell phone surveys In 2020, election polling was often conducted with persons sampled via cell phone numbers. The reason for this is that a growing proportion of Americans have become "cell phone only" in terms of the type of telephone service they own. These persons are not a random segment of the population, and in fact are disproportionately renters, younger, males, and minorities. In 2024, it is estimated that more than 65 percent of those with telephone service in the United States will be cell phone only. Research in the 2004 election indicated that the cell phone only group of voters, as a group, did not vote differently from other voters. However, as the size of the cell phone only group grew, their political attitudes and voting preferences, as a group, began to differ in non-negligible ways from the group who had a landline telephone. (See also ***Landline surveys***; ***Random-digit dialing***)

Census Gathering data from all elements in a population, or trying to do so, rather than just from a sample of elements as in a survey or poll. A census is sometimes called an enumeration.

Closed-ended question A poll question that provides all respondents with a predetermined set of response alternatives from which to choose, rather than allow them to answer in their own words. This can be done explicitly by asking a question and providing answers such as "very likely, somewhat likely, somewhat unlikely, or very unlikely" or implicitly by phrasing the question so that the answers are either "yes or no." The set of response alternatives must be both mutually exclusive and exhaustive. (See also ***Open-ended question***)

Computer-assisted personal interviewing (CAPI) Face-to-face surveys in which the interviewer uses a computer to proceed through the questionnaire and simultaneously enters the answers into a database that is quickly available for analysis. CAPI's advantages are the great control it affords over elements of the design of the questionnaire, such as randomized ordering of certain items and the accurate entry of data in an easy-to-analyze format. CAPI software also may allow for the interview to be recorded so that the supervisors can later judge interviewer quality.

Computer-assisted telephone interviewing (CATI) Telephone surveys in which the interviewer uses a computerized form of the questionnaire, as is done with CAPI.

Computer-assisted web interviewing (CAWI) Interviews employing a self-administered questionnaire that the respondent completes on a computer or smartphone.

Confidence interval In a poll that uses a probability sample, the range of variation around a poll finding within which the poll is likely to be an accurate measure of the population value. Confidence intervals are calculated by taking the poll's margin of sampling error and adding it to and subtracting it from the poll's findings. For example, a poll with a margin of error of 4 percent that finds that 45 percent of the public support Candidate A has a confidence interval on this finding that ranges from 41 to 49 percent. The pollster is then very confident (typically 95 percent of the time) that if a census had been conducted, the true value of the proportion supporting Candidate A would be in the 41 to 49 percent range. Confidence intervals cannot be calculated for polls that are based on nonprobability samples. (See also ***Probability sample***; ***margin of sampling error***)

Confidence level A statement of the likelihood that a relationship observed in a sample is not merely due to chance. This likelihood is traditionally expressed as the number of times in 100 samples that this relationship could occur, usually as 95/100 or 99/100 times.

Confidentiality A pledge by the pollster to respondents that their responses will never be associated publicly with their names or any other identifying information. Confidentiality is not the same as anonymity since the pollster (or at least the interviewer) does know identifying information about the respondent and thus can and does link answers to particular respondents. (See also ***Anonymity***)

Contact attempts When an individual is drawn in a sample for an interview, an attempt is made to make contact with them. This contact could be by an interviewer visiting their home, calling them on the phone, or sending them a questionnaire by mail. They might be contacted in advance by mail or e-mail to let them know an interview is requested. Each time such an effort is made is called a contact attempt, and often it takes multiple tries to get a completed interview.

Context effect The potential consequence of asking a question within the context of other questions such that the effect is to have the answers biased by the context. For example, asking about overall presidential job-approval ratings after asking a series of questions about specific aspects of the president's job performance appears to lower ratings of overall job performance, thereby producing a bias, compared to asking this question first. Context effects also can occur within a question stem or within sets of response alternatives to a question.

Contingency question A question whose answer determines which question is asked next in the questionnaire. For example, answering "Don't know" to a question about which candidate a respondent intends to vote for may lead to a question that asks which candidate the respondent is leaning toward. The leaning question is not asked of those who offered the name of a specific candidate in the earlier question.

Core voters Respondents who indicate strong support for a candidate are unlikely to waiver in their support. This is determined by a series of questions following the measure of candidate preference.

Coverage The extent to which a poll's sampling frame includes (i.e., covers) everyone in its target population. For example, a telephone poll of voters that uses a telephone directory as its sampling frame will not include any voter with an unlisted number, resulting in poor coverage of telephone households.

Cover letter A way to help legitimize contact with sampled persons so as to encourage cooperation. These letters are printed on the letterhead of the polling firm or the poll's sponsor and explain the nature of the poll, how the person was sampled, and information about confidentiality. Such letters have been found to increase response rates. In a mail survey, the purposes of a cover letter are to introduce the study and to include instructions about completing and returning the questionnaire. (See also ***Advance contact***)

Cross-sectional survey A poll that interviews one group of sampled respondents at one point in time. Most polls are cross-sectional, as opposed to panel surveys in which the same people are interviewed more than once. Different cross-sectional polls can be combined to create tracking polls if they ask the same questions. (See also ***Panel studies***)

Demographic question A poll item that measures any of the so-called vital statistics of the respondents. Typically, these are either physiological (such as gender, age, or race) or experiential (such as education, income, or marital status) attributes.

Dependent variable Symbolically represented by the letter Y in equations, the dependent variable is one that is predicted by, and may be caused by, another (independent) variable. In political polls, party affiliation (an independent variable that indicates whether respondents identify themselves as Democrats, Republicans, etc.) often predicts candidate preference. If candidate preference can be predicted by party affiliation, then the preference is thought to be dependent upon affiliation. Originally, these terms (dependent and independent) were associated with experimental research studies in which scientists controlled the levels of exposure that subjects received of an independent variable (such as dosages of a new drug in medical studies) and then observed the effect, if any, on the dependent variable (such as changes in health). (See also ***Independent variable***)

Designated respondent The one person within a household who is systematically chosen to be that unit's respondent. Several techniques are used to make this choice. What they all have in common is that they provide an arbitrary approach to choosing this individual that does not give the interviewer the freedom to choose which person to interview or to ask the questions of the first person who answers the phone or opens the door or whoever is willing to be interviewed. These techniques are all designed to increase the likelihood that the sample will be demographically representative of the population. Lower-quality polls, including those that are conducted overnight, do not employ such techniques because they increase the costs and the time to complete the poll.

Differential nonresponse The notion that unit nonresponse could differ for different types of respondents in a survey. It can create a problem of potential bias, for example, if nonresponding women are different on what is being measured than women who respond and/or nonresponding men.

Double-barreled question Any item that includes two separate concepts that should properly be asked as two different items. For example, *"How would you rate the president's job performance on crime and the economy?"* Answers to double-barreled items are virtually impossible to interpret since the pollster cannot know to which part of the item respondents meant their answers to apply.

Double negative A problem with the wording of a poll item caused by including two negatives in the same question. This makes it difficult for respondents to understand the question and answer it accurately, almost certainly contributing to the error in the data for the item. For example, asking respondents, *"To what extent are you opposed to not allowing prayer in the public schools?"* is very confusing wording and places a great burden on the respondents to figure out what answer to give to reflect their own opinions about school prayer. Experienced pollsters find it easy to avoid creating items with double negatives.

Dual-frame random-digit dialing (DFRDD) This is a sampling technique used in telephone interviewing that involves two samples drawn from separate frames—one of cell phone numbers and another of landline numbers.

Early voting A system of balloting whereby votes can be cast in advance of Election Day. In one form, voting machines are situated in accessible places for up to one month in advance; in another, registered voters are allowed to permanently request an absentee ballot that is mailed to their home. In Oregon and other selected jurisdictions, the entire election is held by mail, and ballots are mailed to voters up to three weeks in advance of when they are counted. In the 2020 presidential election, more than 100 million votes were cast early, representing more than 60 percent of all the votes cast. Some of this high level of alternative ballot use can be attributed to the COVID pandemic, and it is unlikely that the same level of early voting will occur in 2024.

Election night decision team The team of statisticians and analysts at each media organization responsible for analyzing exit poll returns and other data in order to project the winner of each race.

Election night projections On the evening of a primary or general election, television broadcasts now routinely make projections of which candidates will win. Depending on the sophistication of the methods used to gather the information used in these projections, they can be extremely accurate. From 1993 to 2002, VNS (Voter News Service) was the organization created by a consortium of national television networks and the Associated Press to gather the information and provide these projections for major elections. VNS used exit poll data, returns from key precincts, and past voting patterns to formulate its projections. In 2000 and 2002, election night problems associated with VNS led the media sponsors to terminate their funding of the organization. In 2004 and 2006, exit polls for a consortium of major media organizations were conducted by the partnership of Edison Research and Mitofsky International. This new organization is known as the National Election Pool (NEP), and it has conducted the major exit polls since 2008. Research shows that a majority of the public say they find early projections objectionable, including accurate ones. (See also ***Exit polls***; ***NEP***; ***VNS***)

Elements Members of a population or a sample. A sample consists of the selected elements from the population. In a poll, the respondent is the sampled person from whom data are gathered. In most election polls, a household is the unit that is sampled first, and then within the household one person is selected to be the respondent (element).

EPSEM sample A probability sample in which each element has an equal chance of being sampled, thus the name Equal Probability of Selection Method. (See also ***Probability sample***)

Exhaustive A characteristic of a survey question's set of response alternatives that means that all possible answers to the question must fit into one of the closed-ended response choices or one of the code categories for an open-ended question. (See also ***Mutually exclusive***)

Exit polls Originally, face-to-face polling of voters leaving their voting places on primary or general Election Day. As conducted by the network-sponsored election research group NEP, sampled voters are handed a two-page questionnaire, printed back-to-back, on a clipboard. When they have completed the questionnaire, respondents place it into a cardboard ballot box. Data are gathered in a relatively small number of sampled precincts within the geopolitical area being surveyed. Interviewers try to use a selection rule to select every *n*th voter exiting the voting place for an interview. As voting opportunities changed to include absentee ballots during COVID, a majority of votes have recently been cast before Election Day, so pollsters are now employing mixed-mode designs involving telephone and internet interviews with those who have voted already. Exit polls gather data that are used to help make election night projections of winners and to analyze voting patterns in the electorate. Many people hold the view that early projections of winners based on exit polls have affected past election outcomes, although no definitive evidence is available to support that contention. (See also *AP VoteCast*; *Election night projections*; *NEP*; *VNS*)

Face-to-face interviewing Polling in which a human interviewer administers the questionnaire in person to the respondent. Traditionally, this has been done by having the interviewer travel to a potential respondent's home, knock on the door, and ask to come inside to conduct the interview. This mode of data collection is not often used now because of its costs and other practical disadvantages compared to telephone interviewing. Face-to-face interviews allow for longer and more complicated questionnaires compared to other modes of interviewing.

Favorability ratings A type of poll item that measures whether a respondent approves of (is favorable to) or disapproves of (is unfavorable to) an incumbent's performance in office or a candidate's professed policies. The favorability score that is calculated from these data is the difference between the percentage of those sampled who are favorable and the percentage who are unfavorable. For example, if 40 percent of the electorate held a favorable view of the president, whereas 45 percent held an unfavorable view (with 15 percent undecided), the president's favorability rating would be slightly negative (–5 percentage points). (See also *Approval ratings*)

Field period The time that elapses between the start and finish of data collection. Most polls conducted for the news media have very short field periods, ranging from a few hours (as in surveys conducted on the evening of a televised debate) to the more common two or three days. Most polls conducted for candidates also have short field periods because of the need to get data back quickly. Academic surveys of political issues generally use much longer field periods, often a month or more. A general rule is that the shorter the field period, the higher the nonresponse, and thus the greater the chance for serious nonresponse error.

Focus group A moderated small-group discussion, generally with eight to ten participants. A moderator takes the group through a prearranged discussion agenda in a way that tries to simulate a real-world group discussion as much as possible, without the moderator's own opinions biasing the discussion. Unlike polls with scientific sampling designs, information gathered from focus groups has no scientific representativeness. But a focus group can provide richer and more detailed feedback on issues such as reactions to certain types of political advertising than is typically gathered by way of a structured poll questionnaire. Most focus groups are conducted in person, but more are now conducted online, especially since the pandemic.

Frequencies A table or set of numbers that represent the answers given by respondents to one question in a poll. The answers are aggregated (grouped) for each possible response alternative across all possible responses. This aggregation can be done as simple counts (absolute frequencies) or as percentages (relative frequencies). For example, the following aggregation adds to 100 percent and is a distribution of relative frequencies to a question that uses a strongly approve to strongly disapprove response scale: 13 percent strongly approve, 27 percent approve, 42 percent disapprove, 10 percent strongly disapprove, 8 percent are uncertain. (See also *Marginals*)

FRUGing Fund-raising under the guise of legitimate polling. An unscrupulous and unethical practice that tricks people into thinking they are being interviewed for a legitimate poll when instead they are being set up for an eventual fund-raising pitch. In a mail solicitation, the respondent may see a questionnaire composed of leading questions about an issue that concludes with a request for help by making a financial contribution. In a telephone survey, the pitch for money may come days or weeks after the polling is completed, and the respondents whose answers suggest that they would make likely donors may not even make the connection between the two telephone calls. (See also *SUGing*)

Gender Gap A term created by some political analysts in the 1980s and embraced by the news media to refer to the consistent differences observed between women and men in the candidates they favor and their opinions on various policy issues. In the 1992 general election, for example, women's votes divided 46 percent for Clinton, 37 percent for Bush, and 17 percent for Perot, compared to men, who voted 41 percent for Clinton, 38 percent for Bush, and 21 percent for Perot. Thus, there was a Gender Gap of 5 percentage points of women favoring the Democratic candidate. The Gender Gap has appeared in each presidential election since, as well as in many contests for lower-level offices.

Horse race The contest between candidates in an election measured in a pre-election poll by asking respondents for whom they intend to vote and reported as their relative standing in the race. (See also ***Trial-heat question***)

Horse race journalism The tendency of reporters, editors, and producers to focus election coverage predominantly on which candidate is ahead or behind in the race or will be the likely victor. Sometimes this emphasis seems to preclude reporting news related to policy issues that might better educate the electorate and thus advance public discourse in ways that are thought to help democracy. Horse race journalism also includes the proclivity of many journalists to cover an election campaign as a contest or game, often using the language and metaphors of sports reporters to characterize the winning and losing strategies used by the respective candidates' campaign teams. Criticism of this approach notwithstanding, which candidate will win the horse race is a major news story. (See also ***Trial-heat question***)

House effects Differences that are observed in the results of surveys conducted by more than one polling organization (i.e., more than one "house") when they use the same questions at about the same time. The differences might be attributed to differences in such factors as sampling, interviewing, or weighting procedures.

Independent variable Symbolically represented by the letter X in equations, the independent variable is one that predicts, and may cause, another (dependent) variable to change. In the analysis of election polls, demographic and background variables such as gender, age, region of the country, party affiliation, and education often serve as independent variables. They are used to compare, and thus help understand, responses to dependent variables such as candidate preference and political attitude questions. (See also ***Dependent variable***)

Informed consent A standard of ethics practiced by scrupulous pollsters that first informs all respondents about their rights and about any potential harm that may come from their voluntary participation in a poll. Pollsters seek the consent of respondents to participate in the poll before they ask questions. Informed consent can be accomplished through a variety of wordings of a poll's introduction. Often the process is implicit and leads to informal consent on the part of the respondent, instead of using explicit language to ask for the respondent's formal consent.

In-person interviewing A data collection method that involves an interviewer reading questions to the respondent and recording the answers offered in the physical presence of the respondent.

Insert polls Pages inserted in a magazine or newspaper containing questions for a poll. Readers self-select themselves as respondents by tearing out the pages, answering the questions, and then mailing or faxing them to the publication. Insert polls have no control over sampling and thus have little value as accurate measures of anything. Nevertheless, they can serve as vehicles for a newspaper or magazine to engage its readers by courting their opinions. As news consumption moves away from printed media, the use of these polls is dying out.

Instrument Another name for the questionnaire, used on occasion because questions are the tools used to take the measurements that pollsters make. (See also *Questionnaire*)

Interactive Voice Response (IVR) This is sophisticated voice-recognition technology that is sometimes used to administer a questionnaire and then capture respondents' answers. It is very difficult to conduct reliable and valid polls of the public using this technology for a host of reasons, most importantly because of the serious (and expensive) sampling challenges that must be overcome. However, evidence from recent election years suggests that when combined with a rigorous sampling approach, the IVR approach can generate accurate horse race predictions.

Intercept polls/samples Face-to-face surveying that stops (or intercepts) respondents in public areas such as shopping malls, downtown street corners, airports, or the like and asks them to complete a poll or other type of research task. Used mostly for market research, intercept surveys use nonprobability samples and suffer from not knowing with any confidence what target population is represented by the sample.

Internet polls These are currently unscientific polls that use volunteer samples because there are no good frames available that list who owns a computer and has access to the internet. Therefore, it is incorrect to generalize the results from these polls to all adults, all consumers, or all voters. Commercial polling firms have a strong interest in this kind of polling because it has the potential for very inexpensive and rapid data collection. This is a good technique, however, for conducting polls of members of an organization or a firm in which everyone has access to a computer. Some firms draw telephone samples first and supply people with access to the web if they volunteer to participate in future surveys but do not own a computer. (See also ***Log-in polls***)

Internet pop-up polls Single questions or a short series of questions that typically pop up when someone is visiting the website of some news organizations. These polls are not reliable or valid as there is nothing known about the population represented by the respondents who choose to answer them. Often the quality of the question wording in these polls is poor.

Interviewer The person who interacts with the respondent from whom data is collected. An interviewer is present for face-to-face, telephone, or live video interviews but not for self-administered questionnaires used on the internet or for mail surveys.

Interviewer-assisted data collection This term refers to the mode of data collection in which an interviewer is present. (See ***Interviewer***; ***Mode***)

Introductory spiel The words read by an interviewer at the start of contact with a potential respondent. The purpose of the introduction is to structure the information that the interviewer conveys in a persuasive way to increase the chance that the sampled respondent will agree to participate. An introductory spiel typically conveys information about the nature and purpose of the poll, the name of the poll's sponsor, the name of the organization conducting the poll, how the person was sampled, and the confidentiality (if any) of participation. All this can be accomplished in a few skillfully worded sentences that the interviewer can and should honestly and accurately supplement if questioned by the respondent.

Item Another term for a question appearing in a questionnaire.

Item nonresponse Occurs when a respondent does not provide a substantive answer to a specific question.

Landline surveys Telephone surveys that reach people via their landline, sometime called "wired" lines, as opposed to via their cell phones. Landline lines include cordless telephones that sometimes are used to talk on a wired/landline. Currently, only about one-quarter of American households still have a landline telephone available. This low rate severely imperils the generalizability of surveys that only use landline telephone interviewing for their RDD election polling. In addition, cell phone interviews now cost more than twice as much as landline interviews because the cell numbers must be dialed by hand rather than by computer. (See also *Cell phone surveys*; *Random-digit dialing*)

Leaners Persons who say that they have not yet made a final decision about the candidate they will vote for, but who are asked which candidate they are leaning toward. In analyzing the data from a pre-election poll, most pollsters will somewhat discount the reported preferences of leaners when doing the calculations that aim to project the election outcome, by according them less weight than those from respondents with a firm candidate preference. (See also ***Core voters***; ***Undecideds***)

Likelihood of voting The probability that a given respondent will vote in a forthcoming election. Pollsters have developed their own "secret formulas" to measure voting likelihood because a valid method provides the pollster (and the clients) a competitive advantage over another pollster with less valid methods to assess likelihood. The likelihood of voting is usually measured through an index composed of several questions. These usually include registration status, whether a person voted in the last similar election, the respondent's own estimate of his or her intention to vote, and party affiliation. Persons not registered to vote in an election have a zero likelihood of voting, and they will not be eligible for selection to participate in most election polls. (See also ***Probable electorate***)

Likely voter A poll respondent who has provided answers that cause the pollster to conclude that the person probably will, in fact, vote in the upcoming election. This is the criterion that many pollsters use to classify a respondent as likely to vote as the election nears. The ability of pollsters to differentiate likely voters from unlikely voters with accuracy is an important part of the art and science of election polling. (See also ***Probable electorate***)

Log-in polls These are mostly unscientific polls by which users of the internet can self-select themselves to log into a website and register their opinions on an issue. The websites can be sponsored by news organizations or by any of several special-interest groups. The surveys are often limited to only one question, and frequently no information about the respondents is collected. These polls are the equivalent of other kinds of surveys that employ volunteer samples of self-selected respondents, and there are no safeguards on how many times an individual can participate. They are subject to the biases that come from unequal access to and usage of computers and the internet. (See also ***Call-in polls***; ***Internet polls***; ***Mail-in polls***)

Longitudinal studies A form of polling in which the same questions are administered over time so changes in attitudes or other measures can be assessed. When the same respondents are interviewed at more than one point in time, this is called a panel study. Each time interviews are conducted is called a wave; thus, a longitudinal survey has at least two waves of data collection. The passage of time between waves may be fixed (e.g., once each month) or variable (e.g., before election primaries or before the conventions). Another form of longitudinal study involves the same questions being asked of separate samples. These are known as repeated cross sections. Both types of longitudinal designs are used to measure change over time. (See also ***Panel studies***)

Mail-in polls These polls usually involve responses to a printed questionnaire that is included in a publication such as a newspaper or magazine. That usually means that the respondents are self-selected, as a function of their interest in the topic of the survey as well as whether they are readers of a particular newspaper or magazine. This makes a mail-in poll different from a survey, in which there is usually a well-defined sample of respondents who are asked to complete a questionnaire by mail. In an unscientific mail-in poll, the response rate is usually unknown because there was no list or frame from which the sample was drawn, so probabilities of selection and response are unknown.

Mail survey A poll that sends a questionnaire (typically paper) to a household or an individual via the mail. Thus, the questionnaire is self-administered without the participation of an interviewer. Nowadays, mail surveys include those disseminated via fax and/or the internet (e-mail). Insert surveys are a form of mail surveying as the respondents complete the questionnaire at a time of their choosing and mail the questionnaire back. Mail surveys have the advantage of relatively low cost, and they allow respondents to take as much time to think about their answers as they choose. Their disadvantages are the time they take to do well and the uncontrolled setting in which the questionnaire is actually completed. Mail surveys are rarely used by the news media for election polling because they take so long to conduct well, typically a month or longer to achieve an acceptable response rate.

Mall intercept interviews Survey interviews conducted in public places such as malls that are based upon convenience samples. Because there is no form of probability sampling involved, the information gained from such surveys cannot be generalized to the population, and the estimates cannot employ confidence intervals or confidence levels. (See also ***Intercept polls/samples***)

Marginals This term sometimes refers to the frequency distribution for a single variable. It also applies to the frequency counts or percentages that can be summed down each column and across each row of the table that contains the cross-tabulation of two poll questions. For example, the answers to an attitudinal question given by men and women are called the marginals because they appear at the margins of the crosstab table. (See also *Frequencies*)

Margin of sampling error (MOSE) This is a statistical measure that is only meaningful when a probability sample is used. It is a measure of variation, imprecision, or uncertainty, associated with any finding of a poll, because a poll is not a census. Because not everyone in the target population is sampled and measured, there is a chance (a nonzero probability) that the poll findings are in error, even to a very small extent, simply because only a sample of the target population was selected. With a probability sample, formulas can be used to calculate the size of this imprecision within a known degree of confidence—typically the 95 percent level of confidence. Thus, a sample of 1,100 respondents has a margin of sampling error of approximately ± 3 percentage points, indicating that 19 times out of 20 the population or true value lies within the range that includes the sample estimate plus or minus 3 percentage points. The MOSE is often reported by the news media, whereas the fact that there are other likely sources of error in any poll, such as low response rates that result in unrepresentative samples or faulty elements of the questionnaire, is not. (See also *Confidence interval, Probability sample*)

Measurement error Possible sources of bias and variance in poll findings due to the questionnaire (its wording and/or ordering), the interviewers' behavior (purposeful or careless and unintended), the respondent (purposeful or unintended), and the mode (face-to-face, telephone, internet, IVR, or mail). Serious pollsters try to use methods that are likely to reduce these potential causes of error. No matter what is done, however, the likelihood remains that some small level of measurement error will exist. If resources allow, a pollster can try to estimate the size of some potential sources of measurement error—by gathering extra data or doing extra analyses—and then adjusting (correcting) the data before reporting them.

Media polls Election surveys sponsored (and possibly conducted) by news organizations. Most media election polls gather data about both candidate preferences and political attitudes. Critics of the media's use of the data gathered via these polls believe that they contribute to the media's fascination with the horse race. Media organizations sponsor polls to provide themselves with a competitive news advantage and to have access to information that has been gathered explicitly for the organization's own news purposes.

Methods box A sidebar that is often printed in a newspaper or magazine or posted on a website to accompany an article reporting poll results. The methods box provides the reader with information about how the poll was conducted, typically including the mode of data collection, the target population that was sampled, the sample size, the dates of data collection, information about the margin of sampling error, and whether any statistical weighting adjustments were made after the data were gathered.

Mixed-mode surveying The use of multiple modes of data collection in a survey, such as starting by contacting people on the telephone and then using e-mail to try to get them to complete the survey on a website. (See also ***Mode***)

Mode The way data are gathered in a survey, such as in person, on the telephone, through the mail, or over the internet. Sometimes the mode of data collection can produce characteristic differences in responses, known as mode effects. (See also ***Mode effect***)

Mode effect A type of measurement error (i.e., bias or variance) in survey data that is due to the mode by which the data were gathered, as opposed to sampling error, nonresponse error, coverage error, or other types of measurement error. (See also ***Measurement error***)

Mutually exclusive An attribute of a set of response alternatives to closed-ended poll items or the code categories for any open-ended response that makes it logically impossible for a respondent's answer to be coded into more than one of the response choices.

National Election Pool (NEP) The exit-polling operation established in 2003 for the 2004 election cycle, replacing VNS. The current membership consists of ABC News, CBS News, CNN, and NBC News, who have hired them as the data collectors. (See also ***AP VoteCast***; ***Election night projections***; ***Exit polls***; ***VNS***)

Noncontacts A sampled household or person who is never contacted by the poll. In face-to-face and telephone surveys, this results from such factors as addresses or telephone numbers that do not reach the correct household/person, the sampled people never being at home, or people being unable to talk to the interviewer at the times interviewers try to make contact. In mail surveys, this results from incorrect mailing addresses. Noncontacts are a source of nonresponse, and doing several callbacks can reduce them. Noncontacts are more prevalent when trying to reach males and adults younger than age thirty.

Nondirective probing A type of behavior that well-trained interviewers use to follow up responses to open-ended questions and ambiguous responses to closed-ended questions. Nondirective probing requires interviewers to remain neutral while they encourage respondents to answer a question more fully. Nondirective probing strives to eliminate interviewer-related errors that could distort (bias) the answers that respondents provide.

Nonprobability sample Any of several different sampling schemes (such as quota, snowball, or convenience designs) in which the elements in the sampling frame do not have both a known and a nonzero probability of selection. Thus, it is impossible to calculate the size of the poll's margin of sampling error with a known degree of confidence with a nonprobability sample. Of note, this statistical fact does not stop some pollsters from reporting their margin of sampling error with a nonprobability sample—it simply makes their calculations meaningless. Nonprobability samples are useful in the early stages of research or when a pollster needs to gain an impression of the preferences and attitudes of a target population but does not need to be very confident about how well the poll generalizes to the target population. (See also **Quota sample**; **Snowball sample**)

Nonresponse Present in virtually all polls, nonresponse occurs whenever no data are gathered from a sampled element (person or household). The primary sources of nonresponse are noncontacts and refusals. Other minor sources are language or a respondent's physical and mental difficulties. Nonresponse is especially problematic in polls with short field periods because the limited amount of time precludes the use of multiple recontacts to reduce noncontacts and lowers the efficiency of trying to convert initial refusals. It is likely that most media polls achieve a response rate of less than 10 percent (less than 90 percent of those sampled are interviewed), due in part to their relatively short field periods.

Nonresponse error If the sampled persons in a poll who never are interviewed differ, as a group, in meaningful ways in their preferences and attitudes from those who are interviewed, a poll will contain nonresponse error. The size of this error is related to the amount of nonresponse and to the magnitude of the difference between the preferences or attitudes of those who responded and those who did not. Nonresponse error probably is the single most serious cause of inaccuracy in otherwise good-quality polls—ones that use good sampling and data collection techniques.

Nonsampling error A term devised to contrast all sources of survey error (bias and variance) other than those related to sampling error. The sources of nonsampling error include coverage error, nonresponse error, and measurement error. Pollsters can utilize many methodological techniques either to try to reduce the possible size of these errors or to measure their size if they cannot be eliminated or reduced.

Open-ended questions Poll questions that allow respondents to answer in their own words rather than limiting the range of responses to a predetermined set of alternatives. These answers are recorded verbatim. Open-ended answers, while providing information that can be much richer, more detailed, and more valid than closed-ended data, have a very serious disadvantage for most polls in that they may require laborious coding into meaningful categories before they can be analyzed if available coding software is insufficient for a pollster's needs. Sometimes these verbatims are used in news stories to provide juicy quotes to humanize a numerical finding from a closed-ended item. (See also ***Closed-ended questions***; ***Verbatim responses***)

Opinion questions Closed-ended poll questions that measure more transitory or specific beliefs about current political or public policy issues. Although some people use the terms opinion and attitude interchangeably, most social scientists contrast opinions with measures of attitudes, which are thought to be more general and fundamental views. An opinion question is often posed as a statement to which a respondent is asked to agree or disagree, for example, "*Do you oppose or favor the new bill in the state legislature that would make it legal for a woman to get an abortion for any reason of her choice? Do you strongly oppose it, oppose it, favor it, or strongly favor it?*"

Opt-in internet panels A panel composed of individuals who agree to participate in surveys who volunteered to join rather than being recruited. As a result, they do not have a known probability of selection. As a result, drawing a probability sample from an opt-in panel does not produce a representative sample for which a margin of sampling error can be calculated. (See also ***Nonprobability sample***)

Order effect The possible biasing effect that can result from the order (or context) in which a poll item is asked of respondents. Research has shown conclusively that some questions are answered differently depending on what has been asked before them in the poll. Pollsters try to eliminate order effects by doing a considerable amount of pretesting of their questionnaires using different orders. Or they can randomize the order of certain questions and then take different response patterns to these items into account at the time the data are being analyzed. As both these approaches add to the cost of polling, they are not often used to their full potential for making polls more accurate. (See also *Context effect*)

Panel studies A survey design in which the same set of respondents are interviewed at more than one point in time. When they are asked the same questions, this provides an excellent way to measure the full extent of change among the sampled respondents. (See also ***Longitudinal studies***)

Paper-and-pencil interviewing (PAPI) Until the microcomputer revolution of the 1980s, virtually all polling was done using a questionnaire printed on paper with answers recorded on the pages with a pencil. Pencils were preferred over pens because they make it easier for interviewers to change what they record. PAPI is rarely used in telephone polls nowadays, although it is still needed when a polling firm's computer system crashes or when the need to conduct a poll arises so quickly that the software programming required to computerize the questionnaire would take too long. Of note, research has found that, on average, a questionnaire with PAPI takes 10 to 20 percent less time than its computerized version for interviewers to administer because PAPI affords the interviewer more control over pacing.

Poll Literally, a counting of heads. When used to refer to a type of social research, a poll is a form of sample surveying that arose in the early 1800s as a way of canvassing the voting preferences of easily accessible subsets of the electorate (in bars, trains, or at rallies) in order to predict the likely election winner. These early straw polls used unscientific convenience samples to capture public opinion, which was then reported in newspaper stories. Nowadays, the term poll typically is used to represent any political sample survey of the electorate conducted by the media, politicians, or political interest groups that aims for a relatively quick and somewhat cursory tally of the public's political opinions and preferences. Academic survey groups occasionally conduct studies that they call polls, but they usually have longer field periods (thus higher response rates), use more thoroughly pretested questionnaires, and release their findings without the deadline pressures of most other pollsters.

Pollster A person who conducts polls, typically for paying clients.

Population The group that a sample is meant to represent. In election polls, the population may be all adults within a geopolitical unit, such as a precinct or city; all registered adults; or all likely voters. For many practical reasons, a poll's population is almost never entirely included in its sampling frame, the list of all elements in the population. To the extent that the sampling frame does not include all members of the population, the sampling frame and initial sample may lead to considerable coverage error.

Precision The extent to which a poll finding, such as the percentage of likely voters who will support Candidate A, is an accurate measure of the true value in the population. The difference between the estimate derived from the final sample and the population value may be due to several factors. Polls that use probability samples can calculate the size of the poll's imprecision that is due to sampling error with a known degree of confidence. The size of the imprecision caused by potential nonsampling errors, such as those associated with noncoverage, nonresponse, or measurement problems, cannot be calculated as readily or as confidently. (See also ***Confidence interval***)

Pre-election polls Any poll that takes place before an election. Usually this means before a general election but after a primary; sometimes the term refers to a pre-primary poll. Traditionally, one purpose of these polls is to predict the winner of the election. The closer the poll is taken to Election Day, the more likely the poll will be accurate, all other considerations being equal. The past three decades have witnessed considerable criticism of the media's use of pre-election polls as part of so-called horse race journalism.

Pre-primary polls Polls conducted prior to a primary but close enough to primary Election Day to be a reasonable measure of the voting preferences of those who will turn out for the primary. Of note, there is an unfortunate paradox associated with pre-primary polls, especially those conducted by or for the news media. The primary electorate is often more volatile in its preferences because many people have limited information about the candidates early in the campaign process, and it is also more difficult to estimate turnout in primaries than in a general election. At the same time, fewer resources are typically committed to pre-primary polls than to pre-election polls, thus making them even less likely to be accurate.

Presidential approval A type of poll question that was first asked by pollsters in the 1940s, and thus one of the longest-running time series of poll data available. The item asks respondents to indicate the extent to which they approve or disapprove of the way the current president is handling the job of being the nation's chief executive. (See also ***Favorability ratings***)

Pretest The testing of a questionnaire (or other part of a poll, such as its introductory spiel) before regular data collection actually begins. The purpose of a pretest is to improve the way the questionnaire works, including the wording of its items, the order of items within the questionnaire, and the length of the interview. Traditionally this has been done by conducting practice interviews with a small number of respondents (twenty to thirty) who are not necessarily randomly sampled. In the past decade, new approaches to pretesting have included cognitive testing, which gathers in-depth information from a few respondents one at a time about such factors as what they think the poll's questions mean or what range of answers seem appropriate to them.

Primacy effect The tendency for respondents answering self-administered questionnaires to select the first response option offered in a list.

Prior restraint The ability of a government to control the release of certain types of news by a country's news media. As it relates to election coverage, many democratic nations have laws that limit the timing of the media's release of news derived from pre-election polls. The First Amendment to the US Constitution prohibits the nation's federal, state, and local governments from engaging in prior restraint.

Probability sample Any of several different sampling approaches that share two attributes: Each element in the sampling frame (population) has a known probability of being selected and each element in the sampling frame has a nonzero probability of being selected. The great benefit of using a probability sample is that it allows the pollster to calculate the size of the poll's sampling error. Types of probability samples include simple random sampling, systematic sampling, stratified sampling, and cluster sampling. There are at least two commonly held misconceptions about probability samples: (1) all elements must have an equal chance of selection, and (2) no elements may have a 100 percent (that is, a certain) chance of selection. (See also ***Simple random sample***; ***Stratified sample***; ***Systematic sample***)

Probable electorate The group of persons who are thought to be likely voters and thus are the part of the population that will determine the outcome of an election by their voting behavior. (See also ***Likely voter***)

Pseudo polls Any of several misguided and/or unscrupulous techniques that try to appear to be legitimate polls but are not. The primary purpose of these techniques, which often are conducted by political candidates or political interest groups, is to accomplish fund-raising under the guise of polling or to convey partisan propaganda under the guise of polling. Innocent respondents are thus duped into believing that the pollster is sincerely interested in gathering their opinions. These pseudo polls are conducted both via telephone and through the mail. (See also ***FRUGing***; ***Internet pop-up polls***; ***Push polls***; ***SUGing***)

Public opinion As it relates to election polling, public opinion includes the attitudes, preferences, and beliefs of the public (typically defined as adults in a society) about a host of political and public policy issues. Critics of election polling contend that polls reduce public opinion to mere numbers and thereby distort what the public really believes or prefers on political topics. Other pollsters, such as social critic Daniel Yankelovich, contend that traditional polling as it is used by the news media often fails to distinguish the complexity of opinions and judgments held by the public and thereby does not serve democratic discourse very well.

Push polls A method of pseudo polling in which political propaganda is disseminated to naive respondents who have been tricked into believing they have been sampled for a poll that is sincerely interested in their opinions. Instead, the push poll's real purpose is to expose respondents to information, conveyed in the poll questions, that favors a specific candidate or political view to influence how they will vote in an election.

Push to web A legitimate mode of data collection in which a potential respondent is contacted initially by phone or mail and given a website address to go to complete an interview. It is typically used when the research firm does not have a list of e-mail addresses for all their sampled units.

Questionnaire The entire set of items used to gather data in a web or mail survey or in a poll interview. The questionnaire begins after the poll's introductory spiel and its respondent selection method, if one is used. Election polls generally begin with questions that measure political attitudes, then measure voting intentions, and end with items on the respondents' demographic characteristics.

Question stem The part of a poll item that sets forth the substance or focus of the question being asked. The question stem does not include the response alternatives. A question stem may be balanced or unbalanced.

Quota sample A kind of sampling technique in which final respondent selection is usually left to the interviewer, who may be given an assignment to conduct interviews with five men and five women, for example. Because the interviewer decides which men and women to interview, there is no way to determine the probability of selection of any respondent. As a result, a quota sample is a nonprobability sample design. (See also ***Nonprobability sample***)

Random Something that happens without purposeful choice. In random sampling, the selection of an element from a sampling frame is arbitrary (thus unpredictable) and done in such a way that every element has a fair chance (probability) of selection. Randomness provides the underpinnings for representative sampling in that it makes it highly probable that the chosen sample will accurately represent the target population.

Random assignment Not often used in election polling, this is a technique that randomly (arbitrarily) assigns different question wordings or orderings to different respondents who are interviewed in the same poll. By doing this, the pollster can use the data produced to analyze cause-and-effect relationships to learn whether differences in the question wording, for example, cause changes in the answers that respondents give. Random assignment is a very powerful research technique because it provides the most valid way to test hypotheses in an experimental way and thus explain why something has happened.

Random-digit dialing (RDD) A form of random sampling in telephone surveys that for the past two decades has been the predominant method of sampling for election polls because it has avoided the coverage error that would likely result if sampling were done from telephone directories. RDD allows a pollster to sample people who live in households that do not publish or list their telephone numbers. Traditionally, the RDD procedure randomly creates the numbers that interviewers dial by choosing a three-digit prefix (exchange) that rings in the geopolitical area in which the poll is conducted and then randomly assigning digits to the prefix to create a seven-digit local telephone number. This local number may or may not reach a household, regardless of whether the number is listed or in current use. People with unlisted telephone numbers often are concerned that polls can reach them via this method, but nevertheless many choose to participate as respondents in good-quality polls. Starting in 2004, however, the growing trend toward cell phone use coupled with new federal telecommunications policies and regulations created several threats to the long-term viability of this sampling approach in the United States. (See also ***Cell phone surveys***; ***Landline surveys***)

Random sampling Any method that selects poll respondents randomly (arbitrarily) and gives each possible respondent a fair chance of being selected. When used with a probability sampling design, random sampling provides the basis for calculating a poll's margin of sampling error. Without random sampling, it is meaningless to calculate the size of sampling error. There are many ways that random sampling can be accomplished. Nowadays, computers are commonly used to create the randomized order of selections.

Recency effect The tendency for respondents to a survey to select the last response option offered from a series.

Recontact An attempt to complete an interview with a sampled respondent who was previously unavailable. The purpose of recontacts, despite the expense they add to polls, is to increase response rates and the representativeness of those sampled, thereby lessen the chances for nonignorable nonresponse error. Without recontact attempts, most polls will interview a sample that is disproportionately composed of women and older adults and thus is unrepresentative of the population.

Refusal Any time a sampled respondent decides that he or she will not participate in a poll. Refusals are a major source of nonresponse in polls and may lead to a serious level of error in a poll's findings. If time allows in a telephone poll, for example, pollsters can have skilled interviewers call back initial refusals to try to convince them to participate (an attempt to convert them). Experience suggests that women and older adults are more likely than men and younger adults to refuse to participate in polls.

Refusal conversion An attempt to convince a sampled respondent who has previously refused to participate in an interview. Using skilled interviewers, this process typically succeeds in about one in five cases. It is unclear whether this somewhat costly effort reduces nonresponse error, thereby improving the poll's accuracy. If it does not reduce nonresponse error, there is little cost-benefit advantage for a pollster to attempt refusal conversions. It is generally agreed among ethical pollsters that a respondent who explicitly has said, "Don't call me back," should not be the recipient of a refusal conversion callback.

Refusal rate The proportion of sampled persons who are contacted by an interviewer and refuse to participate in a poll. Refusal rates for many polls exceed 50 percent; that is, one-half or more of contacted respondents refuse to participate.

Representative sample The extent to which a sample matches the demographic, attitudes, or other characteristics of a target population it is intended to represent. It is not always understood that random sampling does not ensure that the resulting sample will be representative. This is because even with random samples, chance variation can lead to significantly under- or oversampled subgroups of the target population. In addition, nonresponse in polls often severely threatens representativeness. One way that pollsters try to check on the representativeness of their final samples is to compare the sample's demographic characteristics to population statistics from a recent census.

Respondent burden A term that refers to the effort that a respondent must put in to complete an interview. This burden might be small or large depending on how long the questionnaire is, how difficult the questions are to answer, and whether the questions cause the respondent any emotional difficulty. All these factors contribute to the burden borne by the respondent. But the vast majority of polls do not cause any undue or unpleasant level of burden on participants.

Respondents The people selected to be interviewed for a poll. With most household-based sampling used by election polls, the household is the unit that is first sampled, and then one person is selected from within the household to serve as the respondent. When there is only one eligible person in the household to interview, as is the case for people who live alone, the selection of the respondent is automatic. In households with two or more people who fit the poll's eligibility criteria, some form of within-unit selection is used in high-quality surveys to choose one of these persons as the designated respondent in that household. In many polls, no such selection process is used. People who agree to serve as poll respondents should understand that their participation is entirely voluntary and that no harm will come to them regardless of whether they choose to participate.

Response alternatives The set of answers used in a closed-ended item from which respondents are expected to choose the one that best fits their answer to the question, for example, very likely, somewhat likely, somewhat unlikely, or very unlikely. When the respondent is presented with a set that does not include a "Don't know" or "Undecided" alternative, the alternatives are called a forced-choice set because they force the respondent to choose one of the substantive responses. Sets of response alternatives may be balanced, if they include a true midpoint, or unbalanced.

Response rates Several different measures that reflect various aspects of the proportion of sampled persons who actually completed the questionnaire (see https://aapor.org/standards-and-ethics/standard-definitions/). No poll achieves a 100 percent response rate because there always are people who cannot be contacted during the field period (because they are sick or on vacation, for example) or who refuse to be interviewed. Response rates are affected by such factors as the length of the field period, the quality of the interviewing, and the topic of the poll. There is some disagreement among pollsters and other survey researchers over what is considered a low response rate. Those working for the federal government often consider rates below 80 percent to be low, compared to those in academic settings who generally regard rates below 50 percent as low. In contrast, many pollsters in the private sector think response rates are not low until they fall below the 20 percent level. What really matters from the standpoint of polling accuracy, however, is not what the response rate is, but whether the poll has nonresponse error. If it does not, then the poll's accuracy will not suffer because of its nonresponse. Recent evidence suggests that low response rates in otherwise high-quality election polls may not necessarily lead to inaccurate horse race data. (See also *Nonresponse error*)

Rolling averages A term that refers to the numerical findings of tracking polls, whereby small daily samples of respondents are summed across three-day periods. For example, estimates are calculated for the periods Monday-Tuesday-Wednesday, Tuesday-Wednesday-Thursday, Wednesday-Thursday-Friday, and so on. Then the response averages for each three-day set are compared to see if any change or trend in intentions or attitudes is present. The problem with looking for change in rolling averages is that mere chance variation due to sampling error can make it appear that something has changed when in fact it has not, especially when small sample sizes are involved. (See also ***Trend analysis***)

Sample The group, or subset, of some larger population that is selected to participate in a poll. Depending on how the sample is chosen from the population, the pollster may be able to calculate the extent to which the information collected from the sample is likely to represent the population, as is the case with probability samples. Any group of people who are interviewed can be termed a sample, but that does not mean that anyone (including the pollster) necessarily knows what population they represent if a probability design is not used. Whenever a sample is drawn (chosen) in a way that precludes having confidence about what population it represents, then the resulting data are ambiguous as indicators of the intentions or opinions of anyone other than those who were sampled.

Sample design The method used to select a sample for a poll. A basic and critical distinction in sample designs is whether a probability or nonprobability design is used. With a probability design—one in which each element in the sampling frame has a known, nonzero probability of selection—the pollster can calculate the size of the poll's sampling error. No meaningful calculation of the size of sampling error can be done with confidence in nonprobability samples.

Sample precinct A sampling unit used in exit polling. Within each sample precinct, a random sample of voters are interviewed as they leave their voting places. This is the basic sample design for the exit polls at the state and national levels that the National Election Pool conducted for ABC, CBS, CNN, NBC, and other news organizations on Election Day in November 2020.

Sample size The number of elements, typically people, selected from a population. This may refer to the number of elements at the start of the poll (known as the original sample) or the number of interviews eventually obtained (known as the final sample). The larger the final sample size, the smaller the margin of sampling error, all other factors being equal.

Sampling error When using a probability sample, a pollster can employ statistical formulas to calculate the size of the uncertainty (variation/imprecision) around a poll finding because a sample was drawn rather than trying to gather data from every member of the population. For example, the percentage of the electorate who will support Candidate X may vary from the proportion in the entire population merely because the estimate is based on a poll and not a census. Without a probability sample, it is meaningless to use the sampling error formulas, but that does not stop some pollsters from doing so, because their clients apparently do not know the difference. The size of a poll's sampling error is related to (1) the exact type of probability sample design that is used, (2) how similar or dissimilar (heterogeneous) the public's attitudes or intentions are on whatever is being measured, and (3) the final sample size. There is only a minute relationship between the relative size of the sample and the size of the target population.

Sampling frame The list from which a sample is chosen that contains all of the elements in the population. If any part of the target population is missing from the sampling frame, there exists the possibility that the poll will have coverage error. This would be the case, for example, if a telephone poll used a telephone directory as its sampling frame. Most election polls utilize a random-digit-dialing sampling frame, as these polls are conducted via telephone and want to sample people regardless of whether their telephone numbers are listed. This avoids the possibility of coverage error that might be associated with whether a number is listed or unlisted. Many high quality surveys now use the US Postal Service's Delivery Sequence file containing more than 98 percent of the addresses in the US as the basis for their sampling frames. (See also ***RDD***)

Sampling interval In systematic samples that select every nth element in a sampling frame, the sampling interval is the number of elements that are skipped between sampled elements. For example, if a systematic sample of 200 is drawn from a sampling frame of 2,000 registered voters, then the sampling interval is 10. (See also *Systematic sample*)

Scientific sampling A systematic approach to selecting respondents from whom to gather data. Some would argue that only probability samples are scientific. Others would suggest that nonprobability samples can be scientific if they are implemented in a systematic fashion such that others could reasonably repeat or replicate the sample, but far too often they simply are not.

Screening A process that sometimes is used at the end of a poll's introductory sequence—after the respondent has been told some basic information about the poll—to identify eligible respondents and screen out ineligible ones. For example, shortly before Election Day, pollsters will try to screen in likely voters and screen out unlikely ones by asking a series of questions meant to differentiate those who will vote from those who will not. This allows the pollster to allocate most interviewing resources to gathering data from those who will vote rather than interview everyone. Screening sequences do not always work accurately: When respondents are screened in as eligible to be interviewed when in fact they are not, an error of commission is said to have occurred; when respondents are screened out as ineligible when in fact they were, this is called an error of omission.

Secret ballot A mode of gathering data in a poll that simulates the process used by voters when they cast their votes. Secret ballots are used in pre-election polls very close to Election Day and in exit polls. In the latter case, the respondent who has just voted is typically handed a clipboard and pencil with a short questionnaire to complete. When the respondents finish, they fold the questionnaire and place it in a cardboard ballot box that the interviewer is holding.

Self-administered data collection Any questionnaire that a respondent fills out without the intervention of an interviewer. Traditionally, this has been done via a printed questionnaire that the respondent marks with a pencil or pen. Nowadays, this commonly occurs with the respondents completing the questionnaires on their own via the internet.

Self-selected sample The result from any poll that allows respondents the easy opportunity to decide on their own whether to take the time to complete the questionnaire. Typically, the accuracy of mail surveys has suffered because their response rates are low as a function of no interviewer involvement in trying to encourage people to respond at the time they receive the questionnaire. Self-selected samples are often biased because the motivations that lead certain people to decide to respond and others not to respond may be highly correlated with whatever topic is being measured by the poll. For example, a mail or call-in poll about attitudes toward gun control would most likely get responses from persons at the two extremes of the political spectrum on this issue. Because of self-selection, the pollster will not know how well the sample reflects the target population. (See also *Call-in polls*; *Insert polls*; *Log-in polls*)

Simple random sample A method of choosing a sample from a population that merely bases the selection on a totally arbitrary (random) process. These selection criteria might involve using a series of random numbers to decide whom to include in a sample and whom to leave out. Of note, the use of random sampling does not ensure that it is a probability sample or that it is a representative sample of the target population.

Snowball sample A nonprobability sampling technique that can be very useful when the pollster does not need to be certain about how well those who have been interviewed reflect the attitudes or intentions of a target population. Snowball sampling typically is used to find persons in rare subgroups in the population (e.g., persons who voted for Eugene McCarthy, John Anderson, and Ross Perot in previous presidential elections), by asking such people to nominate others like themselves for the pollster to contact, thus "snowballing" toward a final desired sample size.

Social desirability The tendency of people to want to present themselves in a positive light when someone else is asking them questions about their attitudes, experiences, or background. Many tend to overreport positive things about themselves and underreport negative things. This includes the tendency to give answers that a respondent perceives that an interviewer or pollster will consider correct answers. Social desirability can cause poll data to be biased; how much depends on how strong the effect is. Pollsters concerned about possible social desirability bias can add certain items to their questionnaires that will allow them to do analyses after the data have been gathered to estimate the size of the effects and try to correct for them before reporting the data. Social desirability has consistently been found to occur more with interviewer-administered data collection than self-administered data collection.

Spin A term used to describe a particular interpretation that someone wants placed on a result from a poll. This interpretation has a particular strategic advantage for the person applying the spin, usually the most favorable meaning of the poll. Sometimes spin is created by selecting the results from some questions and ignoring others. Other times, the results of a confidential poll, or part of a poll, will be leaked to journalists for wider dissemination because of the favorable results it contains.

Split-half design The use of a true experimental design within a questionnaire in order to assign different question wordings or orders to different subgroups of respondents at random. By using random assignment of the different questionnaire versions, the pollster can conduct powerful and valid tests of the cause-and-effect relationships between the versions (the independent variable) and the answers that respondents provide (the dependent variables). For example, one subgroup of respondents might be asked their candidate preferences without being reminded about the respective candidates' policy stances, while another group might be told this policy information first. Such a split-half design would allow the pollster to test whether the policy information caused any changes in the respondents' expressed preferences.

Standardized survey interviewing A form of asking poll questions in which interviewers are trained and monitored to ensure that they read the items exactly as they are written in a pleasant but neutral voice and that they follow up open-ended questions with nondirective probes in order to get respondents to give more complete answers in a way that does not bias the responses. The goal of standardized interviewing is more readily achieved in telephone polls than in face-to-face interviews because a supervisor should always be present during a phone poll. This is not practical in face-to-face polling.

Stratified sample A form of probability sampling in which the sampling frame is ordered (or grouped) according to a relevant stratum or strata before the actual sample is selected. Stratified sampling can ensure that the selection of respondents occurs in a way that accurately represents whatever characteristic(s) the frame is stratified upon. Thus, stratification decreases the poll's sampling error compared to what it would have been with an otherwise random but unstratified sampling. For example, if a list of registered voters were grouped by gender, then sampling could be done in whatever proportion the pollster deemed appropriate for females and males. This would not happen if the list were not stratified and simple random sampling was performed.

Stratum A subset of a larger group, such as the categories that compose a demographic characteristic. For example, the four categories 18 to 29, 30 to 44, 45 to 59, and 60 and older make up one set of strata for the age variable. To ensure that sampling is more representative, a sampling frame can be ordered by strata that are relevant to the purpose of the sampling.

Straw polls A form of gathering information about public opinion, about voting intentions, that has been used in the United States since the early 1800s. Straw polls do not use any scientific approach to sample respondents, and therefore their findings cannot be generalized with any confidence to represent the preferences of any group beyond those that were polled. Instead, they gather the opinions of people who are conveniently available in a variety of public and/or private places and gatherings.

SUGing Soliciting under the guise of polling. An unethical form of polling conducted by some telemarketing firms. These firms have their interviewers, who really are their sales staff, lead respondents into thinking that a real poll is being conducted, when instead it is simply the prelude to a sales pitch. The practice persists because of the assumption that the sales pitch will be more successful if the interviewer has had a chance to develop some rapport with the respondent before making the sales pitch. This correctly assumes that many people enjoy being asked to participate in a poll and that they will be more likely to stay on the phone if they think they are being polled than if they think they are being pitched. (See also ***FRUGing***)

Survey As opposed to a census, in which data are gathered from all members (elements) in a population, a survey gathers data from only a subset, or sample, of the population. The use of a sample is one defining characteristic of the research technique called a survey. Surveys can be (and are) conducted of a host of nonhuman and inanimate objects, such as sampling plants in a cornfield, fish in a pond, rocks on a mountainside, or cars on an assembly line. When they are well planned and implemented, surveys are an extremely cost-effective way to gather all types of information that is critical to accurate decision making in both the public and private sectors.

Systematic error Also called bias, this is a constant and directional form of inaccuracy that can occur in research, such as election polling, and leads to a consistent distortion of findings away from the truth, for example by overestimating or underestimating the prevalence of an attitude, perception, or belief. (See also ***Bias***)

Systematic sample A form of probability sampling in which respondents are chosen from a list in a repetitive, yet random, manner. This results by first calculating the size of the sampling interval that will be needed. For example, if a systematic sample of 500 is taken from a list of 10,000, then the interval will be 20. Second, a random number between 1 and the size of the sampling interval, which is 20 in this example, is chosen, such as 17. Thus, the sample will consist of the 17th person on the list, followed by every 20th person thereafter—the 37th, 57th, 77th, . . . 9,997th—to complete the sample of 500. This form of sampling can lead to a slight reduction in sampling error, compared to a simple random sample, because it forces sampling to take place evenly across the entire listing.

Target population The larger group of people, such as the population to which a pollster wants to be able to generalize a poll's findings. For election polls, the target population varies over the course of the election campaign as the size of the probable electorate changes. For pollsters to have confidence that their polls will accurately reflect the desired target population, they must use a sampling frame that covers the target population well, employ some form of probability sampling, and achieve acceptable response rates from those sampled. The target population of most media-sponsored national election polls is likely voters (starting with adult citizens of the United States who are registered) among the noninstitutionalized population that lives in the forty-eight continental states, and who speak or read English.

Telephone households In 2024, 98 percent of households in the United States will have at least one telephone access line that reaches their home. Those without telephone service, so-called non-telephone households, are disproportionately poor, nonwhite, and living in rural areas of the South and Southwest. RDD sampling, the type used by many telephone election polls, utilizes a sampling frame that theoretically includes all telephone households in the geopolitical area being polled. In 2022, it was estimated that 71 percent of US households had only a cell phone for their home telephone service. In 2024, many firms will be designing telephone samples with at least 80 percent cell phone respondents, while some are sampling only cell phone numbers. US cell phone households must be dialed by hand, according to federal regulations, and contact is more difficult because of the patterns of daily life followed by cell phone owners. As a result, it costs more than twice as much to obtain an interview with someone with a cell phone compared to a landline phone.

Telephone surveys Surveys that sample and recruit people via their wired and/or cellular telephone number(s) and have data gathered over the telephone. Due to federal telecommunications regulations that began in the United States in the 1990s and the nature of the US cellular phone industry, it is very difficult to try to conduct surveys on respondents' cell phones, but pollsters now understand that they risk the chance of significant bias if they do not include cell phone respondents in their telephone samples.

Third-person effect An often observed phenomenon whereby individuals are concerned about or expect there to be effects of exposure to some stimulus, such as exposure to polls, on others but not themselves. This is true for both pre-election polls and their impact on candidate preference and for exit polls and their impact on voter turnout on the West Coast when a presidential race is called while the polls are still open there.

Tracking polls A type of pre-election surveying in which relatively small samples of respondents are interviewed each day for several days in a row. Often, each day's sample is independent (different) from the other days. The interviews gathered each day are then aggregated, typically over a three-day period, to look for trends in preferences and opinions. A serious problem of tracking polls is that their daily response rates are low, and daily fluctuations may be due merely to chance (sampling error). (See also ***Rolling averages***; ***Trend analysis***)

Trend analysis Using poll data to try to determine consistent and meaningful changes over some period, such as a week, month, or year. Trend analysis can be accomplished in one of three standard ways. It can be done with the data gathered by tracking polls, but only with great caution. It also can be done with data that come from panel studies, in which the same people are asked similar poll questions at different points during an election year. It can also be done with longitudinal studies in which different samples of people are asked the same questions at different times. Pollsters, reporters, and other political observers then try to link real-world events with the observed changes to explain why they appear to be occurring. (See also ***Longitudinal studies***; ***Panel studies***)

Trial-heat question The item that asks respondents which candidate they prefer or how they intend to vote. Traditionally this is the most important question asked in an election poll, and usually it is asked very early within a questionnaire. This item is typically presented with some variation of the wording "*If the election were held today, . . .* " The responses to trial-heat items provide the data that drive horse race journalism.

True experiment A type of research design that randomly assigns respondents to at least two different conditions to produce data that allow for powerful and valid cause-and-effect analyses. (See also ***Split-half design***)

Unbalanced question A question stem or set of response alternatives that is not balanced. An unbalanced stem presents only one side of an issue rather than both or all sides. This is generally thought to bias responses to the item.

An unbalanced set of response alternatives is simply one that is not symmetrical and therefore does not contain a true midpoint. Unbalanced response alternatives do not necessarily contribute to poll error.

Undecideds Those respondents who report in a trial-heat item that they have not yet made up their minds about which candidate they will vote for. The proportion of respondents who say they are undecided decreases the closer the poll is taken to Election Day. Pollsters often ask undecideds additional questions to determine toward which candidate they are leaning.

Underdog effect A sympathy effect that apparently causes some voters who otherwise might be expected to vote for one candidate to support another candidate when pre-election polls predict that candidate will lose the election. As with the bandwagon effect, definitive research on the underdog effect is very difficult to conduct and, therefore, not much is known with certainty about the effect. (See also ***Bandwagon effect***)

Uniform poll closings A legislative proposal that voting in person at polling places across the United States should take place during the same hours all across the country. This means that polls would close at the same moment, regardless of which time zone(s) the state falls within. The motivation for such a major procedural change is to keep the news media from making early projections based on eastern states whose polling places have closed several hours before voting is completed in western states. There are two groups of supporters for this change. One consists of critics who assume that early projections affect voting in western states. The other consists of media organizations that realize that this may be the only practical solution to the complaints that critics make. Despite what many politicians, journalists, and others in the public believe, however, no definitive research has ever demonstrated the size and direction of the effect of early election night projections on voter turnout or candidate preference.

Unit A sampling term that refers to the entity within which a respondent is selected to be interviewed. In election polls this is almost always a household or a home. In an RDD design and an address-based sampling design, random sampling occurs first at the household unit level, before an individual within the housing unit is selected. In an exit poll, the first unit selected is a precinct, usually followed by a systematic sample of people who voted there.

Unweighted data Data from a poll or survey as they are collected and analyzed (without any weights applied), sometimes called "raw data."

Variable As it relates to election polls, a variable is a question that is used to gather data from respondents. It is termed a variable because it is assumed that respondents' answers will vary from person to person; that is, they will not all be the same. If there were no variation in the answers, the measure instead would be a constant. Then there would be no need to ask the question because everyone's answer would always be known to be the same.

Verbatim responses The exact words used by a respondent to answer an open-ended poll item. In self-administered polls, respondents write down their answers in their own words. In polls that use interviewers, the interviewers are expected to record the answer in the respondent's own words without summarizing them. This may require an interviewer to ask a respondent to slow down his/her speaking rate or to repeat part of the answer to a question so the interviewer can record information correctly and legibly.

VNS (Voter News Service) The company that was formed in 1993 by combining the former Voter Research and Surveys and the News Election Service. It was disbanded in 2003 after a series of operational problems that arose in the 2000 and 2002 elections. The primary purpose of VNS was to gather election statistics, including exit poll data, to support the election analyses of its media sponsors: ABC, CBS, CNN, NBC, Fox, and the Associated Press. This consortium of sponsors all received the same data but analyzed and reported it separately. This joint approach saved these organizations several millions of dollars in data collection compared to what they would have spent if each gathered the information separately. VNS was replaced by the National Election Pool (NEP), run by the partnership of Edison Media Research and Mitofsky International starting with the 2004 exit polls that were conducted for these major news companies. When Warren Mitofsky passed away in 2006, Edison Media Research and Joseph Lenski became the sole collectors of the NEP data. (See also ***Exit polls***; ***NEP***)

Volatility The uncertainty associated with whether poll respondents will go to vote on Election Day as well as whether they will change their candidate preferences when they do. This kind of volatility has been growing in the American electorate, and it makes the prediction of election outcomes from pre-election polls more risky. Careful pollsters gather data within their polls to assess how volatile the electorate appears to be and then take this into consideration when they make their pre-election predictions.

Vote-by-mail A relatively new approach to conducting elections in some jurisdictions that is growing in acceptance. In January 1996, for example, Oregon elected its new US senator entirely by mail; and in a 1998 initiative, the citizens of Oregon voted to hold all of their statewide elections by mail. In an Oregon vote-by-mail election, every registered voter receives the information describing the candidates and a ballot that has to be mailed back to the county office by a set date. This system is now in use for some elections in nineteen states. Voting by mail is creating new challenges for those who conduct both pre-election and exit polls because voting takes place over time and there are no voting places at which to interview a sample of all voters in a given election. Exit pollsters are experimenting with various telephone methods for interviewing people who vote early so as to be able to combine the voting preferences of early voters with information gathered from people voting in person on Election Day via exit poll interviews.

Weighting Statistical adjustments to poll data that are conducted before the data are analyzed. Weighting is used to adjust for respondents' unequal probabilities of selection in probability samples. It is also used by some pollsters to try to adjust for nonresponse in a final sample whose characteristics do not match those of the target population very well. Sometimes, weighting is used to count the answers of certain respondents more heavily than others, such as when formulating the prediction of an election outcome from pre-election poll data. In such a case, a pollster attaches greater weight to the answers of those respondents who are most likely to vote, compared to the answers of those whose likelihood of voting is less certain.

Selected References

The following list of selected references will provide the reader with additional information about the main topics addressed in this volume. They provide either further background or additional methodological details the reader might find useful. Some of the entries provide important historical or background context, while others provide current information about methods and analysis.

THE HISTORY AND ROLE OF POLLS IN THE MEDIA AND DEMOCRACY

Barbara A. Bardes and Robert W. Oldendick. 2017. *Public Opinion: Measuring the American Mind* (Lanham, MD: Rowman & Littlefield).
This book provides a useful summary of where public opinion comes from and the current state of American public opinion on several important policy issues. Of particular interest will be the first part, especially chapters 2 through 4, which cover the origins of public opinion, how opinions are measured, and how the data are used by several important but different audiences or consumers of poll results.

Leo Bogart. 1985. *Polls and the Awareness of Public Opinion* (New Brunswick, NJ: Transaction).
This book contains a broad and useful discussion of the way in which the widespread use and acceptance of polls changed public debate in the United States and the relationship between citizens and the leaders they elect.

Rosalee Clawson and Zoe M. Oxley. 2020. *Public Opinion: Democratic Ideals, Democratic Practice*, 4th edition (Washington, DC: Congressional Quarterly Press).

This volume consists of a thorough treatment of the basic concepts underlying democratic government, especially public opinion. This includes the measurement of such politically relevant terms as trust in government and other institutions as well as trends in public attitudes about civil liberties and civil rights.

Jean Converse. 1987. *Survey Research in the United States* (Berkeley: University of California Press).
This is the essential history of the early development of survey research in the United States. It is based on extensive archival research and extended interviews with many of the central figures in the field. The research underlying this work emphasizes both the individuals and institutions that were critical to the development of the survey-based social and policy research enterprise we know today.

Robert M. Eisinger. 2003. *The Evolution of Presidential Polling* (Cambridge: Cambridge University Press).
This book presents a brief history of the use of polling in the White House since Franklin D. Roosevelt's first term. It contains a discussion of the relative use of polls by the president and members of Congress, and it looks at the combining of information gathering and the public relations functions of the White House in promoting a president that the current era of polling has facilitated. After describing the rising trends in the use of polls, it also discusses prospects for polling as a White House activity.

Robert S. Erikson and Kent L. Tedin. 2023. *American Public Opinion: Its Origins, Content, and Impact*, 10th edition (Milton Park, UK: Routledge).
The latest edition of this book contains a discussion of the significance of public opinion in contemporary America and the central role of the media in disseminating information about it.

George Gallup and Saul Forbes Rae. 1940. *The Pulse of Democracy: The Public Opinion Poll and How It Works* (New York: Simon and Schuster).
At the advent of polling in the United Sates, these authors justified its role in advancing democracy while supporting Gallup's entry into this business.

Susan Herbst. 1993. *Numbered Voices: How Opinion Polling Has Shaped American Politics* (Chicago: University of Chicago Press).
In this book, Herbst traces the history of quantification in American journalism as it is inextricably linked to coverage of campaigns and elections. She covers straw polls and problems of crowd estimation, as precursors to the movement toward polling as we know it today. In that regard, she sees polls

as sociological phenomena that are a natural development of other forces that have been at work in our political system. This part of the book is enhanced by the results of interviews with journalists who represent different cohorts of political reporters.

Jeff Manza, Fay Lomax Cook, and Benjamin I. Page (Editors). 2002. *Navigating Public Opinion: Polls, Policy, and the Future of American Democracy* (New York: Oxford University Press).
This book discusses the relationship between public opinion and public policy. More explicitly, it contains a series of essays on whether there is such a connection and the pitfalls of relying on polls as a linkage device.

L. John Martin (Editor). 1984. "Polling and the Democratic Consensus," *Annals of the American Academy of Political and Social Science*, 472 (March).
This volume is an early compendium of articles on the role of polls in the democratic process. The work consists of thirteen articles covering methods; the relationships between public opinion, polling, and political behavior; polls and politicians; and polls and the media.

David W. Moore. 1995. *The Superpollsters* (New York: Four Walls Eight Windows).
This is an important book because it personalizes the historical polling business through fascinating accounts of several important figures in the business. In addition to chapters about such major public pollsters as George Gallup and Louis Harris, the reader can find information about the major Democratic pollsters—Pat Caddell, Peter Hart, and Irwin Tubby Harrison—as well as Republican pollsters Robert Teeter and Richard Wirthlin. On the media side, the major figures portrayed include Warren Mitofsky (CBS and VRS), Richard Morin (*Washington Post*), Michael Kagay (*New York Times*), Kathleen Frankovic (CBS), and Jeff Alderman (ABC).

HOW POLLS ARE CONDUCTED

Floyd J. Fowler Jr. 2015. *Survey Research Methods*, 5th edition (Thousand Oaks, CA: Sage).
This best-selling brief text is part of a series on Applied Social Research Methods. It is highly readable as a first book on survey research and requires no real statistical sophistication in order to follow or benefit from its instruction. The book takes a broad approach to various aspects of survey research instead of going into depth on any single one, employing the Total Survey Error perspective. It includes sections on sampling, nonresponse, and modes

of survey data collection, questionnaire design, and preparing data for analysis. Ethical issues in survey research are also discussed.

Robert M. Groves, Floyd J. Fowler Jr., Mick P. Couper, James M. Lepkowski, Eleanor Singer, and Roger Tourangeau. 2009. *Survey Methodology*, 2nd edition (New York: John Wiley and Sons).
This volume is the most comprehensive and accurate introduction to current best practices in survey methodology for someone who already has basic knowledge in the field. The book uses the Total Survey Error framework to present and explain the major issues in survey research related to coverage, sampling, measurement, and nonresponse.

Eleanor Singer and Stanley Presser (Editors). 1989. *Survey Research Methods: A Reader* (Chicago: University of Chicago Press).
This edited volume consists of some of the best articles on survey methodology that have appeared in *Public Opinion Quarterly*, the journal of the American Association for Public Opinion Research. Singer and Presser, in addition to being accomplished survey methodologists, have also been editors of the journal.

SAMPLING

Edward Blair and Johnny Blair. 2014. *Applied Survey Sampling* (Thousand Oaks, CA: Sage).
Another in the "little green books" written to provide detailed and comprehensive information about survey sampling but in a relatively nontechnical and thus accessible way for those who are not advanced statisticians. The authors use many real-world examples to illustrate the concepts they are presenting and show how these sampling concepts are used.

Graham Kalton. 2020. *Introduction to Survey Sampling* (Thousand Oaks, CA: Sage).
This volume in the Sage "little green books" series provides a brief introduction covering all the main topics in sampling.

Leslie Kish. 1995. *Survey Sampling* (New York: John Wiley & Sons).
The bible for advanced students and practitioners of survey sampling, this classic text remains important more than seventy years after its first edition was published. Although the author intended it to be a simple book on sampling methods, advanced statistical and methodological training is required before someone can fully comprehend and appreciate its depth and rigor.

Sharon L. Lohr. 2022. *Sampling: Design and Analysis* (London: Chapman & Hall).
This book provides a modern introduction to the field of survey sampling. It concentrates on the statistical aspects of taking and analyzing a sample, incorporating a number of applications from multiple disciplines. In addition to describing a range of different sampling procedures, it also contains an extensive discussion of how to account for different designs in data analysis, including estimation, inference, and statistical approaches like regression with complex survey designs.

Richard Valliant, Jill A. Dever, and Frauke Kreuter. 2013. *Practical Tools for Designing and Weighting Survey Samples* (New York: Springer).
This volume presents important information about how to weight data derived from complex sample designs currently in use. For most surveys, weighing is a necessary step prior to analysis.

INFORMATION ABOUT ELECTION AND POLICY POLLS

Larry M. Bartels. 1988. *Presidential Primaries and the Dynamics of Public Choice* (Princeton, NJ: Princeton University Press).
This book offers the best description of how the current presidential nomination process works. It focuses on the post-1972 period in which the candidates have been required to enter primaries and caucuses to secure pledged delegates at their parties' national nominating conventions. Bartels deals with the concept of momentum—its value to candidates and its impact on voters.

One of the key concepts explaining voter choice in the primaries is the set of expectations created by the candidates and the press in concert. Voters are looking for cues about whom to support, which can come from various sources, including political elites, the results in previous primaries or caucuses, and polls. The quantification of the opinions of others in polls has become one of the greatest contributors to the media's propensity to engage in horse race coverage that describes who is ahead and who is behind. And this makes a substantial contribution to momentum and perceptions of viability.

Albert H. Cantril. 1991. *The Opinion Connection: Polling, Politics, and the Press* (Washington, DC: CQ Press, 1991).
This highly readable book was written under the auspices of the National Council on Public Polls (NCPP), a now defunct professional organization of survey firms dedicated to improving both the quality of polls and the

quality of poll-based information that is publicly disseminated. The book is both scholarly and comprehensive. It is informed by expert opinion and by research findings on the effects of poll methods and it reports many of these opinions and findings; and it provides a historical perspective on the issues it addresses.

Robert Chung. 2012. *The Freedom to Publish Opinion Poll Results* (World Association for Public Opinion Research).
This monograph represents the fifth compilation of restrictions on the ability to conduct and publish opinion survey data. Jointly sponsored by WAPOR and ESOMAR, the study is based upon expert informants in sixty-six countries about the restraints or constraints on the public opinion profession and organizations. In general, the latest version suggests a general reduction in these limitations. This report has been updated many times, each with more countries covered. The latest version can be found at https://wapor.org/publications/freedom-to-publish-opinion-polls/.

POLLS AND POLITICAL CANDIDATES

Jeffrey M. Stonecash. 2008. *Political Polling: Strategic Information in Campaigns* (Washington, DC: Rowman & Littlefield).
This book is written by a political pollster and highlights the aims of such research, how to design questionnaires, analyze the data, and make presentations of the results from that perspective.

PRESIDENTIAL POLLING, THE MEDIA, AND DEMOCRACY

Paul J. Lavrakas and Michael W. Traugott (Editors). 2000. *Election Polls, the News Media, and Democracy* (New York: Seven Bridges Press).
This volume covers the media's use of polls, trends in reporting of election polls, election poll accuracy, and controversial issues in election polling.

Paul J. Lavrakas and Jack K. Holley (Editors). 1991. *Polling and Presidential Election Coverage* (Newbury Park, CA: Sage).
This book focuses on the use of poll-based coverage in the 1988 Bush-Dukakis election campaign. Three themes unite the chapters: (1) How did the news media use pre-election polls to cover the Bush-Dukakis election? (2) What effects did this coverage likely have on the public? (3) What might the media and journalists do better in using polls as part of their future election coverage?

Paul J. Lavrakas, Michael W. Traugott, and Peter V. Miller (Editors). 1995. *Presidential Polls and the News Media* (Boulder, CO: Westview).
This book focuses almost entirely on the 1992 Bush-Clinton-Perot election campaign. The various authors cover developments in media polling; the methods of media polls; media polls in the 1992 elections; and the public's reaction to media polls. There are four common themes in the book: the power of the polls; the notion that the media are mostly data rich but analysis poor; the need for a new approach to using polls and related research techniques, in the form of focus groups, to both frame and make news; and the need for the news media to exercise greater responsibility in using and reporting election poll-based news so as to further, not hinder, democratic processes.

QUESTIONNAIRE DESIGN

Norman M. Bradburn, Seymour Sudman, Timothy Johnson, and Brian Wansink. 2023. *Asking Questions: The Definitive Guide to Questionnaire Design,* 3rd edition, (Newbury Park, CA: Sage).
Another in the series of Sage "little green books," this volume provides an introductory guide to questionnaire design. First published more than thirty-five years ago, the third edition provides significant updates to cover designing questionnaires for web surveys and multimode surveys.

Jean M. Converse and Stanley Presser. 1986. *Survey Questions: Handcrafting the Standardized Questionnaire* (Newbury Park, CA: Sage).
Another in the series of Sage "little green books," this volume is the standard for a brief introduction to designing and evaluating questionnaires. It consists of three chapters that the authors describe as concentric circles that move from the general to the specific and focus on the reader's particular research problem. The first deals with strategies for creating questions and highlights a long list of cautions that a researcher should keep in mind. In the second, the focus is on research findings about the impact of question wording and form. Finally, the authors deal with evaluations of questions designed for a specific task—the importance of pretests, consulting with others, and listening to the comments of interviewers who conducted the pretest interviews.

Willem E. Saris and Irmtraud N. Gallhofer. 2007. *Design, Evaluation, and Analysis of Questionnaires for Survey Research* (Hoboken, NJ: John Wiley & Sons).
This book is devoted to the development of reliable and valid questionnaires, with an emphasis on how to deal with these issues in cross-national comparative research. It employs an evidence-based approach to questionnaire

design and evaluation. In addition to the authors' own research results, it is based upon meta-analyses of research on question design and the effects of response scales.

Howard Schuman and Stanley Presser. 1981. *Questions and Answers in Attitude Surveys* (New York: Academic Press).
This book is the single greatest collection of experimental results that clearly demonstrate that survey responses are a function of what you ask and how you ask it. Schuman and Presser present the results of more than two hundred question wording and order experiments that they conducted in multiple surveys. It covers question wording and question order, open-ended versus closed-ended questions, assessment of no opinion by altering question form, measuring middle positions and issues of balance and imbalance in questions, and problems of response acquiescence.

They also report results on intensity of opinions and attitude strength, and there is a very good chapter on tone of wording that includes discussions of the impact of question wording when asking about hot topics such as abortion (or ending pregnancy as an alternative).

Roger Tourangeau, Lance J. Rips, and Ken Rasinski. 2000. *The Psychology of Survey Response* (Cambridge: Cambridge University Press).
Although this is not a book on questionnaire design per se, it provides a very wise and invaluable perspective on the entire process of how respondents make sense of the questions that pollsters and other survey researchers ask of them. By focusing on the respondent's task in the polling process, interested practitioners as well as casual readers will learn much about the characteristics of a survey question that likely will generate accurate data.

DATA COLLECTION AND ANALYSIS

Lonna Rae Atkeson and R. Michael Alvarez (Editors). 2018. *The Oxford Handbook of Polling and Survey Methods* (Oxford: Oxford University Press).
A compendium of all of the main concepts associated with polling and survey methodology described in detail.

Mario Callegaro, Katja Lozar Manfreda, and Vasja Vehovar. 2015. *Web Survey Methodology* (London: Sage).
This is the most extensive treatment of design and implementation concepts for this newer mode of data collection. It treats pre-fielding topics in great deal as well as the requirements for the successful implementation of a web survey to ensure maximum data quality.

Donald A. Dillman, Jolene D. Smyth, and Leah M. Christina. 2023. *Internet, Mail, Phone and Mixed-Mode Surveys: The Tailored Design Method*, 4th edition (Hoboken, NJ: John Wiley & Sons).
This is the latest update of Dillman's 1978 classic, which became a widely respected book about the practice or application of survey research methods in mail and telephone surveys. This edition focuses on self-administered modes for conducting surveys, thus the telephone mode is mostly replaced by the internet mode. The book provides step-by-step instruction on how to determine the mode of data collection to use, how to choose the best sampling design for the mode chosen, how to write survey questions, and how to lay them out for a mail survey or computer-assisted web interviewing (CAWI) questionnaire.

Wolfgang Donsbach and Michael W. Traugott. 2008. *The SAGE Handbook of Public Opinion Research* (London: Sage).
This is an edited volume on various aspects of public opinion research, and part 3 deals with methodology. The first part, consisting of thirteen chapters, deals with the design of surveys; and the second part, consisting of six chapters, deals with the measurement of public opinion. In each chapter, there is a discussion of recent research on subjects like surveys by telephone or sampling, including an extensive bibliography of the latest published research on the subject.

Paul J. Lavrakas, Michael W. Traugott, Courtney Kennedy, Allyson L. Holbrook, Edith D. de Leeuw, and Brady T. West. 2019. *Experimental Methods in Survey Research: Techniques That Combine Random Sampling with Random Assignment* (Hoboken, NJ: John Wiley & Sons).
This volume focuses on the use of experiments in all aspects of survey data collection and analysis, including surveys with many different sampled populations and topics of interest. The authors of individual chapters are academics, government researchers, and individuals who work in the commercial sector.

DATA ANALYSIS

Earl Babbie. 2021. *The Practice of Social Research*, 15th edition (Boston: Cengage Learning).
This very well written classic textbook has been used to teach more college students about research methods in the social sciences than any other. It is an easy read and does not presume any previous training in research methods or statistics. Although its primary focus is on conceptualizing, planning,

and implementing social science research designs, including data collection methods such as surveys and polls, it also provides a very clear explanation of the basic thinking and statistical procedures that researchers must use to analyze their data. The analytic chapters cover cross-tabulations, correlations, and other analytic techniques commonly used by pollsters.

Steven G. Heeringa, Brady T. West, and Patricia A. Berglund. 2017. *Applied Survey Data Analysis* (London: Chapman & Hall).
This book is highly recommended in reviews appearing in the major survey research journals and contains information about and examples of analysis techniques for data derived from complex survey designs.

HOW TO EVALUATE POLLS

Norman M. Bradburn and Seymour Sudman. 1988. *Polls and Surveys: Understanding What They Tell Us* (San Francisco: Jossey-Bass).
This nontechnical book is aimed at newcomers to public opinion measurement and various postsecondary-level students of public opinion and market research. While somewhat similar in purpose to the present volume, the structure is different. Bradburn and Sudman have provided answers to the questions frequently asked by respondents in surveys, by those who have not yet been selected as participants, and by journalists, businessmen, and many others who have to deal with survey data. It shares the mission of the present volume, and several other of the books reviewed here, in trying to educate consumers of polls.

George H. Gallup. 1948. *A Guide to Public Opinion Polls* (Princeton, NJ: Princeton University Press).
In many ways, this volume is the forefather of the current *Voter's Guide* text. It used a question-and-answer format and was produced with nontechnical language for a popular audience. For Gallup, this volume was also a way to promote the new method that he was working with and make its details more accessible to the general public. The reader will find it entertaining to compare the treatment of the same topics in the current book to Gallup's work of more than seventy-five years ago.

George H. Gallup. 1972. *The Sophisticated Poll Watcher's Guide* (Princeton, NJ: Princeton Opinion Press, 1972).
This volume is dedicated to the daily newspapers of America that had the foresight to make public opinion data available to the masses, through Gallup's weekly columns and those of his contemporaries. This volume is only

broadly organized around questions that serve as focal points for Gallup's commentary on public opinion and its role in democracy, the importance of polls as measures of public opinion, and election polls and the prediction of elections.

WHAT ARE SOME COMMON PROBLEMS AND COMPLAINTS ABOUT POLLS?

Jelke Bethlehem. 2020. *Understanding Public Opinion Polls* (London: Chapman & Hall/CRC).
This is an easily accessible introduction to the conduct of polls, including a discussion of their strengths and weaknesses. It includes a checklist of considerations in the evaluation of the quality of a poll.

G. Elliott Morris. 2022. *Strength in Numbers: How Polls Work and Why We Need Them* (New York: W. W. Norton & Company).
Written by a data journalist, this book contains a history of ways to assess public preferences, including polls, with an emphasis on the importance of such measures in a democracy. There is an emphasis on educating poll consumers rather than criticizing those who collect the data and disseminate the results.

Daniel Yankelovich. 1991. *Coming to Public Judgment: Making Democracy Work in a Complex World* (Syracuse, NY: Syracuse University Press).
Yankelovich, a social critic and pollster, presents a bleak assessment of the effects the news media have on America's search for public policy solutions to the nation's and the world's problems. He believes that a crucial concept missing from American democracy is a set of terms to describe the quality of public opinion and to distinguish good public opinion from bad. He details the barriers formed by devising public policies that rely too heavily on the "judgment of experts" and relying too little on the wisdom of the public. Yankelovich challenges the news media to help develop this wisdom in the citizenry.

Index

1948 election, 27, 48
1992 election, 32, 34, 42, 74, 180, 181, 209, 249
2000 election, 5, 28, 30, 37, 41
2004 election, 1, 5, 6, 10, 32, 41, 46, 57, 107, 203, 207, 216, 235
2012 election, 1, 6, 29, 39, 54, 55, 59, 170
2016 election, 27, 38, 41, 59, 79, 124, 140, 190
2020 election, 1, 3, 6, 10, 11, 26, 27, 29, 35, 39, 40, 41, 43, 45, 49, 64, 78, 79, 82, 83, 92, 101, 106, 120, 124, 132, 136, 138, 155, 158, 159, 197, 206, 227
2022 election, 2, 10, 11, 72, 77, 82, 83, 108, 132, 136, 137, 176
2024 election, 11, 38, 41, 54, 57, 77, 78, 79, 80, 82, 89, 96, 118, 129, 132, 186, 207
800 numbers, 18, 69, 167, 186, 199, 201
900 numbers, 69, 167, 180, 199, 201

ABC News, 11, 66, 114, 216
abortion, 113, 114, 176, 200, 201
absentee ballot, 9, 28, 29, 63, 206, 208
absentee voters, 10
advance contact, 141, 193, 199, 205

African American candidate, 38, 122, 123
age as an analysis variable, 25, 71, 77, 94, 97, 103, 105, 127, 131, 139, 151, 152, 170, 201, 205, 210, 217
aggregated opinions, 3
Alderman, Jeff, 239
allocation method, 32
Alvarez, Michael, 244
American Association for Public Opinion Research (AAPOR), 2, 7, 9, 15, 35, 48, 49, 60, 99, 164, 166, 173, 178, 187, 191, 199, 240; Best Practices, 164, 191–195; Code of Ethics, 164, 191–195; Standards for Disclosing Information about Public Poll Method, 164, 191–195; Transparency Initiative, 48, 164, 165
American Community Survey (ACS), 19
AmeriSpeak, 81, 92
anonymity, 38, 134, 149, 200
approval rating, 72, 85, 119, 157, 158, 159, 169, 200, 204, 208
AP VoteCast, 6, 11, 41, 44, 67, 92, 200, 208, 216
Associated Press (AP), 40, 41, 47, 48, 67, 72, 99, 176, 200, 207, 235
Atkeson, Lonna Rae, 244

attitudes, 14, 19, 20, 23, 24, 39, 51, 75, 77, 86, 97, 104, 106, 112, 113, 120, 121, 129, 138, 151, 155, 156, 160, 161, 168, 172, 176, 177, 178, 189, 203, 210, 214, 215, 217, 218, 222, 224, 227, 229, 231, 238, 244
attitudinal question, 136, 200
auto-dialer, 129

Babbie, Earl, 245
balanced question, 108, 109, 179, 200
balanced wording, 108
ballot box, 39, 42, 127, 207, 228
bandwagon effect, 36, 46, 201, 234
Bardes, Barbara, 237
Bartels, Larry, 241
base electorate, 31
battleground states, 10, 35, 53
Berglund, Patricia, 246
Bethlehem, Jelke, 247
bias, 20, 35, 42, 43, 44, 70, 93, 97, 99, 101, 104, 107, 108, 109, 115, 121, 122, 123, 124, 137, 138, 139, 140, 142, 145, 146, 148, 167, 171, 201, 204, 206, 215, 216, 217, 229, 230, 231, 232, 233
biased question, 60, 122, 124, 176, 179, 201
Biden, Joe, 1, 3, 14, 28, 32, 36, 40, 45, 57, 70, 72, 78, 79, 85, 92, 104, 106, 112, 113, 118, 121, 138, 153, 154, 155, 157, 158, 159, 160, 161, 169, 197
big data, 139
bivariate frequencies, 70, 201
Blair, Edward, 240
Blair, Johnny, 240
blogs, 6, 26, 44, 46
Bogart, Leo, 237
Borg, Marian J., 124
Bosnia, 114, 124
Bradburn, Norman M., 243, 246
Bradley effect, 123
Buchanan, Patrick, 2, 43
Bureau of the Census, 19

Bush, George H. W., 32, 34, 43
Bush, George W., 7, 32, 41, 72, 182

Caddell, Pat, 239
Callegaro, Mario, 244
call-backs, 186, 201
call-in poll, 69, 167, 180, 181, 182, 184, 194, 213, 229
campaign coverage, 47, 64, 74, 189
campaign polls, 10, 13, 24, 51, 55, 56, 57
candidate polls, 24, 51, 53, 57, 170
candidate preference/support, 15, 24, 30, 31, 34, 36, 38, 47, 63, 86, 91, 118, 120, 131, 132, 140, 155, 189, 202, 204, 205, 210, 213, 215, 230, 233, 234, 235
candidate recall, 118, 119, 202
candidate recognition, 55, 56, 119, 202
candidate viability, 55, 202
Cantril, Albert H., 241
Carter, Jimmy, 27, 40
computer-assisted personal interviewing (CAPI), 131, 141, 193, 202
computer-assisted telephone interviewing (CATI), 68, 103, 133, 148, 152, 153, 202
computer-assisted web interviewing (CAWI), 134–135, 144, 148, 153, 193, 202, 203, 245
CBS News, 40, 66, 67, 111, 156, 181, 216, 227, 235, 239
cell phones, 5, 9, 10, 37, 38, 81, 83, 89, 90, 128, 129, 132, 133, 139, 141, 167, 168, 186, 203, 206, 212, 213, 223, 231, 232
cell phone surveys, 133, 203, 213, 223
census, 18, 19, 48, 95, 193, 203, 215, 225, 227, 231; Bureau of the Census, 19
Christina, Leah, 245
Chung, Robert, 242
Clawson, Rosalee, 237
Clinton, Bill, 32, 34, 98, 109,110
Clinton, Hillary, 35, 38, 110, 140

closed-ended question, 70, 106, 107, 115, 140, 143, 149, 203, 217, 244
cluster sampling, 221
CNN, 40, 67, 73, 114, 216, 227, 235
Commitment to America, 176
complex language, 110
complex structure, 109, 110
complicated language, 109
conceptual midpoint, 108
confidence interval, 86, 87, 91, 92, 139, 154, 197, 198, 203, 214, 215, 220
confidence level, 85, 86, 154, 204
confidentiality, 134, 149, 156, 187, 199, 200, 204, 205, 212, 230
constant, 152, 159, 235
contact attempts, 33, 34, 141, 143, 204
context effect, 118–120, 204
contingency question, 144, 204
Contract with America, 176
Converse, Jean, 238
Cook, Fay Lomax, 239
core voters, 31, 204, 213
Couper, Mick, 240
coverage (of a population), 18, 76, 82, 137, 193, 204, 205, 216, 218, 220, 223, 227, 240
cover letter, 183, 205
credibility interval, 91, 92
Crossley, Archibald, 4
cross-sectional poll or survey, 15, 159, 205
cross-tabulations, 70, 83, 157, 215, 246
cynicism about government, 74

data aggregator, 45, 46
data analysis, 5, 8, 26, 123, 176, 241, 245, 246
data collection, 4, 5, 6, 8, 9, 13, 15, 16, 18, 20, 23, 24, 26, 29, 39, 40, 41, 55, 60, 66, 67, 68, 69, 82, 84, 92, 97, 103, 117, 123, 127, 128, 129, 130, 131, 132, 133, 134, 135, 136, 137, 141, 142, 144, 145, 194, 200, 208, 211, 212, 214, 216, 217, 220, 222, 228, 229, 235, 240, 244, 245, 246

data entry, 20, 148
Dean, Howard, 1
debates, polling after, 182
de Leeuw, Edith, 245
deliberative poll, 1
demographic characteristics/question, 39, 80, 86, 90, 93, 101, 104, 105, 111, 121, 129, 131, 143, 147, 151, 152, 156, 170, 184, 192, 201, 205, 210, 222, 225, 230
demonstrations, as a reflection of public opinion, 17
dependent variable, 154, 201, 205, 210
designated respondent, 42, 89, 90, 142, 143, 146, 205, 225
Dever, Jill, 241
differential nonresponse, 124, 135, 206
Dewey, Thomas E., 27
Dillman, Donald, 245
dirty tricks, 2
disclosure standards, 99
Dole, Bob, 32
Do Not Call list, 5, 10, 52, 180
Donsbach, Wolfgang, 245
don't know, 116, 117–118, 153, 171, 177, 204, 225
double-barreled question, 109, 112, 206
double negative, 109, 111–112, 206
dual-frame random digit dialing (DFRDD), 88, 89, 206
Dukakis, Michael, 242

early voting, 9, 10, 28, 29, 34, 43, 63, 83, 206
Edison Media Research, 11, 41, 42, 235
editorial control, 5, 64
education, as an analysis variable, 103, 105, 110, 129, 170, 205, 210
effective sample size, 87
Election Day, 3, 4, 6, 10, 14, 24, 25, 26, 27–29, 30, 31, 37, 39, 41, 43, 44, 46, 53, 58, 59, 63, 65, 76, 77, 78, 83, 95, 103, 130, 157, 158, 172, 206, 207, 208, 220, 227, 228, 234, 235, 236
election night decision team, 49, 207

election night projections, 1, 39, 46, 47, 207, 208, 234
election polls, 5, 7, 9, 14, 23, 24, 25, 28, 39–40, 46–47, 58, 63, 65, 73, 76, 77, 78, 79, 80, 81, 82, 84, 85, 88, 95, 96, 97, 100, 102, 119, 127, 128, 129, 130, 131, 136, 137, 138, 143, 144, 148, 158, 168, 169, 175, 176, 189, 190, 201, 207, 210, 213, 215, 219, 222, 223, 225, 226, 227, 232, 234, 235, 242, 247
election projections, 6, 36, 37
Electoral College, 27, 35, 40, 45, 53
elements, 52, 76–77, 93, 203, 207, 217, 219, 221, 222, 223, 226, 227, 228, 231, 234
enumeration, 18, 203
EPSEM sample, 93, 207
Erikson, Robert, 238
ESOMAR (World Association for Marketing, Social and Opinion Research), 7, 48, 242
estimate(s), 15, 18, 19, 25, 27, 28, 30, 31, 32, 33, 35, 36, 37, 38, 39, 42, 43, 44, 45, 46, 54, 63, 75, 76, 78, 83, 84, 85, 91, 98, 101, 124, 130, 138, 139, 154, 168, 169, 170, 189, 194, 197, 213, 214, 215, 220, 226, 227
exhaustive, 106, 152, 203, 207
exit poll(s), 1, 4, 6, 14, 24, 25–26, 29, 30, 39–48, 63, 67, 78, 82–83, 99, 124, 127, 130, 137, 170, 207–208, 216, 227, 228, 233, 235, 236; bias, 43; leaks, 6, 44

face-to-face interviewing, 8, 10, 14, 15, 23, 27, 31, 65, 127, 128, 131, 132, 134, 139, 150, 208, 211, 230
factoid, 69
fake polls, 13
favorability ratings, 55, 208
Federal Communications Commission (FEC), 5, 10, 129, 133
field period, 19, 25, 208
Finkel, Steven E., 124

First Amendment, 47, 221
first-call respondent, 68
focus group, 54, 176, 192, 193, 209, 243
Forbes, Steve, 1, 2
Fowler, Floyd J., 239, 240
Fox News, 6, 40, 41, 44, 45, 67, 72, 73, 200, 235
Frankovic, Kathleen, 49, 239
frequencies, 69, 70, 153, 155, 157, 201, 209
FRUGing, 18, 60, 180, 209

Gallhofer, Irmtraud, 243
Gallup, George, 4, 27, 65, 238, 239, 246
Gallup Poll, 4, 21, 28, 32, 34, 35, 49, 63, 72, 73, 109, 110, 111, 114, 119, 157, 160
gender as an analytical variable, 37, 103, 124, 131, 132, 139, 140, 151, 152, 155, 170, 205, 209, 210, 230
Gender Gap, 140, 154, 155, 209
get out the vote (GOTV), 59, 77
Gingrich, Newt, 176
Google Trends, 138
Gore, Albert E., 32, 35, 38, 41, 182
government agencies, polling by, 62
Greve, Frank, 176
Groves, Robert M., 240
Growth and Opportunity Project, 59
Guterbock, Thomas M., 124

hanging chads, 42
Harris, Louis, 65
Harrison, Irwin Tubby, 239
Harris Poll, 63, 129, 239
Hart, Peter, 239
Heeringa, Steven, 246
Herbst, Susan, 21, 238
herding, 2
Hickman, Harison, 166
Holbrook, Allyson, 245
Holley, Jack K., 49, 242
Holocaust, 111, 124
horse race, 1, 7, 49, 62, 84, 138, 156, 169, 210, 211, 215, 226

horserace journalism, 1, 7, 26, 33, 36, 73, 158, 210, 220, 233, 241
hostage crisis, 40
house effects, 166, 210
Huffington, Arianna, 98–99
Hussein, Saddam, 72, 177

image, candidate, 52–53, 58
impact of polls, 1, 20–21, 69, 189, 233
independent variable, 154, 201, 205, 210, 230
informed consent, 142, 210
initial contact, 143, 141, 146–147
in-person interviewing, 6, 37, 42, 82, 131, 132, 141, 142, 144, 211
insert polls, 183, 184, 211
instrument, 103, 192, 211
Interactive Voice Response (IVR), 15, 67, 68, 104, 127–128, 130, 134, 135–137, 144, 193, 211
intercept polls/samples, 211
interest groups, 17, 20, 23, 59, 60, 63, 74, 165, 175, 180, 181, 219, 221
Internet data collection, 29, 127, 133–135, 167, 169
Internet polls, 30, 81, 96, 97, 128, 135, 147, 150, 166, 167, 211
Internet pop-up polls, 82, 184, 212
interviewer-assisted data collection, 16, 212
interviewers, 14, 25, 27, 38, 42, 75, 82, 83, 90, 91, 96, 104, 107, 117, 123, 124, 127, 129, 131, 132, 133, 135, 139–149, 179, 185, 187, 192, 201, 208, 212, 215, 216, 217, 219, 223, 230, 231, 235, 243
interviewing: face-to-face, 23, 75, 127–128, 131–132, 139, 144, 150, 208; in-person, 37, 42, 82, 139, 211; interviewer-administered, 16, 167; monitoring, 140–141; self-administered, 8, 10, 15, 16, 25, 29, 39, 75, 108, 110, 117, 120, 127, 132, 134–135, 137, 167, 228; standardized, 145–146, 230;

telephone, 132–133, 139, 185, 186; training, 140–141, 212
introductory spiel, 142, 212, 220, 222
IPSOS/Knowledge Panel, 21
Iran, 1, 40
Iraq, 56, 73, 177
item, 13, 14, 30, 103–108, 112, 113, 115, 116, 118–124, 137, 143, 149, 163, 164, 191, 192, 202, 205, 206, 208, 212, 216, 218, 220, 222, 225, 229, 233, 234, 235
item nonresponse, 212

Johnson, David, 2
Johnson, Timothy, 243

Kagay, Michael, 239
Kennedy, Courtney, 62, 245
Kerry, John, 1, 106, 107
Kish, Leslie, 240
Knight-Ridder, 176
Kreuter, Frauke, 241

landline only, 38
landline (phone) surveys, 212
Landon, Alf, 27, 80
last birthday method, 90
Lavrakas, Paul J., 242, 243, 245
leading phrase, 109, 113
leaks, 6, 44, 57, 74
leaners, 31, 118, 213
legibility, 108
Lepkowski, James, 240
Lewinsky, Monica, 40, 56
likelihood of voting, 28, 30, 120, 213, 236
likely voter, 25, 28, 34, 35, 37, 54, 59, 77, 88, 89, 97, 98, 172, 213
Literary Digest, 27, 80
log-in polls, 2, 69, 167, 181, 182, 213
Lohr, Sharon, 241
longitudinal design/studies, 15, 214, 233

mail-in polls, 69, 213, 214

mail surveys, 27, 59, 90, 127, 130, 133–135, 147, 149, 200, 205, 212, 214, 216, 222, 228, 245
mall intercept interviews, 91, 214
Manfreda, Katja, 244
Manza, Jeff, 239
marginal, 70, 157, 209, 215
margin of error, 85, 95, 194, 203. *See also* margin of sampling error (MOSE)
margin of sampling error (MOSE), 34, 83–84, 87–88, 89, 91, 94–95, 97, 101, 154, 168, 182, 193, 197–198, 203, 215, 227
Martin, Elizabeth, 62
Martin, L. John, 239
McDermott, Monika L., 49
measured opinion, 16, 177
measurement error, 177, 215, 216, 218
media polls, 19, 51, 57, 58, 66, 67, 68, 69, 70, 71, 87, 98, 147, 149, 151, 152, 156, 166, 189, 201, 215, 217, 243
methods box, 156, 164, 216
midterm election, 2, 10, 35, 41
Miller, Peter V., 49, 62, 74, 243
Mitofsky, Warren, 11, 41, 43, 49, 207, 235, 239
Mitofsky International, 207, 235
mixed-mode designs, 6, 9, 10, 41, 43, 68, 128, 130, 137, 208, 216, 245
mode, 14, 23, 38, 69, 75, 82, 117, 127, 128, 129, 132, 135, 136, 137, 143, 145, 148, 164, 166, 167, 183, 191, 193, 194, 208, 212, 215, 216, 222, 228, 239, 244, 245
mode effect, 216
mode of data collection, 23, 82, 130, 131, 136, 137, 166–167, 194, 208, 212, 216, 222, 244, 245
momentum, in the nominating process, 58, 62, 241
Moore, David W., 239
moral values, 106–107

Morin, Richard, 74, 124, 239
Morris, Dick, 56
Morris, G. Elliott, 247
MSNBC, 67
mutually exclusive, 106, 152, 203, 216
Mutz, Diana, 62
NAFTA. *See* North American Free Trade Agreement

National Council of Public Polls, 99, 241
National Election Pool (NEP), 6, 11, 39, 41, 45, 106, 207, 216, 227, 235
National Opinion Research Center (NORC), 6, 21, 41, 67, 81, 92, 200
NBC News, 40, 156, 216, 227, 235
New Hampshire, elections in, 42, 49, 53
news aggregators, 67
news coverage, 2, 4, 7, 13, 24, 26, 54, 63, 65, 189
News Election Service (NES), 40, 235
newsworthiness, 19, 170, 176
New York Times, 41, 66, 67, 85, 156, 206, 239
next birthday method, 90
no opinion category, 73, 244
noncontact(s), 96, 147, 148, 216, 217
noncoverage, 100, 220
nondirective probing, 140, 146, 217
nonprobability sample, 5, 15–16, 77, 85, 88, 90–92, 168, 169, 184, 193, 194, 203, 211, 217, 222, 226, 228
nonresponse, 95–99, 100–102, 146, 186, 208, 216, 217; differential, 124, 135, 206; error, 96–99, 186, 201, 208, 217, 224, 226; item, 137–138, 212
nonsampling error, 97, 217, 218, 220
North American Free Trade Agreement (NAFTA), 111
number portability, 10, 89

Obama, Barack, 1, 53, 72, 170, 181
Oldendick, Robert, 237
on the job training, 140

open-ended question, 4, 56, 68, 105–108, 127, 135, 140, 149, 217, 218, 230, 235
opinion questions, 146, 177, 218
opt-in internet panels, 96, 97, 100, 135, 168, 192, 218
order effects, 37, 118–121, 218
Oxley, Zoe, 237

Packwood, Bob, 29
Page, Benjamin I., 239
panel studies, 15, 16, 129, 159, 160, 214, 219, 233
paper and pencil interviewing (PAPI), 25, 108, 145, 148, 193, 219
party identification, 32, 70, 103, 151, 156, 158, 170
Patterson, Thomas, 74
Perot, Ross, 59, 180, 209, 229, 241
Pew Research Center, 21, 49, 35, 38, 71, 106, 160
political consultants, 24, 139
poll-based news, 243
polls, analysis of, 8, 36; call-in, 69, 180, 181, 182, 184, 201; estimate, 26, 42, 44; exit, 1, 4, 5, 6, 10, 14, 24, 25, 26, 29, 30, 38, 39, 40, 41, 42, 43, 44, 45, 46, 47, 48, 63, 67, 78, 82, 83, 99, 106, 117, 124, 127, 130, 137, 155, 170, 207, 208, 216, 227, 228, 233, 234, 235, 236; insert, 183, 184, 211; instant, 181; intercept, 211; Internet, 30, 81, 96, 97, 128, 141, 147, 150, 166, 167, 211; issue, 179; log-in, 2, 69, 167, 181, 182, 213; mail-in, 69, 167, 214; media, 19, 51, 57, 58, 67, 68, 69, 70, 87, 98, 99, 147, 149, 151, 152, 156, 166, 189, 201, 215, 217, 243; post-debate, 182; pre-election, 5, 10, 14, 15, 24, 26, 27, 28, 29, 30, 31, 34, 35, 36, 37, 38, 46, 48, 57, 62, 63, 81, 87, 89, 92, 95, 96, 97, 99, 101, 122, 124, 128, 129, 130, 154, 155, 158, 166, 201, 210, 213, 220, 221, 228, 233, 234, 235, 236, 242;

pre-primary, 89, 118, 220; private, 51, 135, 150, 178; pseudo, 1, 18, 51, 60, 180, 187, 221, 222; push, 1, 2, 57, 165, 179, 222; sponsor, 6, 44, 135, 178, 179; state-level, 27, 45, 53; straw, 91, 127, 219, 231, 238; telephone, 38, 68, 80, 90, 96, 133, 143, 150, 166, 167, 185, 186, 201, 204, 219, 224, 227, 230; tracking, 10, 25, 32, 33, 34, 35, 49, 205, 226, 233; 800- polls, 18, 199; 900- polls, 18, 199
pollster, 2, 5, 6, 10, 15, 16, 23, 26, 27, 28, 29, 30, 31, 32, 33, 34, 35, 37, 41, 42, 43, 45, 51, 69, 75, 77, 78, 79, 82, 84, 85, 86, 88, 89, 90, 91, 92, 94, 95, 96, 99, 100, 101, 102, 103, 104, 105, 106, 107, 109, 110, 111, 112, 113, 115, 116, 117, 118, 119, 120, 121, 122, 123, 124, 128, 132, 133, 134, 135, 136, 137, 138, 140, 141, 142, 143, 145, 146, 166, 178, 200, 247
population, 5, 9, 13, 14, 15, 16, 17, 18, 19, 23, 28, 30, 37, 38, 42, 48, 51, 54, 67, 69, 71, 75, 76, 77, 78, 79, 80, 81, 84, 85, 86, 87, 88, 89, 91, 93, 95, 97, 99, 100, 101, 105, 121, 124, 132, 135, 142, 152, 154, 155, 164, 167, 168, 169, 170, 172, 176, 177, 184, 192, 193, 197, 199, 201, 203, 204, 206, 207, 211, 212, 214, 215, 216, 217, 219, 220, 221, 223, 224, 225, 226, 227, 229, 231, 232, 236, 245
Poynter Center for Media Studies, 7
precision, 76, 84, 87, 220
presidential approval, 72, 158, 172, 220
pretest, 109, 122, 220
Price, Vincent, 124
primacy effect, 136, 137, 218, 221
prior restraint, 47, 221
probability sample, 15, 17, 27, 76–77, 83–84, 88–89, 92, 100, 169, 192–193, 221
probable electorate, 28, 77
public mandate, 39

public opinion, 3, 4, 7, 9, 16–17, 54, 60, 61, 62, 72, 74, 86, 111, 113, 115, 138–139, 146, 157, 158, 164, 171, 176, 177, 184, 191, 192, 195, 199, 202, 219, 222, 231, 237, 238, 239, 242, 245, 246, 247
push poll, 1, 2, 57, 165, 179, 222
push to web, 183, 222

quarantine room, 6, 44, 46
question manipulation, 115
question stem, 112, 115, 116, 200, 204, 222, 233
questionnaire, 5, 6, 89, 13, 14, 15, 17, 18, 20, 23, 24, 25, 26, 27, 28, 39, 42, 60, 68, 69, 71, 75, 78, 79, 81, 84, 87, 90, 95, 97, 103–113, 115, 116, 117, 118, 119, 120, 121, 122, 127, 130, 131, 133, 134, 135, 136, 137, 143, 144, 145, 146, 148, 150, 152, 156, 167, 178, 182, 183, 184, 189, 192, 202, 203, 204, 205, 207, 208, 209, 211, 212, 214, 215, 218, 219, 220, 221, 222, 225, 228, 229, 230, 233, 240, 242, 243, 244, 245; complex language, 110–111; experiment, 105, 110, 122–123; format, 103–104, 105–106; length, 143–144; order, 60, 103–104, 118–121, 171; self-administered, 15, 108; (un)biased questions, 60, 124, 176, 179
question wording, 37, 56, 60, 72, 109, 111, 113, 115, 116, 122, 123, 145, 161, 165, 171, 172, 201, 212, 223, 230, 243, 244
quota sample, 27, 48, 193, 217, 222

Rae, Saul, 238
random, 19, 88, 90, 93, 94, 105, 106, 110, 122, 124, 136, 141, 202, 203, 218, 222, 223, 229, 230, 231, 233, 245
random assignment, 122–124, 223, 230, 245

random digit dialing (RDD), 83, 88–89, 128, 142, 150, 182, 185, 206, 212, 223, 227, 232, 234
random sampling, 93, 94, 124, 197, 221, 222, 223, 224, 229, 230, 234, 245
random start, 94
Rasinski, Ken, 244
RDD. *See* random digit dialing
RealClearPolitics.com, 45, 157, 159
recency effect, 137, 224
recognition, aided, 119
recontact, 33, 67, 71, 132, 133, 147, 149, 194, 217, 224
refusal, 96, 147, 193, 224
refusal conversion, 147–148, 193, 224
refusal rate, 121, 224
registered voters, 5, 25, 28, 29, 30, 34, 73, 77, 79, 80, 88, 94, 172, 193, 206, 228, 230
registration-based sampling (RBS), 30, 82, 83
reliability, of measurement, 194
repeated cross-sections, 158, 214
representative sample, 54, 91, 94, 128, 137, 142, 161, 172, 186, 224, 229
respondent burden, 108, 131, 206, 225
respondents, 2, 6, 14, 15, 17, 18, 23, 24, 27, 30, 31, 33, 34, 36, 37, 38, 39, 42, 59, 60, 67, 68, 69, 70, 71, 73, 75, 85, 87, 89, 91, 92, 95, 100, 101, 103, 104, 105, 106, 107, 108, 109, 110, 111, 112, 113, 115, 116, 117, 118, 119, 120, 121, 122, 123, 124, 127, 128, 131, 132, 133, 134, 135, 136, 137, 138, 139, 140, 141, 142, 143, 144, 145, 146, 147, 148, 149, 150, 151, 152, 153, 154, 155, 156, 158, 159, 164, 165, 166, 167, 170, 171, 172, 177, 178, 179, 180, 181, 182, 184, 185, 187, 189, 192, 194, 197, 199, 200, 201, 202, 203, 204, 205, 206, 207, 209, 210, 211, 212, 213, 225, 226, 228, 230, 231, 232, 233, 234, 235, 236, 244, 246

Index   257

response alternatives, 105–106, 107, 108, 109, 112, 113, 115–117, 119, 136, 171, 180, 203, 204, 207, 209, 216, 222, 225, 233, 234. *See also* response options

response options, 73, 107, 172, 177, 192. *See also* response alternatives

response rate(s), 9, 16, 27, 67, 69, 76, 95–99, 100, 134, 135, 141, 164, 166, 167, 169, 170, 184, 186, 189, 201, 205, 214, 215, 217, 219, 224–226, 228, 232, 233

Rips, Lance J., 244

rolling averages, 33, 226

Romney, Mitt, 1, 53

Roosevelt, Franklin D., 27, 61, 80

Roper, Elmo, 4

Roper Organization, 111

sample, 13, 76, 192, 226; design(s), 5, 60, 76, 77, 83, 87, 192, 222, 226, 227, 241; EPSEM, 93, 207; frame, 38, 76, 79–83, 91, 93, 94, 100, 133, 167–168, 192–193, 219, 227, 228, 230, 232; hybrid, 92; opt-in online, 100; precinct, 39, 42, 43, 83, 227; random, 65, 76, 83, 87, 88, 93–94, 139, 197, 223, 224, 229, 232; RDD, 83, 128; recruitment, 192; representative, 37, 54, 60, 91, 93, 94, 100, 128, 132, 135, 142, 161, 167, 170, 172, 184, 186, 224, 229; scientific, 14, 17, 18, 23, 25, 28, 54, 69, 75, 76, 81, 127, 129, 130, 156, 228, 231; self-selected, 18, 43, 69, 82, 91, 128, 135, 167, 180, 181, 228; simple random, 87, 93, 197, 221, 229, 232

sampling interval, 93–94, 227

Saris, Willem, 243

Schuman, Howard, 244

screening, 5, 9, 164, 194, 228

secret ballot, 29, 31, 37–38, 228

self-administered data collection, 117, 134, 228, 229

sensitive topics/questions, 104, 109, 113–114, 132

shy Trump voters, 35, 124

Silver, Nate, 2, 45, 166

Singer, Eleanor, 11, 240

Smith, Tom W., 124

Smyth, Jolene, 245

snowball sample, 88, 217, 229

social desirability, 38, 118, 121–122, 123, 134, 136, 137, 167, 229

social media, 17, 54, 55, 61, 138, 139, 181, 192, 194

spin, 40, 42, 58, 65, 229

split-half design, 106, 122–123, 230, 233

sponsorship, 20, 164, 165, 179

sports metaphors, 73

standardized survey interviewing, 145, 230

statistical software, 70, 148, 152

Stonecash, Jeffrey, 242

Strategic Vision LLC, 2

stratum, 83, 94, 230

straw polls, 91, 127, 219, 231, 238

Sudman, Seymour, 243, 246

SUGing, 18, 60, 179, 231

super PAC, 1

survey, 2, 3, 4, 13, 14, 231; cross-sectional, 15, 205; longitudinal, 15, 214; mail, 27, 59, 90, 130, 134, 135, 149, 205, 214, 222, 245; research, 4, 8, 10, 18, 19, 23, 60, 164, 170, 180, 189, 240, 243, 245, 246; sampling, 9, 240, 241

SurveyUSA, 137

systematic error, 35, 122–124, 201, 231

systematic sample, 93, 228, 231, 294

target population, 42, 67, 69, 76–79, 81, 85, 87, 88, 89, 91, 95, 97, 99, 100, 101, 105, 132, 135, 142, 154, 167–168, 170, 184, 193, 199, 201, 204–205, 211, 215, 216, 217, 223, 224, 227, 229, 232, 236

Tedin, Kent, 238

Teeter, Robert, 239
telemarketers, 96, 179
Telephone Consumer Protection Act, 129
telephone directories, 80, 223
telephone households, 30, 88, 205, 232
telephone surveys, 5, 10, 65, 75, 78, 89, 105, 117, 128, 133, 202, 211, 222, 232, 245
third-person effect, 46, 233
timing, of calls, 186
topline results, 70, 71
total survey error, 239, 240
Tourangeau, Roger, 240
tracking polls, 10, 25, 32, 33, 34, 35, 205, 226, 233
Transparency Initiative, 48, 49, 99, 164
Traugott, Michael W., 48, 49, 62, 74, 124, 242, 243, 245
trend analysis, 24, 158, 160, 233
trial-heat question, 25, 30, 31, 35, 36, 38, 53, 55, 63, 73, 118, 158, 172, 202, 210, 233, 234
true experiment, 28, 30, 36, 47, 105, 106, 111, 123, 205, 230, 236
TrueNorth, 92
true value, 84, 121, 122, 154, 203, 215, 220
turnout, 1, 2, 28, 29, 31, 32, 45, 46, 58, 74, 77, 79, 94, 95, 121, 154, 170, 220, 233, 234
tweets, 17, 61, 138, 139
Twitter (now known as X), 54, 138, 139, 181, 192

unbalanced question, 108–109, 179, 180, 225, 233
undecideds, 24, 28, 31–32, 116–117, 118, 213, 234
underdog effect, 36, 46, 201, 234
unequal chance of selection, 100

uniform poll closings, 48, 234
unit, 88, 225, 227, 234
University of Chicago, 11, 41, 81, 92, 200
unlisted household, 168
unlisted phone number, 168, 185, 205, 223, 227
unrepresentative sample, 37, 93, 170
unweighted data, 100, 101, 235
US Bill of Rights, 48

Valliant, Richard, 241
variable, 152, 153, 154, 156, 201, 205, 210, 214, 215, 230, 235; dependent, 154, 201, 205, 210; independent, 154, 201, 205, 210, 230
verbatim responses, 107, 149, 218, 235
video-assisted data collection, 132–134, 139
volatility, 28, 34, 37, 235
vote-by-mail, 10, 29, 235, 236
Voter News Service (VNS), 5–6, 40–42, 99, 207, 216, 235
Voter Research and Surveys (VRS), 40, 42–43

Wall Street Journal, 156, 176, 200
Wansink, Brian, 243
Washington Post, 66, 124, 239
weighting, 92, 99, 100–101, 164, 167, 190, 194, 210, 216, 236, 241
West, Brady, 245, 246
Whitman effect, 123, 125
World Association for Public Opinion Research (WAPOR), 7, 48, 242

X (formerly known as Twitter), 54, 138, 139, 181, 192

Yankelovich, Daniel, 222, 247

About the Authors

Michael W. Traugott is a political scientist and survey methodologist. He is professor emeritus of Communication Studies and Political Science and research professor emeritus in the Center for Political Studies at the Institute for Social Research at the University of Michigan. His main research areas of interest are public opinion and political communication, and he has studied the use of polls in the media. Currently his research focuses on how members of the public understand and interpret poll results through the process of motivated reasoning. He has served as the president of the American Association for Public Opinion Research and the World Association for Public Opinion Research, and he has been recognized for distinguished lifetime achievement by both organizations. He has served as a consultant to media organizations and is interviewed frequently about electoral politics and polling issues.

Paul J. Lavrakas is a research psychologist and since 2007 has served as an international methodological research consultant for several universities, not-for-profit and for-profit companies, and government agencies. He was a tenured full professor at Northwestern University (1978–1996) and Ohio State University (1996–2000) and was the founding faculty director of the Northwestern University Survey Lab (1982–1996) and the OSU Center for Survey Research (1996–2000). From 2000–2007 he was vice president and chief methodologist for Nielsen Media Research. He played a major role in introducing dual frame RDD surveying in the United States, Australia, and Japan. In the past decade, he has helped to develop methods for the creation of probability-based online panels in the United States and in Australia. Among his many publications, he is the editor of the *Encyclopedia of Survey Research Methods*. He has conducted preelection polls and served the American Association for Public Opinion Research (AAPOR) as its President in 2012–2013, was co-winner of the AAPOR Innovators Award in 2003, received the AAPOR Award for Exceptionally Distinguished Achievement in 2019, and was the co-winner of the 2021 AAPOR Book Award.